THE NEW
NEIGHBOURHOOD
OF DUBLIN

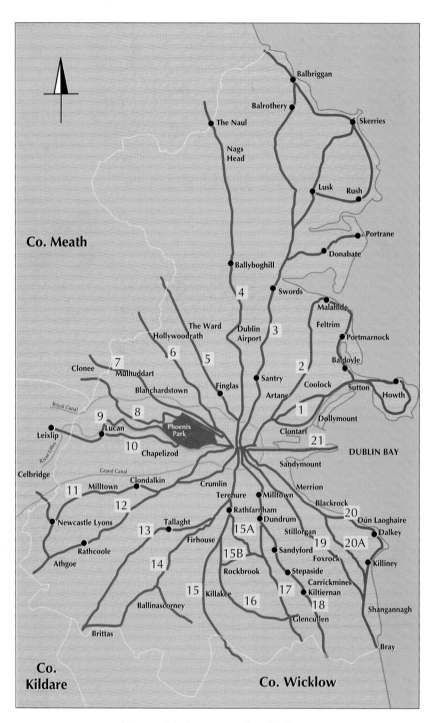

Key map showing routes referred to in text

THE NEW
NEIGHBOURHOOD
OF DUBLIN

JOSEPH HONE   MAURICE CRAIG

MICHAEL FEWER

A. & A. Farmar

© Joseph Hone, Maurice Craig (original text) 2002
© Michael Fewer (additional text) 2002

British Library cataloguing in Publication Data
A CIP catalogue record for this book is available from the British Library.

Cover design by Alice Campbell
Designed and set by Bookworks
Printed and bound by Colourbooks

The publishers would like to thank the Irish Architectural Archive for permission to reproduce numerous photographs from their collection. Other photos are by Maurica Craig Brendan Grimes and Michael Fewer.

Maps by Fiona Fewer and Michael Fewer.

Picture credits:
Irish Architectural Archive: pages 11, 15, 25, 35, 41, 51, 57, 59, 75, 85, 89, 95, 97 (nunciature), 109, 119, 153, 161, 189, 197, 203, 205, 213, 217, 223, 225, 229, 233, 239 and 241.
The Maurice Craig Collection: pages 45, 55 (Santry Court), 73, 81, 121, 131 and 145.
The Patrick Healy Collection: pages 5, 9, 27, 29, 37, 49, 69, 123, 135, 137, 141, 143, 147, 149, 157, 159, 169 (north elevation), 173, 181, 187, 195, 207, 221 and 243.
Michael Fewer: pages 7, 17, 19, 21, 23, 33, 39, 67, 79, 87, 91, 93, 97 (towerhouse), 99, 105, 111, 113, 151, 163, 165, 167, 169 (south elevation), 177, 185, 191, 193, 201, 209, 219, 227, 231, 237, 245 and 247.
Brendan Grimes: pages 3, 31, 55 (portico), 65, 71, 77, 103 and 175.

The image on the title page is of Kenure Park, for which see page 51.

ISBN 1-899047-78-6

First published in 2002
by
A. & A. Farmar
Beech House
78 Ranelagh Village
Dublin 6
Ireland
Tel: + 353 1 496 3625
Fax: + 353 1 497 0107
Email: afarmar@iol.ie
Web: farmarbooks.com

CONTENTS

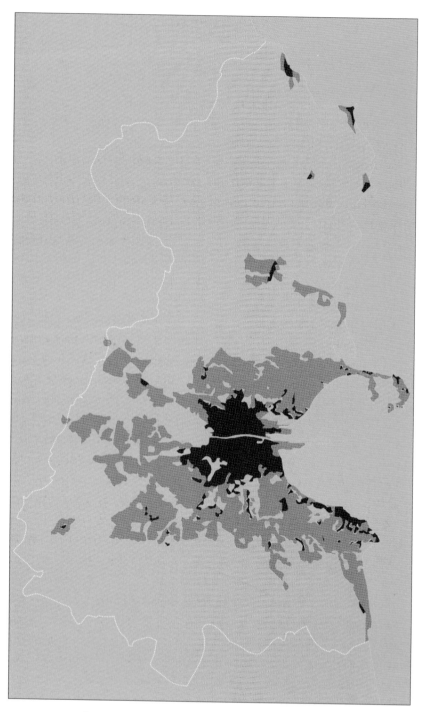

The Expansion of Dublin City Suburbs 1948–98
Footprint of built-up areas

Dublin 1948   Dublin, expansion 1948–98

Original Preface, 1949

The intention of this book is to bring the *Post-Chaise Companion Through Ireland* (1776) up to date on a larger scale over a smaller area. The inevitable differences are many. The *Post-Chaise Companion* restricted itself, on the whole, to the seats of noblemen and gentlemen, with here and there a 'Danish Fort'. But the revolutions of time have swept away many of the noblemen and gentlemen, though hardly so thoroughly as modern archaeology has disposed of the Danes. Many of the houses remain, and others have arisen; and we feel that it is time that someone should record their present occupants, especially when they have, as in so many cases, attained distinction in comparatively recent years.

The *Post-Chaise Companion* covered the whole of Ireland by following roads radiating from Dublin. We have adopted the same principle, and the limits of a single county allow us to go into much greater detail. The most convenient single book on the district is Weston St J. Joyce's *Neighbourhood of Dublin*, on which we have drawn extensively for information. But this book is not intended to supersede Joyce; rather, we have tried to combine a difference of treatment with a readjustment of perspective. Joyce wrote some forty years ago. Some of the things he recorded have disappeared. Others are (to us) less interesting than they were to him. Others (and this applies particularly to houses built after 1700) have become interesting by the secular revolution of taste. And of course other features of interest have appeared since Joyce's time. Many places in the county have acquired historical associations during the eventful period which separates us from him.

We have tried, so far as possible, to satisfy these changed conditions. Though we do not claim originality in documentary research, we have investigated, at first hand and often on foot, most of the places mentioned. Similarly we have incorporated a good deal of verbal information which might otherwise have become obscured by time.

The Routes are designed, as the time demands, for motorists, with the exception of the last Route. We would add, however, the warning that even the simplest forms of sight-seeing take longer to do than appears on paper. In County Dublin, thickly populated and pre-eminent in history for so long, this is especially true.

We apologise in advance for any inaccuracy concerning living persons, though we have done our best to verify the information given in current works of reference.

Joseph Hone and Maurice Craig

INTRODUCTION

The original text of this book was written by J. M. Hone and myself during 1949. Lord Clonmore, later Earl of Wicklow, who was in partnership with a man called Reynolds, was a publisher and had given Joe Hone the impression that their firm, Clonmore and Reynolds, might publish such a book.

Joseph Maunsel Hone (Joe Hone to his familiars but not, at this stage, to me) was a very distinguished man of letters, the friend of Yeats and his chosen biographer, author of the *Moores of Moore Hall*, and of the lives of George Moore, the painter Henry Tonks and others, including Berkeley and Swift. He had been the partner of George Roberts in the firm of Maunsel and Roberts, the most important Irish publishing house of its time. He was the President of the Irish Academy of Letters, and initiated a dictionary of Irish writers which never got beyond the stage of specimens being published in 1944 under the auspices of the Abbey Theatre.

He was born in 1882 and was at that time sixty-six, thirty-seven years my senior. I was naturally very gratified and flattered at being asked to collaborate. My Charlemont book had already appeared and I had nearly finished the text of my *Dublin 1660–1860* which was to take three years to grind its way through the publishing process. I cannot remember exactly how we divided the work. Parts of it clearly reflect Joe's intimate acquaintance with the professional and commercial classes, many of whose big houses were still there in their grounds, especially in the South County, and many of whom were related to him.

He was then living at Ballyorney beside the Dargle beyond Enniskerry. I recall much work done on the kitchen table of that house. It was, for me at least and I think also for him, a very enjoyable undertaking.

In the event, not altogether to my surprise, Clonmore and Reynolds declined to take the book. There were two typescript copies. Joe gave me his and told me I could have whatever benefit there might be from the book. I put it out of my mind, but many years later gave one of the copies to the National Library.

When my agent Jonathan Williams suggested that it might, fifty years later, have some life in it, I could see the point. Everything topical in it had become out of date, but with the lapse of time it had perhaps become a 'period piece'. There was a new, and perhaps larger, audience. The population of the county was vastly greater than it had been. Thousands of people now lived in the areas through which the twenty-one routes ran. The essential thing was to find a collaborator who could cover the ground again and report on what was now to be seen.

Michael Fewer, with an established reputation as an architect and an author of books on walking travel, was ideal casting for the part, and, fortunately for us, was keen to play it. To my surprise, and I think also to his, much more of what we mentioned half a century ago was still there, though sometimes less easy to find. In finding and describing all this, Michael has given the book whatever value it may turn out to have.

I have not tampered with our original text, except very occasionally to correct a gross error or a piece of ignorance of which I should now be ashamed. I was very young.

Maurice Craig, November 2001

The original Hone and Craig manuscript provides a remarkable record of the built environment of County Dublin just over a half-century ago. Within a decade of its completion, development of many new housing areas in the county had begun in earnest, a trickle of suburban development that turned into the deluge of the nineteen-sixties, followed by the comprehensive urbanisation of many square miles of rural areas which has continued up to the present day. While the 546 buildings and installations mentioned in the original manuscript are by no means a comprehensive listing, I found the list sufficiently thorough to provide an excellent baseline for a survey of what has happened in the region since 1949. Between October 2000 and June 2001, with the assistance of the Faculty of the Built Environment of the Dublin Institute of Technology, I carried out that survey, and it forms the basis of the accompanying notes in this publication.

The Ireland of 1949 was very different to the Ireland of today. Four years after World War II rationing was still in force, covering such foodstuffs as butter, bread, tea and flour, and there continued to be a shortage of fuel for cooking and heating. It was a pre-antibiotic era, and infectious diseases such as tuberculosis and influenza were widespread and often fatal; average life expectancy in Ireland was approximately 25 per cent lower than it is today. The arrival of television was more than a decade away, and society in Ireland remained deeply conservative, with the Catholic Church wielding great influence at all levels of society. The Free State had been in existence for a mere twenty-six years in 1949; it was still a pre-Lemass Ireland, sixteen years before the Planning and Development Act (1963) was enacted, and twenty years before the publication of Myles Wright's Dublin region advisory plan and report, the harbinger of the future development of Dublin's suburbs. Probably the most significant statistic having bearing on the development of County Dublin between 1949 and 1999 was the increase in population from about 130,000 to 577,000.

With this last statistic in mind, one would expect that the destruction of the existing built environment in the region would have been considerable, but my findings indicate a much higher survival rate than I had anticipated. Of the buildings and installations mentioned in the original manuscript, I was unable to locate the sites of five. Of the remaining 541, I found that 94, or 17 per cent, had been demolished, 49 in north County Dublin, and 45 in south County Dublin. Houses were by far the main building type affected; 71 houses out of the 284 listed, or 25 per cent, had been demolished. Besides unique classic houses such as Allenton in Tallaght, Frascati in Blackrock, and Kenure Park in Rush, the significance of which was clear to all concerned, this number also includes many commonplace rural houses in perfectly good order at the time of their destruction. Retained and used imaginatively for community purposes they could have enriched the new suburbs instead of being unnecessarily sacrificed in the clearance of lands for new housing developments, parks and roads.

Like Maurice over fifty years ago, I was gratified and flattered at being asked to be involved in this book, and it was for me too a most enjoyable undertaking. I benefited from the assistance of many during the course of my research, but I would like especially to thank David Griffin of the Irish Architectural Archive, Susan Rowntree, Conservation Officer of Dublin Corporation, and Fionnuala May, Conservation Officer of Fingal County Council, the Dublin Institute of Technology, in particular John Ratcliffe, Director of the Faculty of the Built Environment and James Horan, Head of the School of Architecture, Dr Brendan Williams and Brendan Grimes. I would like to thank Peter Healy for his assistance in my search for period photographs and his permission to use many taken by his late brother, Patrick Healy. I also thank my daughter, Fiona Fewer for her assistance regarding graphics, and Jonathan Williams, whose guidance and advice were most valuable.

Michael Fewer, November 2001

ROUTE 1

HOWTH

Amiens Street Station, ½ mile from the General Post Office, is the Dublin terminus of the Great Northern Railway. It occupies the site of the house in which the novelist Charles Lever was born. On the right is Sheriff Street leading towards the Alexandra Basin.

The street called Amiens consists chiefly of small shops and houses. It leads into the North Strand and crosses the Royal Canal at Newcomen Bridge. Just before the Canal, at the left, off Portland Row, stands the palatial Aldborough House, built in 1793 by the eccentric Edward, 2nd Earl of Aldborough (whose second title was Amiens), but never occupied by him.

A descendant of a Robert Stratford, a seventeenth-century English adventurer, who settled at Baltinglass, County Wicklow in 1660 and acquired great landed estates, Aldborough had a passion for building. He inherited country seats at Belan in County Kildare and at Baltinglass, at Glenhammin, Suffolk, and a mansion in Denmark Street, Dublin. To these he added Stratford House on Oxford Street, London, built for him by Adam, and Aldborough House in Dublin. He also founded the town of Stratford-on-Slaney, near Baltinglass, which in 1786 consisted of, at least in principle, four squares and twelve streets and possessed several factories, and erected a residence for himself, called Amiens Park and Lodge. It was intended to augment the town by laying out five more squares and another

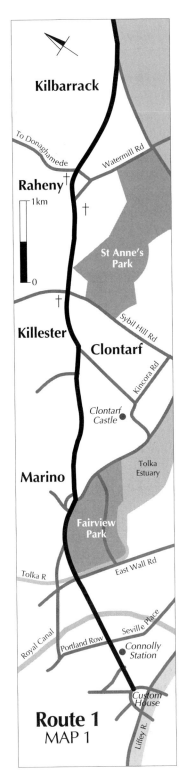

Kilbarrack

To Donaghamede

Watermill Rd

Raheny †

1km

†

St Anne's Park

†

Sybil Hill Rd

Killester

Clontarf

Kincora Rd

Clontarf Castle ●

Tolka Estuary

Marino

Fairview Park

Tolka R

East Wall Rd

Royal Canal

Portland Row

Seville Place

Connolly Station ●

Custom House

Liffey R.

Route 1
MAP 1

0

At the south end of Amiens Street is **Busáras**, Ireland's first urban public building in the international style, completed in 1951. Opposite it are the western blocks of the **International Financial Services Centre** of the early 1990s.

Aldborough House has a beautifully proportioned three-storey façade and tall, slender piano nobile windows over a portico supported on four Tuscan columns. It is in remarkably good condition considering the uses and abuses it has suffered over the last two hundred years. Recently architects Howley and Harrington received planning permission to restore it as the headquarters of the Irish Musical Rights Organisation, but the scheme has since been abandoned and at time of writing the property is on the market again.

Aldborough House

3

twenty streets. Aldborough House was begun in 1793, but when finished, Lady Aldborough refused to enter it.

The house remained empty until 1813 when it was purchased by Professor von Feinagle of Luxembourg as a school for 'the higher classes of youth'. The Professor was an educational theorist who claimed that his system developed the reasoning powers above the ordinary without enlarging the time usually devoted to the Greek and Latin languages alone, and his course included mathematics, modern languages, fencing and dancing. On the Professor's death in 1820, the school was continued for some years under a deed of trust. During the Crimean War, the building was converted into a barrack, but subsequently remained unused for nearly fifty years until taken over by the General Post Office, in the possession of which it still remains as stores. The front is stone, with curved wings, one now demolished, and the chief feature of the interior is a winding, white stone staircase in a great hall of the same height as the building. This so often unwanted house escaped damage from the bombs dropped in its vicinity in the summer of 1941.

The district on the left of North Strand is known as Ballybough (*Baile-bocht*, the town of the poor). It was a favoured quarter in turn of the Quaker, Huguenot and Jewish settlers during the seventeenth and eighteenth centuries. Just north of the bridge over the Tolka at Ballybough is the earliest Jewish cemetery in Ireland.

Ballybough was very probably the central point of the Battle of Clontarf, which took place on Good Friday, 1014, and ended in a great Irish victory over the Norse adventurers into Ireland under King Sitric. The Danish front extended to the mouth of the Tolka, and the Irish advanced from Drumcondra. The fight lasted from sunrise until the dusk of the evening when the full tide carried the ships away—the words are Malachi's, who, after the fall of Brian Boroimhe in the battle, took on the kingship of Ireland.

> *When Malachi wore the collar of gold,*
> *Which he won from the proud invader*
> Thomas Moore

After the Norman invasion the lands of Clontarf were granted to Adam de Feypo by Hugh de Lacy, Earl of Meath.

From Newcomen Bridge the North Strand road enters Fairview after crossing the Tolka. On the right is Fairview Park, which is bounded by the railway on the far side. The Park was created in recent years out of the

At the junction of Portland Row and Amiens Street are the **Five Lamps**, erected in 1797 as a memorial to General Henry Hall of the Indian Army.

The old **Jewish cemetery** is still there, shaded by a great sycamore tree and hidden from view of the street by a gable-fronted sexton's house with a granite plaque bearing the inscription 'Built in the year 5618' (1858) above the door. Burials in the cemetery began about 1718, and the last interment took place in 1958.

House at Jewish Cemetery

sloblands. Inland, on the left, are modern building estates which bear the general name of Marino (see Route 2).

At Marino Crescent, a group of eighteenth-century houses, a road to the left leads to Malahide by Coolock (see Route 2). Beyond the Crescent is the Howth road, also inland to the left. The Dollymount road continues along the shore and rejoins the Howth road at Raheny. It is at present (1948) being re-engineered as a modern concrete road, on the site of the old tramway.

Detour: Dollymount and St Anne's to Raheny

	Miles
Clontarf Sheds	3½
Bull Wall	4
Dollymount & St Anne's	5
Raheny	5¾

This detour passes under the railway bridge, near which is the site of the Royal Marine Charter School, formerly conspicuous with a large dome. On the sloblands opposite are the remains of a lead mine. Clontarf Castle is reached from Clontarf Avenue to the left of the Dollymount road.

The Castle dates from the early English Pale. It was created by one of Hugh de Lacy's followers (in the reign of Henry II). The lands of Clontarf were a commandery of the Knights Templars in the same reign; later they were an appanage of the Priory of Kilmainham. Sir John Rawson, the last Prior, was created Viscount Clontarf by Henry VIII. Subsequently the possessions of the establishment were conferred on a Cromwellian soldier who sold them to John Vernon, ancestor of the Vernon family. The last vestiges of the ancient castle were taken down by J. E. Venables Vernon in 1853 when the present neo-Gothic structure was created to the design of Morrison, who was also the architect of Kilruddery, Bray. The house is at present occupied by J. G. Oulton, Esq.

We now come to the Sheds of Clontarf, so called from several sheds or penthouses erected for the preserving of fish; and just beyond them are three or four houses with very pretty wrought-iron balconies.

Kincora Road is at a turn to the left; on it, at 26, lives Erwin Schrödinger, the famous physicist. The Bull Wall is on the right, leading to the North Bull, a sickle-shaped sandbank, which has gradually appeared in the past 100 years (see Route 20 for North Bull). On it are the Royal Dublin Golf Club, the premier Irish Golf Club, and a bird sanctuary; it is the scene of

Marino Crescent continues in use two hundred years after it was built, as offices and apartments. It has a comfortable scale and the variety of parapet heights and doorcase types give it a pleasant informality. Unfortunately, few of the original elements such as windows, fanlights and garden railings have survived, and some front gardens have been turned into carparks. Bram Stoker was born at No. 15 on 8 November 1847.

Marino Crescent

The **sloblands** and the remains of the lead mine are gone today and the view across the mouth of the Tolka has changed significantly since 1949. Up until then, only a small area of land between the Liffey and Tolka rivers had been reclaimed. By the end of the twentieth century, the area of land reclaimed had been quadrupled and densely built upon, dramatically altering the skyline visible from the Clontarf shore. The name Fort View can still be seen on a Clontarf gate pier, but not since the 1930s has it been possible to see the Pigeon House fort from here.

Clontarf Avenue is today called Castle Avenue. Morrison's **Clontarf Castle** is now a hotel, and the tower-house is still the major feature of the building, externally and internally, where it forms two walls of the tall, glazed Reception atrium.

The **Schrödinger** house, where the scientist lived between 1939 and 1956, is a pleasant, red brick semi-detached dwelling. Beyond is a terrace of semi-detached, flat-roofed **international style houses**, the first of their kind to appear in Ireland, designed in 1930 by J. V. Downes.

a chapter in Joyce's *A Portrait of the Artist as a Young Man*. Half of it belonged to the Vernons, half to the Guinnesses; it is now municipal property. Beyond Kincora is Baymount, a private school for girls, and adjoining Baymount is the property known as St Anne's. The immense mansion here was built for Sir Benjamin Lee Guinness, and was lived in for many years by his son, Lord Ardilaun, a great benefactor of Dublin. The gardens are magnificent. St Anne's was inherited by the late Benjamin Plunkett, Bishop of Meath, a relative of the Guinnesses, from whom it was ultimately purchased by Dublin Corporation for housing purposes. The house was used as a civil defence depot during the war, 1939–44, when it was largely burnt by an accidental fire. At a corner of the estate, Watermill Bridge, the road turns inland to meet the Howth road at Raheny.

Return to the main route

Returning to the main route, we pass through the inland parts of Clontarf, one of the earliest suburbs of Dublin, consisting of 'a complicated system of roads and by-paths, meandering pleasantly along under a continual canopy of green foliage, broken only by the shrubs and foliage of an occasional villa' (D. A. Chart's *Dublin*, in Medieval Towns Series, Dent & Co.) Modern building has, however, destroyed much of the old charm of Clontarf, and indeed of the road to Howth as a whole.

At Ashbrook, one of the 'occasional' villas of the older Clontarf, lived the Rev. John Gwynn, Regius Professor of Divinity at Trinity College and editor of the *Book of Armagh* (d. 1917). He married a daughter of Smith O'Brien and was father of a notable family which included a Provost of Trinity (E. W. Gwynn) and the author, soldier and sportsman Stephen Gwynn.

Killester, an ex-serviceman's settlement, is a little off the Howth road on the left. It has a fine, new Catholic church, and a convent school (St Brigid's) in red brick of elegant eighteenth-century design. Beyond Killester, on the right, is Furry Park, one of the most attractive of the smaller residences in the neighbourhood of Dublin. During the War of Independence, it was occupied by the late Mrs Llewellyn Davies, who acted as hostess and protectress to Irish political leaders, and was also a benefactress of Irish literature.

At Raheny, 5 miles north-east from the GPO, are two churches, St Assin's of interesting modern design, and All Saints' (Church of Ireland). All Saints' was rebuilt in 1609, and again about 1880, on another site, by the Guinness family.

Down on the seafront road, although the Sheds are gone, I was surprised to find how many of the houses shown on the 1870 OS map are extant, among them **Mount Vernon**, and hidden behind a screen of modern houses, **Baymount**, now called Manresa. Originally known as Granby Hall, it was renovated in 1838 by Robert Warren in the castellated Gothic style popular at the time. It was later bought by the Loreto Sisters, who established a girls' school there. In 1898 it came into the possession of Lord Ardilaun, as did a number of the properties that surrounded his demesne at St Anne's. About 1914 William Lucas Scott established a preparatory school for boys there for a time, and it was later lived in by J. T. Gwynn, one of the literary and academic family. It was acquired by the Jesuit order in 1949 as a novitiate; the modern extensions have, thankfully, not interfered with the original house. The Prayer Room built in 1992 has five stained-glass windows by Evie Hone which had been in the Jesuit house at Rahan, Co. Offaly. The ornate, castellated Gothic gate-lodge, although cut off from the main house, still survives in very good order, fronting onto Mount Prospect Avenue.

St Anne's (1952)

What remained of the great house of **St Anne's** deteriorated under an onslaught of vandalism during the 1950s and 1960s, and it was eventually demolished by Dublin Corporation in 1968. A grassy mound marks where the house was, but the quality of the surviving gate-lodge and elaborate Tudor-style red brick stables hint at the splendour of the original house.

Although there are plenty of the 'occasional' villas of old Clontarf such as Beverly Hall still remaining, **Ashbrook** is no longer there; only its name lives on at the entrance to a recent, pleasant, well-planted development of town houses.

Furry Park, a 5-bay, 3-storey house with granite string courses and doorcase, was a frequent hiding place of Michael Collins during the War of Independence. It was saved by local protestors when it was in danger of demolition a few years ago. Today it is in office use and in a setting that could be improved.

St Assam's ceased to be used as a church when the new, more spacious Catholic church was opened on the other side of the road in 1962.

Raheny derives its name from an ancient rath in the village, and formed part of the lands granted by a Danish king of Dublin to the Holy Trinity Church. In this vicinity survive a few country seats established by the merchant princes of eighteenth-century Dublin, such as Sybil Hill, Raheny Park and Manor House. Raheny Park is now the residence of G. L. Jameson, Managing Director of John Jameson & Co. The Manor House was built by a member of the Grace family and was later owned by W. Sweetman, a brewer, who built a school in the village for the Catholic poor. A Protestant public school had been erected by Samuel Dick, governor of the Bank of Ireland 1797–9, who bequeathed the rents of eight houses for its support.

Detour: The Donahies

At Raheny is a road to the left, leading to the 'Hole-in-the-Wall' where it meets a road joining the Dublin and Malahide road with that from Sutton to Portmarnock. On the road is The Donahies, a beautiful house in red brick, long and low, with a sunken fence or 'ha-ha' before it. It was formerly owned by the Caseys and is now in the possession of the Kennedys, of the firm of bakers. It was originally called St Donagh's, and there is a holy well of that name in a field opposite. About fifty years ago there was a tree in the lawn of Donahies with an iron hoop and chain on it; it was said to be the tree to which James II tied his horse on the way to Dublin, and the district between Donahies and the Malahide road is known as the 'Cry Helps' because the remnants of the king's army had passed through it.

Return to the main route

Upon leaving Raheny, the Howth road rejoins the sea coast, with Sutton strand on the right. On the left is Kilbarrack Cemetery. Here was buried Francis Higgins, the informer known as the Sham Squire, who betrayed Lord Edward Fitzgerald and the Sheares brothers to the Government in 1798. Higgins, who started his life as a waiter in a tavern, inveigled a girl of position and wealth into marriage, and then became a spy and journalist. His grave at Kilbarrack had to be protected from the fury of the mob, and the body was removed for sale to a hospital. Kilbarrack Abbey, or Chapel of Mone, formerly belonged to St Mary's Abbey and is thought to have been built to assist to shipwrecked sailors.

Sutton is a modern suburb situated on the well-populated isthmus connecting Howth to the mainland. Facing the strand is Warren Villa, residence of J. McDowell Esq., jeweller, who owned the winner of the

Raheny is a bustling modern village centre surrounding a small hill on which stand the ruins of the old church. Nearby is a fine granite cross commemorating Marie Hayes, a missionary doctor who died in 1908 in the service of the poor in India. Across the road in the midst of valuable real estate, it is a pleasant surprise to find a surviving crescent of tiny Gothic cottages with leaded windows. In the middle of the village, the building housing Luigi's Restaurant began life in the late eighteenth century as Samuel Dick's Charity School. Dick, a one-time Governor of the Bank of Ireland, lived in nearby Edenmore House (formerly Violet Hill); he was also responsible for the crescent of cottages mentioned above, which date from the last years of the eighteenth century.

Farther along the Howth Road, **Sybil Hill** (which first appears on Taylor's Map of 1816) became the nucleus of St Paul's College run by the Vincentian Fathers; the coach house is now a community centre.

Manor House, built as a dower house by the St Lawrence family, was demolished in 1956 to make room for the red brick buildings of Manor House School run by the Poor Servants of the Mother of God; the original Portland stone gate piers still survive on Watermill Road. **Raheny Park** was also demolished about that time. The majestic line of holm oaks that line the southern side of the Howth road here, planted about 100 years ago along the northern boundary of St Anne's, are a surviving legacy from the days of the great demesnes.

Nothing remains of **The Donahies** now except the name; it was demolished in 1969. A vast desert of housing, occasionally punctuated by schools and featureless grassland 'open spaces' covers the landscape. A large shopping centre of the 1980s does little to alleviate the visual poverty of the Donaghmede area. The old name 'Hole-in-the-Wall' also still lives on, attached to the new, broad road heading north.

Warren Villa has gone, its place taken by St Fintan's High School and a varied row of latter-day villas.

The Donahies

Grand National of 1947. Near the railway was discovered in 1927 the site of a cemetery of stone-lined graves.

Detour: Baldoyle & Portmarnock to Malahide 3½ miles

The road follows a creek or inlet formed between the mainland and the long tract of sand north of Howth. On it are situated the villages of Baldoyle and Portmarnock.

Baldoyle is mentioned in the Register of All Hallows as the subject of a grant (*c.* 1152) to the Bishops of Louth made by Dermot MacMurrough, the King of Leinster who brought the Normans into Ireland. Some historians identify it with Baldough where, in 1369, William de Windsor held a parliament on his arrival in Ireland as King's Lieutenant. Lodging was so difficult in the poor village that the Commons granted de Windsor £3,000 for permission to disperse.

Baldoyle is now chiefly known for its racecourse, which is owned by Dublin Corporation; it is also a popular bathing resort. The principal public building is the Catholic Church of St Peter and St Paul, rebuilt about 1831 with a portico of four Tuscan pilasters surmounted by a pediment. At the Grange are the picturesque ruins of an old church.

At Portmarnock, nine miles from the General Post Office, also conveniently reached by the Hole-in-the-Wall, or from Malahide, the Castle on the rock close to the shore is called Rob's Walls or Robuck's Wall and was founded by a sept of the de Birminghams. The manor belonged for centuries to a branch of the Plunkett family, which still has a seat at Portmarnock House. About a mile from the railway station near the magnificent 'velvet strand' of Portmarnock is St Marnock's, a mansion built by John Jameson, son of John Jameson of Prussia Street and the Bow Street distillery. John Jameson was succeeded here by his brother, William, after whose death in 1938 it was purchased by the Corporation. It is now a luxury hotel.

Return to the main route

The peninsula of Howth is two miles in length and 1½ miles broad, and comprises an area of close to 5,000 acres, the greater part of which is occupied by the hill, a landmark of unusual interest.

'All to the west of Dublin,' writes Stephen Gwynn (*Fair Hills of Ireland*), 'and all to the north is a plain stretching away westward almost to the dead level of the Shannon, and north with very slight undulations to the

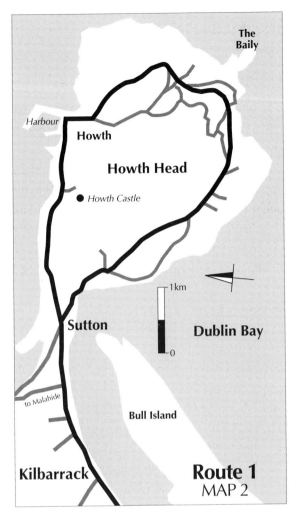

The Baily

Harbour

Howth

Howth Head

● *Howth Castle*

1km

Sutton

Dublin Bay

to Malahide

Bull Island

Kilbarrack

Route 1
MAP 2

Baldoyle racecourse, established in 1860, was closed in the 1970s, and awaits development.

Baldoyle church of about 1830 is still an impressive edifice, standing against the background of the Baldoyle inlet. The granite used for the pilasters and pediment came from Lambay Island, and it is said that the original communion table, altarpiece and windows were provided from the Protestant church of St Nicholas Within in an unusual ecumenical gesture. The ceiling decoration, probably carried out in the nineteenth century, has motifs of a ship's wheel and lifejackets, referring to Baldoyle's maritime background. The original local Boys' and Girls' National Schools, to the left and right of the church and built around the same time, have been converted into a dwelling and a parish centre.

The ruins of **Grange Abbey**, designated a National Monument in 1985, are extant, standing in a grassy open space on the site of an early Christian foundation.

Robuck's Wall is extant and occupied; farther on is a **Martello tower** called locally 'Pa Hick's Tower', converted in 1910 by architect Frederick Hicks, incorporating a pyramidal roof of terracotta Wollscroft tiles, topped by a cast-bronze weathervane depicting a galleon in full sail. After Hicks's death in 1963 the weathervane was stolen.

Portmarnock House was burnt in 1954, and subsequently demolished.

St Marnock's is still in use as a hotel.

13

Carlingford range of hills. But here, on the northern limit of Dublin Bay, is flung down this detached block of mountain—for if cliff and rock and heather and bold outline make a mountain Howth is surely one, though barely half a thousand feet in height; and rising abruptly from sea and plain, it dominates the landscape.'

About 1½ miles from Sutton railway station, on the Burrow road, which takes the northern side of the peninsula, are the town and harbour of Howth, with a population of about 1,500. Previous to the construction of the Harbour of Dunleary, Howth was the chief packet station for Holyhead, over £400,000 having been expended upon it between 1807 and 1810. The piers consisted of rock quarried from the hill above, and rested on foundations of red-grit stone from Cheshire; the work was characterised as a 'beautiful product of English thought and Irish taxation'. With the application of steam, the passage to Holyhead took seven hours on average from Howth, as contrasted with fourteen from the old station at the Pigeon House. Howth remained a packet station until 1832, and then the harbour, choked with sand and mud from the bank on the west side, resumed its former character, when the chief sight of the day was the going and coming of the fishing fleet.

George IV landed at Howth in 1821, immediately after his coronation. 'the first view of a King that Ireland had had since the Boyne' (Curtis, *History of Ireland*). The visit aroused great enthusiasm, which was encouraged by Daniel O'Connell, the Catholic and Repeal leader. Of more important ultimate consequence to Ireland was the arrival at Howth, on 26 July 1914, of Erskine Childers's yacht, the *Asgard*, conveying 1,500 rifles from Hamburg to the Irish Volunteers; for this event may be considered as the start of the physical force movement which ended seven years later with the British withdrawal from the twenty-six counties. The Volunteers collected the arms without hindrance, but on the way to Dublin were intercepted at Marino by Government troops (see Route 2).

To the right of Howth is Howth Castle, the seat of thirty successive barons of Howth. Prior to the Norman conquest, Howth was in the hands of the Ostman family of MacTorcaill; Strongbow gave it to Almeria, the first of the St Lawrences, who became the barons of Howth. Almeria is said to have taken the name of St Lawrence because he beat off an Irish attack on St Lawrence's Day. The Castle is now inherited by the Gaisford St Lawrences. Unlike many Norman barons, the St Lawrences never joined an opposition to an English king, and they held their lands without

Howth Castle is today in need of restoration. For some years the **Dublin Transport Museum**, brainchild of architect James Kilroy, has been housed there; among the restored vehicles on display is one of the original Howth trams, which ran around the Head from Sutton Station to Howth Station until the line was closed in 1959.

Howth Castle

diminution or accretion through the centuries. According to a tradition from the Elizabethan period, Grace O'Malley, the rebel princess of Connaught, being refused hospitality by the then Baron of Howth, kidnapped the young heir in his cradle, and restored him only when the family engaged never again to close the Castle at dinner hour; and there is still always an empty chair at Howth.

The present building is an irregular, mid-eighteenth-century mansion, flanked by square towers at each extremity—the combinations, a writer in the 1860s observed, indicated clearly that its proportions were 'the result of additions made from time to time with more regard to convenience than style'. Many of the contents of the house are of great historical interest, such as a two-headed sword said to have been used by Sir Armoricus and a painting of the young heir who was carried off by Grace O'Malley. Swift was a friend and frequent visitor of the 26th baron, by whom he was persuaded to sit for the famous full-length portrait by Bindon, which represents him holding one of his Drapier letters in his hand, while prostrate at his feet is the naked figure of William Wood, writhing in agony and clutching the patent which empowered him to loose a debased coinage upon Ireland. The demesne of the Castle is very large and the pleasure grounds are celebrated for their rhododendrons and flowering shrubs. In a dip in the ground adjoining the east side of the demesne is a cromlech or giant's grave, which legend connects with Aideen, the wife of Oscar, who died of grief when Oscar fell with other Fenians, and also with the love legend of Diarmuid and Grania. Grania, daughter of King Cormac Mac Art, fled from Finn, the Fenian chief, with Diarmuid across Ireland to Sligo; and cromlechs are said to mark their resting-places. The table is a huge quartz of irregular form, eighteen feet in length and twelve in breadth, and it had supporters—now collapsed—which were seven feet in height.

In the centre of the town of Howth is the Abbey of St Nessan, which was originally founded on Ireland's Eye, where was preserved the Book of Gospels known as the Garland of Howth, now to be seen in the Library of Trinity College, Dublin. The establishment was removed to the mainland in 1228 by Archbishop Luke of Dublin. The enclosure in Howth contains the remains of two buildings called the Abbey and College, and among the monuments is one of marble to Christopher, 13th Baron of Howth, and to his wife; it was erected in 1438, and is decorated with sculptured elements of the Crucifixion. The College consisted of a hall, kitchen and seven cells.

Howth Abbey

In these days of usually paying an entry fee into 'heritage monuments,' it is a pleasure to find that **Howth Abbey** is one of the few places remaining where a sign on the gate gives you the address nearby where you can obtain the key of the church, and make your own personal tour. There is an occupied dwelling, with aluminium windows in medieval stone surrounds, in a part of the old monastery.

Ireland's Eye

Facing Howth Harbour lies the little island of the sons of Nessan called Ireland's Eye, and beyond this islet out to sea lies the much larger Lambay (for which see Route 3). The Eye (Norse for island) is mainly composed of a high rock and produces medicinal plants. Some vestiges of the old Abbey remain, much restored in the nineteenth century.

In 1852, William Burke Kirwan, a professional artist in comfortable circumstances, was tried, convicted and sentenced to death for the murder of his wife while they were alone together in an excursion to this island. Kirwan's defence was that his wife, whose body was found on a rock from which the tide had receded, took a seizure while bathing. His case was prejudiced by the common knowledge that he had lived for twelve years with a Miss Kenny in Sandymount, by whom he had a family of seven children. The medical evidence as to signs of violence on the body was unsatisfactory; but the judge passed sentence of death which was commuted by the Lord Lieutenant to penal servitude for life. During the trial, the unhappy Miss Kenny suffered dreadful persecution, and was driven with her children from lodging to lodging. Kirwan was immured on Spike Island, and for many years his house at 11 Upper Merrion Street remained untenanted. It was said to be haunted, and when it was at last taken, the new tenant found two skeletons, on digging up the back garden. Kirwan was released after twenty-seven years; there is a tradition among the fisher folk of Howth that he revisited the scene of the tragedy before sailing to America to join the mother of his children. (See *Famous Irish Trials* by Judge Bodkin.)

The poet Yeats spent some years of his boyhood at Howth, first at Balscadden Cottage, a low, thatched house above the cliff, and then at Island View, overlooking the harbour. He composed his first plays and poems while wandering about the glades and hill paths of the Head. He has told how he would often sleep out at nights, sometimes in a cave below the cliffs and sometimes among the rocks and rhododendrons in the wilder parts of the grounds of the Castle. He was absorbed at that time in natural history; and, fresh from the study of Darwin and Haeckel, he used to 'plague' a geologist from Guinness's Brewery, who came with a hammer to seek for evidences against Darwin's theory in the bowels of Howth (Yeats *Autobiographies*).

Another poet of Howth was Sir Samuel Ferguson (see his poem 'Congal'). He died at Strand Lodge in 1886.

Balscadden House, Howth

Balscadden Cottage has become Balscadden House, and the thatch has been replaced by slates. In the 1980s it was the home of the late Phil Lynnott, rock singer and musician. **Island View** on Harbour Road is also extant.

Strand Lodge can be found on Claremont Road.

From Howth railway station an electric tramway (GNR) crosses the hill and leads back to Sutton along its southern brow. Near the Baily post office is Earlscliff, the country retreat of Professor Mahaffy (d. 1920), Provost of Trinity, philosophical divine, wit, scholar and sportsman. Away to the east are Puck's Rock and the precipitous headland known as the Nose of Howth. At the south-eastern extremity of the hill is the Baily lighthouse which appears from the shore through a vista of two pointed rocks known as the Needles. Here in the first century was the stronghold of King Crimthan, whose sepulchral cairn crowns the summit of Sliabh Martin, 560 feet above the sea, the highest pinnacle of Ben-Eadair, as Howth was anciently called until at the Danish invasions the name was supplanted by Hovud. From the Baily the electric tramway conducts inland in a gradual descent towards Sutton by the Carrickbrack and Ceancor roads, on the latter of which is situated Tansey House, formerly the residence of C. Twistleton-Wykeham-Fiennes Esq., and now of Hugh Pack Beresford Esq. Here the residents enjoy the southern aspect and grand prospects of Dublin Bay, which sweeps for twelve miles in a continuous background of hills, ending where Bray Head drops into the sea, like a last musical note. At the right, on the cultivated lower slopes of the hill, is situated the little estate known as the Cliffs, where Sir William Orpen, RA, spent several painting holidays in the years before the First World War. Next door, at Carrickbrack, lived Margaret Stokes, the celebrated archaeologist. Nearer Sutton, at Barren Hill House, a road to the left of the railway tramway road leads to the coastguard station and to Sutton House, which was built on the site of an older property by the late Right Hon. Andrew Jameson, who was chairman for many years of Jameson's distillery and a Senator of the Irish Free State. The house has been lately purchased by Mrs Van der Elst, a prominent figure in the agitation against capital punishment. At the foot of the hill, where the tram rejoins the railway, is the Marine Hotel, Sutton.

The **Baily Post Office** is gone, but the nearby **Eastcliff**, Earlscliffe on the nineteenth-century maps, is still there. **Tansey House** nestles beautifully in its fine gardens, and although not visible from the road, **The Cliffs** is extant, as are **Carrickbrack House** and **Barren Hill House**.

Barren Hill House, Howth

The **Coastguard Station** and its dwellings have been converted into a terrace of much-sought-after private dwellings; and **Sutton House** is now in use as a luxury hotel.

Although there has been a lot of luxury villa development on Howth during the last fifty years, a considerable area of the peninsula remains untouched, in pasture or heath.

Robinson Keeffe and Devane's church at Sutton, completed in 1973, with a copper roof and cast-in-situ walls, was one of the earlier churches designed to take into account the liturgical innovations of the Second Vatican Council.

ROUTE 2

MALAHIDE

	Miles from the GPO
Fairview	1
Marino Crescent	1¾
Donnycarney	2
Artane	3
Coolock	4
Belcamp	5
Balgriffin (St Dolough's)	6½
Malahide	9

The road to Malahide from the General Post Office issues by Talbot Street at Amiens Street Station, the terminus of the Great Northern Railway, and takes its course along the North Strand road, over the Tolka and past Fairview to Marino Crescent (see Route 1).

It was at Marino Crescent, on 26 July 1914, that the Irish Volunteers of 1913–14 first came into conflict with Government troops. They were carrying rifles landed at Howth (see Route 1), and, news of the operation having reached Dublin by telephone, a force of police with 200 Scottish Borderers was sent to intercept them. The Volunteers refused to surrender the guns, and, after a slight conflict, took to the fields, taking the arms with them. The Scottish Borderers marched back to Dublin, and, while passing Bachelor's Walk, were greeted by the crowd with jeers, stones and sticks. Some of the soldiers fired, and three men were killed, and others, including women and children, were injured. The shooting caused a great sensation, and greatly embarrassed the Liberal Government which had allowed the Orangemen in the North to run arms without interference.

On the left, farther on, is the well-laid-out Griffith Avenue, leading towards Glasnevin. The Avenue is of modern construction and takes its name from Arthur Griffith (d. 1921), the journalist and editor who founded the Sinn Féin movement and was head of the Provisional Government after the Treaty of 1921.

Beyond Griffith Avenue and before Donnycarney are the grounds of Marino, now in part built over with small villas, and in part occupied by the O'Brien Institute of the Christian Brothers, a great pile in red brick.

On the left opposite **Marino Crescent** is the **Marino housing scheme** of the late 1920s, the earliest such scheme to be embarked upon by Dublin Corporation after the foundation of the Free State. For scale, colour and variety it has seldom been equalled since.

Marino housing scheme

The **O'Brien Institute** is now owned by Dublin City Council Fire Department, and is used as a training centre for brigade personnel.

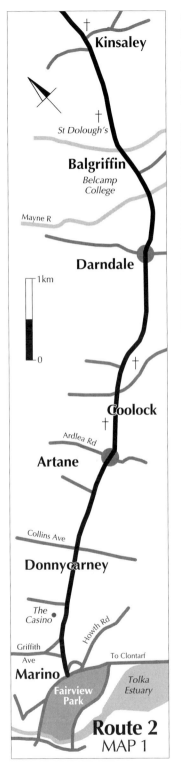

Marino was once the seat of Lord Charlemont, a leader of the Volunteers in 1782. This remarkable nobleman was never put to either school or college, but was accompanied to Italy by his tutor, Edward Murphy, who directed his tastes towards the fine arts; and it is fitting that his town house in Parnell Square should now be the Municipal Art Gallery. The Marino property, earlier the residence of a Cromwellian Attorney General, was a gift to Charlemont from his stepfather, but he carried out upon it extensive additions and alterations, and filled it with artistic treasures. On the grounds he erected, after a design by Sir William Chambers (the architect of the house in Parnell Square), a beautiful temple called the Casino, in which he placed many treasures. The building is visible from the road and is well worth a visit. It is a National Monument in the charge of the Board of Works. Inside and out it is a gem of the eighteenth century, and known as such to all connoisseurs of architecture, and, although too little care was formerly taken to preserve the interior from strolling vandals, one can still admire the fine carvings of the woodwork, and the handsome ceilings. Marino House was demolished in 1930; the family had lived there till 1870.

The village of Donnycarney is passed immediately after the Marino demesne. It is memorable for its mention in a poem by James Joyce (*Chamber Music*):

> *O, it was out by Donnycarney*
> *When the bat flew from tree to tree …*

There is a golf course here. At Cherrymount lives M. J. McManus, Esq., the bibliographer and Literary Editor of the *Irish Press*. In the early eighteenth century, Donnycarney was one of the country seats of the patriotic Sir John Perceval (later First Earl of Egmont), who was the friend and only patron of the philosopher Berkeley.

At Donnycarney, Collins Avenue is on the left of the Santry Road (see Route 3). This is called after General Michael Collins, who was shot in 1922 while operating as Commander-in-Chief of the forces of the Provisional Government. He was commemorated, with Arthur Griffith, in a temporary monument on Leinster Lawn, now removed.

At Artane, three miles from the General Post Office, is a large Industrial School and a burial ground, where there is a tombstone of the Hollywood family, to which belonged the manor for many years. A noted seventeenth-century Jesuit was a member of this family, to which also may have belonged Johannes de Sacro Bosco, the thirteenth-century natural

The Casino passed into the care of the State when **Marino House** was demolished in 1930. On completion of substantial refurbishment work, it was re-opened to the public in 1984. The exquisite building stands in an unfortunate palisaded compound and is in great need of suitable landscaping. The building's decorative stone carving represents the finest and most intricate work in the country, but erosion is beginning to take its toll.

The Casino

I could find no trace of **Cherrymount**.

Artane Boys' School is famous for its band, which plays at all major GAA fixtures at Croke Park. Although much of the land surrounding the school, originally an extensive farm that allowed the place to be self-sufficient in food, was sold for housing developent in recent years, the main school building, a great Victorian granite-faced pile, is extant.

philosopher, who was a Professor at the University of Paris, and the corrector of the Julian Calendar.

On the left at Artane, Skelly's Lane leads into Beaumont Road, Drumcondra, where, on the right, is Beaumont Convalescent Home (see Route 3).

To the right, after Artane, a road leads to Killester (see Route 3).

Just before Coolock, 4 miles from the General Post Office, is Coolock House, formerly the residence of the late R. F. S. Colvill, a member of the well-known Dublin business family, four of whose members were, in succession, Governors of the Bank of Ireland. It is now a nursing home. In the village, on the right, is St Brendan's Catholic Church, with a belfry over the entrance. To the left is another road to Santry; on the right, in the direction of Raheny, are St Brendan's Well and the Church of Ireland church. On a common near this church were assembled in 1803 a great concourse of people connected with Emmet's rebellion, ready to march upon Dublin. Many handsome seats and villas with fine views of the city and the bay in the vicinity of Coolock were built in the late eighteenth and early nineteenth centuries for Dublin citizens; among them may be noticed Brookville, formerly the residence of the banking family of Law, now of Mr Reynolds, the chairman of Córas Iompair Éireann (Great Southern Railways).

About half a mile beyond Coolock, on the left, is the Transvaal Poultry Farm and three-quarters of a mile beyond the farm is a third road to Santry, which passes Belcamp Park, recently bought by Mr Griffith. The oldest part of this house was built in 1681 by the Rev. Patrick Grattan. Here lived, in the early eighteenth century, the widow of Rev. Patrick Grattan, with her seven sons, the eldest of whom was the grandfather of Henry Grattan, who, in 1782, accomplished the independence of the Irish Parliament. Swift was a frequent visitor of the Grattans, and commemorated the family in verse:

> O! were but you and I so wise
> To see with Robert Grattan's eyes!
> Robert adores that spot of earth,
> That literal spot that gave him birth;
> And swears Belcamp is to his taste,
> As fine as Hampton Court at best.

Opposite to Belcamp Park is Belcamp House, and farther west is the property, formerly Clinshogh, now known as Woodlands. Built by the Rev. John Jackson, vicar of Santry, who was another of Swift's friends, Woodlands

Beaumont Convalescent Home is still there, next to the modern **Beaumont Hospital**, opened in 1988.

Coolock House is extant, in use as a convent, and although it has been considerably altered, its fine doorcase has survived.

The original **St Brendan's church** is now a parish hall. Nearby stands the **Tayto factory**, a highly regarded *in situ* concrete design of the early 1970s by David Watkins Cronin.

St John's Church of Ireland church stands forlorn on an eminence in the midst of modern housing and sterile green spaces, with a backdrop of the vast and bland rere wall of the Omni Centre. Of **St Brendan's Well** I could find no trace.

In the midst of a housing estate **Brookville** can still be found; the Sisters of the Holy Rosary run a retirement home here for their nuns. The house is probably older than it looks, and in spite of being much altered, retains some good interior features and a claire voie balcony screen which barely survives the modern addition of an entrance porch. The house has been recently re-roofed; during the work, the original covering was found to be thin stone slabs rather than traditional slates.

The **Transvaal Farm** has disappeared, built over with a bleak suburbia. The site of **Belcamp Park**, now a large public park, can be found to the west along the M50 extension. The house came into Corporation ownership in 1969, and was burnt down in 1977.

Across the road from the site of Belcamp Park, at time of writing, **Belcamp House** stands bare-chimneyed and roofless after another fire. **Woodlands**, a house of unusual design by Lovett Pearce, can be seen in a sylvan setting west of Clonshaugh Road.

Belcamp Park, 1975

was probably designed by Sir Edward Lovett Pearce. It is a red-brick structure, surmounted by a glass observatory with chimney stacks at each corner of the roof, and used to be called locally Swift's house (see *The Correspondence of Swift*, edited by Elrington Ball, vol. 5, p. 295). It now belongs to Major-General McKenna, Irish Army Staff.

High up on a field, on the left, at the entrance to Balgriffin village, is Belcamp Hall, a Junior College of the Oblates of St Mary Immaculate. It was the seat of the eighteenth-century politician Sir E. Newenham, who flourished during the American war of independence and had a great admiration for George Washington, in whose honour he built a tower which still stands beside the dam that holds the lower pond. In this pond his heir was drowned. Adjoining Belcamp Hall is Belcamp Hutchinson, owned by A. Blair White. The house was built by Hely Hutchinson, Provost of Trinity College Dublin (1774).

Balgriffin, 6½ miles from the GPO, formerly belonged to the ancient family of de Burgos, who held the manor in the fourteenth century. It afterwards became the property of the O'Neills and de Bathes, and the castle, out of the materials of which Balgriffin Park was built, was for some time the residence of Richard Talbot, Earl of Tyrconnel, Lord Deputy of Ireland under James II, who sought to make Ireland a Kingdom under French protection. On the Mayne river is Balgriffin Park which was partially destroyed by fire forty years ago. It has been restored, and the grounds are now a part of a fruit farm for Scott's factory. The land in this vicinity is remarkably rich.

Just beyond Balgriffin, on the right, is St Dolough's Park, where lived for many years the Irish landscape painter, Nathaniel Hone, RHA (d. 1917).

On the left, close to the road, is St Dolough's Church, a unique building. The hermit's cell is its oldest part and is said to date from the fifth century, when St Dolough (otherwise St Olave) built and inhabited it as its first hermit. He was succeeded by many others, who lived, died and were buried in the cell. They received their food through a small aperture, if the neighbours did not forget them. If they received food, they thanked God and ate; if not they still thanked God but went hungry. Through another aperture they heard Mass in the church. The present church however was not built until the eleventh century, when the reputation of the hermits for sanctity was so great that a small monastery was added to the cell. The church, the living room or refectory and the cell are all in perfect condition. The remains of such small stone churches are to be found all over

Belcamp Hall can be found in a wooded demesne north of the M50 extension. It is a fine eighteenth-century seven-bay, three-storey house with round-arched windows on the ground floor and a single-storey granite-faced breakfront around the entrance door. Bought by the Oblate Fathers in 1885, the top of the house was damaged by fire in 1921, and the roof was replaced with a flat roof. The nearby chapel, which was designed by Ashlin & Coleman and completed in 1903, has two Harry Clarke windows. The **Washington Tower** still stands overlooking the pond, although it is losing its stucco and has a shroud of ivy.

Belcamp Hall in 1976

Beyond Balgriffin village a narrow lane to the left leads to **Belcamp Hutchinson**, a fine late-eighteenth-century house with modest sweeps around a gravel fore-court. Described in 1801 as a 'large handsome brick house', it has a stucco finish today.

Balgriffin Park is no more, but **St Dolough's Park** is still there.

St Dolough's church and its surroundings are well worth a visit: the Gothic Revival addition was designed by W. H. Lynn and completed in 1865. North of St Dolough's is **Bohomer**, a pleasant five-bay Georgian farmhouse with a curious and tiny gate lodge with a triangular pediment.

29

Ireland; they are said by some antiquarians to be imitated from the original Christian churches of the southern countries. They seldom exceed 40 feet in length and 20 in breadth, being covered with stone roofs. Very few of these now exist in perfect condition, and St Dolough's is not only a perfect example of an ancient Irish foundation but has many other features which puzzle all antiquarians.

Attached to the cell and ancient church is a modern church in the same style, built in the nineteenth century and in use for Church of Ireland services.

Visitors should not miss the Baptistery in the adjacent field. St Patrick is said to have been baptised here, and the seat for the converts can still be seen. The octagonal stone cover to the well was erected in the early seventeenth century and, until recently, the remains of mural paintings could be seen within. These were the work of a member of the ancient family of Fagan, whose ruined house lies under the Hill of Feltrim.

On an eminence above St Dolough's Church is Lime Hill, described in *Dodds's Traveller's Guide Through Ireland* (1801) as one of the best-designed houses in the kingdom, and reflecting additional credit on the justly established reputation of Mr Pentland, the architect. It is now the residence of Mr George Symes.

Three-quarters of a mile from St Dolough's Church is Kinsaley village with, on the right, St Nicholas' Catholic Church and a road leading to the ruined church.

To the left of Kinsaley Bridge is Abbeville, the seat of Major Cusack. This is an early-eighteenth-century house, greatly enlarged by John Beresford, head of the Revenue Board in the years before the Union. He proposed to entertain lavishly and built a large reception room which is decorated with murals reputedly by Angelica Kaufmann. Amongst other additions was that of a kitchen with fourteen fireplaces.

Behind Abbeville, on a byroad, is Greenwood, where the Misses Montgomery, famous beauties, lived. Handel is said to have visited Greenwood during his Irish visit, and gave his name to Handel's Walk in the grounds.

A little beyond Abbeville, a turn to the left leads to Feltrim Hill, where bones were latterly discovered; at the back of it is Drynam House (see Route 3). Half a mile farther, the road begins to skirt Malahide Castle grounds.

A mile and a half farther on, where there is a turn to the left, stood a house called La Mancha, the scene of a murderous fire in 1922. Two houses

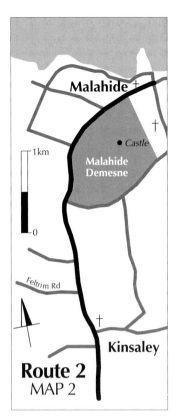

Malahide ✝

✝

● *Castle*

**Malahide
Demesne**

1km

0

Feltrim Rd

✝

Kinsaley

Route 2
MAP 2

I could not get to see **Lime Hill** but understand it is extant. **Kinsaley (Kinsealy) village** is intact, and consists of a row of cottages, an early nineteenth-century school that is now in use as a parish hall, and **St Nicholas's church** of similar date. Nearby, in the ruins of the old Kinsaley church the burial vault of the antiquary Austin Cooper, who died in 1830, can be found. Opposite the church ruin, on a hill, is **Kinsaley House**, an early-eighteenth-century brick-fronted house with a limestone Gibbsian doorcase.

Abbeville, currently the home of former Taoiseach Charles Haughey, is hidden in trees to the west of the main road.

Greenwood is no more.

Feltrim Hill has all but disappeared also, through the agency of Roadstone, and has contributed, in the form of concrete blocks, to the recent buildings of the Dublin area.

The ruins of **Drynam** have disappeared under a scheme of modern private houses.

St Nicholas's church, Kinsaley

(semi-detached, one a petrol station) are now in the former grounds. This eighteenth-century house belonged to a Mrs Robertson of Hogg and Robertson, who sold it to country farmers called MacDonnell, passing on to them her gardener. It is supposed that the latter believed that there was treasure in the garden (a former bulb farm, in which the MacDonnells allowed their neighbours dig for bulbs) and that, after murdering the MacDonnells, he set the house on fire with petrol. As the windows were left unopened, the fire failed to complete its work, and the bodies were found— two brothers, two sisters, a servant and a yard man. The gardener, who reported the fire to the police, was arrested, tried and executed. Mrs Robertson was convinced of her late gardener's innocence.

At the approach to Malahide, on the right, is Malahide Castle, the seat of Lord Talbot de Malahide. The building, hidden from the road by fine plantations, is large, irregular and unequal in height; among its treasures are a triptych belonging to Mary, Queen of Scots. It has two circular towers, but little remains of the original except the main hall. The manor and Castle were designated in 1274 to Richard Talbot, the common ancestor of the Earls of Shrewsbury and the Lords of Malahide, who accompanied Henry II to Ireland. This is a rare instance of a baronial estate continuing upwards of 650 years in the male line. Cromwell handed the property to his follower, Miles Corbett, who resided at Malahide until, at the Restoration, the Talbots regained possession of their estates. They supported James II and it is said that, after the Battle of the Boyne, nine Talbots of Malahide were laid out on the dining-room table. In the nineteenth century, the most notable member of the family was the eccentric astronomer Monsignor Talbot (d. 1886), Chancellor to Pope Pius IX, who was accused of acting for Manning in an intrigue against Newman. The mother of the present Lord Talbot de Malahide was a daughter of Sir James Boswell, second baronet of Auchinleck, through whom important papers of Boswell, Johnson's biographer, reached the Castle. These have lately been given to the world.

Near the Castle is an ancient church, with a decorated altar tomb of the Talbots, containing the remains of Maud Plunkett, maid, wife and widow in one day.

Malahide, a maritime town, with an area of 1,200 acres, lies 9 miles north of Dublin, on a narrow inlet of the sea, between Lambay Island, Ireland's Eye, and the promontory of Howth. The railway station is on the main line to Belfast, which here crosses the estuary. In 1570, Holinshed enumerated Malahide among the principal post-towns of Ireland, and in the eighteenth

Malahide Castle is now owned by Fingal County Council and is, with its gardens and extensive demesne, open to the public.

Malahide town has expanded greatly in recent decades, particularly along the waterfront, where a very large and densely planned development of apartments extends out into the Broadmeadow Estuary.

Malahide Castle

century it manufactured cotton on an extensive scale and had also an oyster fishery. The effort made in the nineteenth century to turn Malahide into a grandiose seaside resort failed to reach completion, although some handsome terraces and a large hotel were then built. Among the present residents are the poet Patrick MacDonogh, and Lynn Doyle, the Ulster humorist. There is also an exclusive golf club and a bird sanctuary at Malahide. The grave of Edmund Curtis, the historian, is in the churchyard of St Andrew's Church (Church of Ireland).

For Ireland's Eye, see Route 1. For Lambay see Route 3.

A return to Dublin may be made by Portmarnock (see Route 1).

Woodlands, Clonshaugh

	Miles from the GPO
Drumcondra	1½
Whitehall	2½
Santry	3¾
Collinstown	5
Swords	8
Donabate	12½
Lusk	13
Rush	16
Skerries	19
The Man of War	18

N.B. Balbriggan 23 by Skerries, 22 by the Man of War

From the GPO the route leads up Parnell (formerly Rutland) Square East. Down Hardwicke Street a fine view is obtained of St George's Church (Protestant), designed by Francis Johnston and finished in 1813. The turn to the right is taken down Dorset Street, and a closer view of the church follows immediately. The North Circular Road is crossed, and the Royal Canal at Binn's Bridge (1 mile). Drumcondra Road is a broad thoroughfare, attractively planted with trees. On the right, 1¾ miles along, is the entrance to Holy Cross College, in the grounds of which is the town residence of the Catholic Archbishop of Dublin. Also in the grounds is Clonliffe House. This was originally called Fortick's Grove, after its owner, Tristram Fortick, who founded Fortick's asylum, extant in Little Denmark Street, in 1765. It later came into the possession of Frederick Jones ('Buck Jones'), owner of the Fishamble Street music hall, and later of Daly's Theatre in Crow Street. Jones, like Lundy Foot (Route 15), was an energetic magistrate, and Clonliffe House was besieged by highwaymen in November 1806. Clonliffe House also figures in 'The Ghost's Promenade', a poem by Thomas Caulfield Irwin. From 1845 to 1857, it was used as a depot for the Revenue Police. In 1859, Holy Cross College was founded here, and the newer and larger building was begun in the following year. Archbishop's House was built during the archiepiscopate of Dr Walsh, about 1890.

At 1½ miles, the Tolka is crossed by Drumcondra Bridge. Shortly after

The delicate spire of **St George's church** developed structural problems in the late twentieth century and at time of writing is still sheathed in scaffolding. The nave and vaults are now devoted to the religion of music, dance and alcohol; the church has become a nightclub and disco.

St George's church during the demolition of the tenements in 1965

Clonliffe House is extant in the extensive grounds of Clonliffe College.

Little Denmark Street was cleared in the early 1970s as part of the site on which the ILAC Centre was built.

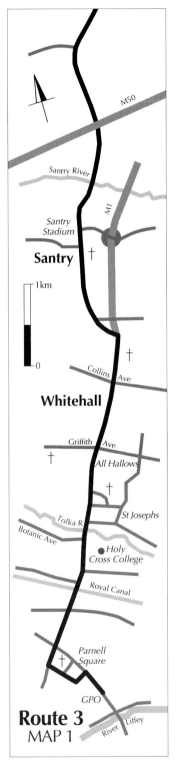

Route 3

MAP 1

this, on left, is St Patrick's Training College occupying Belvedere House. Almost opposite this, at the 'Cat and Cage' public-house, Church Avenue leads to Drumcondra Protestant Church, an unpretentious old building of the early eighteenth century, with a more than ordinarily interesting grave-yard. Here are buried Francis Grose, the antiquary (who died on a visit to Dublin in 1792), and his friend James Gandon, architect of the Four Courts, the Custom House and other buildings, who died in 1823 and was buried in the same grave. The Wexford poet Thomas Furlong, who died in 1827, is also buried here. In the Church is a very fine monument to Sir Marma-duke Coghill, judge of the Prerogative Court.

Behind the Church, with an entrance facing east, is Drumcondra House, the former home of the Coghills, which since 1842 has been part of the Missionary College of All Hallows. The south front by Sir Edward Lovett Pearce is about 1730, the east perhaps twenty years earlier. There are some very fine early panelled rooms inside. In the garden is a Temple by Alessandro Galilei, now used as a burying-place.

Old Drumcondra (which lies north of the Tolka) was in 1591 the scene of the marriage between Hugh O'Neill, Earl of Tyrone, and Mabel Bagenal, sister of the Bagenals, who were among the leading Elizabethan adventur-ers into Ireland. O'Neill carried the girl away from an English house nine miles to the north, and rested at Drumcondra, where he persuaded the Protestant Bishop of Meath to perform the ceremony. Marshall, one of the Bagenal brothers, was killed seven years later in 1598 at the Yellow Ford near Armagh, in battle against O'Neill's forces.

East of and parallel to Drumcondra Road lies Grace Park Avenue, Formerly Goose Green Avenue, on which is situated St Joseph's Asylum for the Male Blind, formerly Drumcondra Castle, Beaumont, formerly resi-dence of the second Arthur Guinness. In the district, at Elm Park, lived Thomas Hutton, the coachbuilder, whose daughter was the fiancée of Thomas Davis.

Beyond St Patrick's College is Home Farm Road, after which Griffith Avenue is reached. Half-way along it to the left is the modern Catholic Church of Corpus Christi, a fine building embodying a free treatment of elements of both Gothic and Renaissance. It is set in a green space, and is cruciform, built of mountain-granite, with a leaden dome at the crossing. The interior is lofty and well lit, the huge crossing-arches and the harmony of all the fittings making a very fine impression. It is now one of the most conspicuous objects in the northern suburbs. The architects were Messrs

Belvedere House is extant at the centre of St Patrick's College.

The **Cat and Cage**, originally established about 1750, is still a prominent landmark on Drumcondra Road; Ormond Road and Church Avenue to the east retain the feel of the winding country lanes they originally were. In the graveyard of **Drumcondra church** Thomas Furlong's monument is easily identified, a slightly eroded pyramidal form in granite with ivy forcing the blocks apart. Also buried here is Patrick Heaney, who composed the music of the National Anthem to accompany the words written by his friend Peadar Kearney.

Outside the churchyard, to the right of the church entrance gate, a rare Saorstát Éireann postbox is still in use.

The **All Hallows Missionary College** occupies a series of substantial buildings of a variety of dates in an extensive and well-maintained parkland. Little has changed here since 1949, other than the loss of the two-hundred-year-old chestnut tree called Pompey, which fell in 1952, and the proliferation of carparks that have sprung up. The Lovett Pearce building has had a Latin inscription with the date 1842 (when the college was officially opened) insensitively incised in very large letters into its façade.

All Hallows College

The **Galilei temple** is partially hidden by the trees to the right of the entrance drive.

St Joseph's School for the Blind occupies another extensive campus: the original house is dwarfed by the later buildings, and has been insulted with plastic windows. A notable, possibly original, feature which survives, however, is the intricate wrought-iron claire-voie at the entrance door.

Other than the rearrangement of altar furnishings following the Second Vatican Council, the **Catholic church of Corpus Christi** has been little altered since it was constructed, and still retains the original Connemara marble altar and tabernacle.

Robinson and Keeffe.

Crossing Griffith Avenue, the road passes on the left a new housing estate called Gaeltacht Park. The fine trees which grew here were almost all cut down during the fuel famine of early 1947, and the district has a starkly denuded appearance. Whitehall, a bus terminus, is at the entrance of Collins Avenue, on the right.

At 2¾ miles, on the right, is Belfield Park, which formerly belonged to the Belvedere family (Rochfort) and was lately occupied by Mr A. M. Sullivan. It was burned by Parliamentarian forces in 1641, and in its present form it consists almost entirely of *cottages ornées*, Swiss chalets, etc., built by Lady Domville two hundred years later. These are kept whitewashed, and present a picturesque appearance. The Parish Church (Protestant) was built in 1790, and contains many tombs of the Barry and Domville families. On the left is the Demesne of Santry Court, first the seat of the Barrys, and later the Domvilles, who were intermarried with them. Both families bore the title of Lord Santry. The Domvilles moved here from Templeogue (see Route 13) in the eighteenth century. The most distinguished resident of Santry at present is Myles na gCopaleen of *The Irish Times*, but his exact location is a matter of some mystery.

Santry Court stands in a demesne (visible on the left) of 140 acres. The centre block was built about 1700, and the wings forty or fifty years later. It was, until 1942, one of the earliest surviving large houses in the county. In the latter year, being in military occupation, it was accidentally burnt and largely destroyed. In the demesne are an obelisk to the memory of a favourite horse, another giving the mileage from Dublin, a graceful column closing a fine avenue of trees, a bridge flanked by four sculptured lions, some fine, old walled gardens, and the Temple, which was brought from Templeogue. This last had been pushed over by some unknown agency in recent years, and for a while lay on the ground beside its base. The entire dome, of solid masonry but without cramps, remained intact, however, after its fall, and it was later removed for a second time to Luggala, County Wicklow. The demesne was set aside after the fire as the site of a new Consumptive Sanatorium, but the project was abandoned in 1947, when £25,000 had already been spent on foundations. The new runways at Collinstown Airport would have interfered with its fitness for its purpose.

The Santry river is now crossed, and a little later Furry Park is seen on the left. At 4¾ miles, a fork on the left leads to Collinstown Airport, visible from the main road.

Gaeltacht Park is still there, a tight and comfortable development well-endowed with mature trees.

Lady Domville's **Swiss cottages** numbered eleven originally, and were part of a model village with a shop, a post office and a forge with a horseshoe-shaped door. The last survivor has been so absorbed into the modern streetfront that it is almost unrecognisable.

Swiss cottages c. 1940

The local parish **church of St Pappins**, erected in 1790, is still in use. The most significant monument in the graveyard is a Portland stone funerary casket with an inscription commemorating Sir Compton Domville, who died in 1857. His son, Sir Charles Compton Domville, carried out the last great renovations to Santry Court, and commissioned Sir Ninian Niven to design the gardens.

Beyond the old gateway to **Santry Court** is **Morton Athletics Stadium**, which owes its existence to the tireless efforts of the late Billy Morton. Work on a large new indoor stadium is currently under way. The walled gardens of Santry Court are extant, and it is to be hoped that they will be restored when Fingal County Council develops what remains of the demesne into a public park. Santry Court itself, an extensive nine-bay, red brick mansion, was demolished in 1957, and the rubble used to create the embankment around the running track of the infant stadium.

Beyond Santry Stadium a sea of signs, office blocks and factories, and a bewildering battlefield of roadworks extend northwards, a confusion of seemingly ill-planned development.

Where **Furry Park** was is now an estate of great, bland, steel-clad warehouses.

Collinstown Airport (Dublin Airport) is, by common consent, the most distinguished modern building in Ireland. It was completed in 1941, and the architect was Desmond FitzGerald, son of the Free State Cabinet Minister. The main building is crescent-shaped, approached, on the concave side, by a fine avenue. At a little distance on either side are blocks of subsidiary buildings. The convex side faces west to the runways. It is magnificently sited, and is seen to advantage from any angle. On a good day, it is distinctly visible from the Dublin mountains, over 13 miles away. The combined simplicity and grace of the building, relying as it does on the use of concrete, metal and glass, is a very striking feature. The public are admitted on most occasions to the entrance hall and restaurant, and to the balconies on the wings. A small charge has recently been imposed for this privilege.

Swords may be reached in a little over 2 miles by byroads from Collinstown, passing Little Forrest and Cremona, two attractive old houses.

Continuing on the main road, we reach (6 miles from the GPO) the village of Cloghran. The church (Protestant) stands on 'a lofty eminence composed of limestone rock, the prospect of the surrounding country and the sea is delightful' (*New Traveller's Guide to Ireland*, 1801).

Swords, 8 miles from the GPO, is situated on the steep bank of a stream which flows into the creek of Malahide, to which a road on the right also leads. The town of Swords, which now has a population of about 1,000, is said to be the oldest in the county of Dublin. It owes its origin to the monastery founded in 512 by St Colmcille, who presented to it a missal written by himself, and appointed St Finian Lobhair (the Leper) its first Abbot, and blessed the well there. Chapels were dedicated to St Finian and St Bridget; the bodies of Brian Boroimhe and his son reposed here after the Battle of Clontarf, on their way to Armagh. On the foundation of the Collegiate establishment of St Patrick's (Cathedral) in 1190, Swords was constituted a prebend of that church, and called 'The Golden Prebend similar to that of Sarum in England'. Among its holders was William of Wyckham. During the Middle Ages, the Archbishops of Dublin had a residence at Swords. It was sacked by the Bruce in 1316, and in 1641 was the scene of a battle in which the Cromwellian Sir Charles Coote defeated an Irish army of the Pale. Before the Union, the town sent two members to the Irish Parliament, and enjoyed the 'potwalloper franchise'—that is to say, every Protestant who owned a hearth could vote. The usual £15,000 compensation, therefore, went not to the borough-owner (as in most cases),

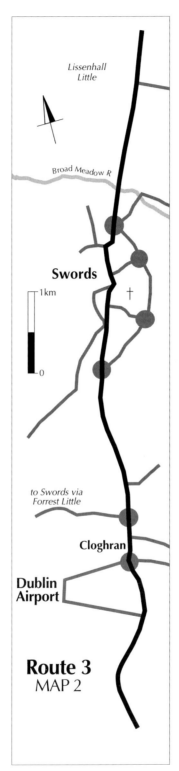

Lissenhall
Little

Broad Meadow R

Swords

1km

0

to Swords via
Forrest Little

Cloghran

**Dublin
Airport**

Route 3
MAP 2

The route passes under the M50 and through the aviation city surrounded by vast carparks that **Collinstown Airport** has become in recent decades. Now called Dublin International Airport, it handled 14 million passengers in the year 2000. The original terminal building, although dwarfed by later buildings, is extant, and, recently renovated, reopened in 1998 as a terminal and offices.

Little Forrest has been replaced by the Little Forrest Golf Clubhouse. Only two massive gate piers and some outhouses remain of what was before.

Although housing estates and development works for more housing have spread southwards into the countryside from Swords in recent years, **Cremona**, a modest five-bay, two-storey over basement house, is still there.

The village of **Cloghran**, now surrounded by busy major roads, is reduced to a few small cottages perched on the southern side of the 'lofty eminence'—the Protestant church, erected on the site of an earlier church in 1712, was demolished in the mid-twentieth century. To the east is **Glebe House**, a fine but run-down old Georgian farmhouse with a good doorcase; recently purchased by Aer Rianta, it has a doubtful future.

Swords has absorbed a deluge of commercial development over the last thirty years, an assembly of the good, the bad and the ugly. In spite of this, some of the older buildings still survive along the 800-metre length of Main and North Streets. The newest building at time of writing is the **Fingal Council Headquarters**, designed by Friel, Bucholz, and McEvoy. A structure of glass and warm-tinted terracotta tiles, its newness is softened on the street front by a cluster of carefully retained mature holm oaks.

but to the potwallopers, who chose to devote part of the sum to the erection of schools under the Incorporated Society. These schools, now called Borough National Schools, are still to be seen. In 1819, Swords was described as 'abounding with houses for the entertainment of visitors with the vending of liquors, its only traffic' (*New Traveller's Guide to Ireland*).

The Round Tower and the tower of the fourteenth- or fifteenth-century Abbey stand close together in the grounds of the Protestant Church, which was built in 1819. Both are well preserved, though the last few feet of the Round Tower, including the cap, are not ancient. The tower tapers rather more rapidly than most, and the masonry is rather crude. The cross which now surmounts it is eighteenth century. The Abbey tower is of four storeys, square and strongly battered, with curved battlements. The remaining ruins of the Abbey were cleared away in 1818.

At the north end of the town is the gate of the castle, or Archbishop's Palace. This consists of a well-preserved curtain-wall, enclosing an area of perhaps two acres, with river-meadows under the walls, and an orchard inside. Inside the gate, on the right, is the Chapel, and there are a number of corner-towers and other buildings, some in good preservation, around the perimeter of the enclosure. The buildings date from 1200 to 1500 (Leask, *Irish Castles*, p. 72). Though not the most interesting, it is one of the most attractive near Dublin.

In the vicinity of Swords are a number of good old houses. Drynam, 1½ miles south-east on the Feltrim road, is now a ruin but was inhabited until thirty years ago. It was of Jacobean date, and the old stone fireplaces can still be seen. It was the residence of the Cruise family, who lived in it in 1913. Two miles west-north-west is Rathbeale Hall, formerly Catherine's Grove, a fine eighteenth-century house with curved wings, built as the residence of the Gorges family, a member of which, General Richard Gorges, married the Dowager Lady Meath, and survived her but two days, an event which caused Swift to write an *Epitaph*, with the lines:

> *Dick sighed for his Doll, and the jointure he lost*
> *The first vexed him much, the other vexed most.*

Rathbeale Hall now belongs to Lady Mary Corbally and Miss Corbally. It is occupied by Lady Mary Corbally. Near it are the ruins of Glasmore Abbey, where St Cronan and his monks are said to have been massacred by the Danes. Half a mile north-east, on the little road leading down to the 'Meadow Water' is Mantua, a fine house of *c.* 1740, now the residence of Dr Cuffe.

At the south end of the Main Street, the austere and dignified **Old Borough School**, designed by Francis Johnson in 1802 and completed in 1809 for a cost of £1,800, seems to be awaiting a use that will ensure its restoration.

Swords Castle was purchased from the Cobbe family of Newbridge House in 1985 by Dublin County Council. The Constable's Tower has been restored and is open to the public. Restoration work continues on the walls and on the **Archbishop's apartments** on the east side of the complex.

Rathbeale Hall was in poor condition when it was sold by the Corbally family in 1958 to Mr and Mrs Julian Peck, who carried out extensive refurbishment works. It is now in the ownership of Mr Joseph Keeling of Keelings Fruit Ltd. It has a fine Palladian front with curved sweeps and wings with venetian windows. The present front is dated c. 1751, but the original house is thought to be c. 1680, incorporating an earlier tower-house.

Rathbeale Hall c. 1960

The ruins of **Glasmore Abbey** are extant but under threat, surrounded by recently built housing.

Mantua is no longer there, its place taken by a business park.

A mile and a half north of Swords, the road crosses the head of the 'Meadow Water' near Meudon and Lissen Hall. Down a side road a mile to the right is Seafield House, built about 1730, perhaps by Benedict Arthur, later the seat of the HelyHutchinson family, and now of Captain Corry. It has a fine situation looking south across the water. The same side road leads, if the left fork is taken, to Donabate and Ballisk, two places little more than ¼ mile apart, and 5 miles from Swords. In Donabate are the remains of a castle, and a ruined tower near the Protestant Church, containing monuments of the Barnewall family. The church itself is a particularly attractive specimen of an eighteenth-century country church. Inside the porch is a seventeenth-century Barnewall monument, but the most noteworthy internal feature is the west gallery, entirely taken up by the Cobbe family pew, which has an octagonal ceiling with highly decorative plasterwork, incorporating swans (in a punning allusion to the family name) and the motto 'MORIENS CANO'. At the north-east corner of the Church stands the mediaeval tower. The Rev. Matthew Pilkington, incumbent here during the eighteenth century, was author of a famous dictionary of painters, and collected pictures for the Cobbe family of Newbridge House, which adjoins Donabate and was designed by Cassels in about 1737. Frances Power Cobbe, the feminist and theological writer (1822–1904) was a member of this family. Between Donabate and the sea is Portrane Lunatic Asylum, an extremely large establishment founded in the late nineteenth century, and completed at a cost of £250,000. From the distance, it presents the appearance of a fair-sized town. On the shore is a tower erected to the memory of Mr George Evans of Portrane House, by his widow, sister of the first Lord Congleton and great-aunt of Charles Stewart Parnell. A number of stories about this eccentric lady and about the neighbourhood generally will be found in Miss Cobbe's autobiography. Also at Portrane are a ruined church and a fairly well-preserved castle.

Opposite Portrane, and about three miles out, is the island of Lambay, an elevated oval in form, four miles long and two miles broad. In the reign of Edward VI, the island was rented by the Archbishop of Dublin to a John Chaloner and his heirs for the use of a colony which he had brought to inhabit it, on condition that within six years he would build a village for fishermen and a harbour for their boats. In the reign of Elizabeth, it passed into the possession of Archbishop Ussher, the biblical chronologist, who resided on it and is said to have here written a considerable number of his works.

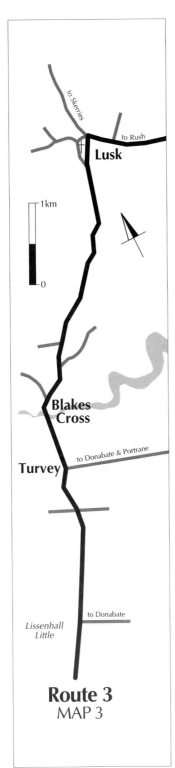

Route 3
MAP 3

Meudon was demolished c. 1998 to make way for Maryfield, a centre for the handicapped.

Lissen Hall is extant, as is **Seafield**, a mixture of Palladian villa and Victorian Italianate mansion, considered in 1892 as a possible location for the new north Dublin lunatic asylum which was eventually sited at Portrane. At that time the asking price was £13,000; in 1996, it was sold with eighty acres of land by Sir Robert Goff to an English businessman for just over £1 million. Sir Robert and his wife moved to Lissenhall.

Donabate church was refurbished in the 1990s.

Newbridge House, the home of the Cobbes, is now owned by Fingal Council and is open to the public.

The red brick buildings of **Portrane Lunatic Asylum**, now **St Ita's Hospital**, are still a dramatic sight in the shoreline landscape, and the round tower erected in 1844 by Sophia Evans in memory of her husband is extant.

The **ruined church at Portrane**, dedicated to St Catherine, with its battlemented tower displaying carved stone heads, has been stabilised by the Office of Public Works and is in quite good condition.

The **castle of Portrane**, a thirteenth-century tower-house, is known locally as **Stella's Tower** after Dean Swift's friend, Esther Johnson, who stayed there in 1712. Last lived in about 1740, it stands ivy-covered and roofless in the middle of a field.

A comprehensive archaeological survey was carried out on **Lambay Island** in 1996 under Professor Gabriel Cooney of UCD. The fauna of the island now includes introduced wallabies.

James Ussher, whom Dr Johnson described as 'the greatest luminary of the Irish Church', was born in Dublin in 1581. He entered Trinity College of the new Elizabethan University of Dublin at the age of thirteen, when he made a deep study of the Fathers, and in 1607 he was appointed Professor of Divinity. In 1620 he became Bishop of Meath, and in 1625 Archbishop of Armagh. He took part in the Convocation of 1634, which established the canons of the reformed Irish Church. He was hostile to Wentworth's policy of crushing all Irish independence, and left Ireland before the Rebellion of 1641. Mahaffy (*An Epoch of Irish History*) defines him as 'an evangelical yet episcopalian'. He was present at the execution of Charles I, when he fainted, but he had the respect of Cromwell, who wished to give his great library to Dublin. The books, however, were offered for sale by Ussher's daughter, Lady Tyrrell, and, in the result, the Restoration having supervened, reached Trinity College, and became the nucleus of the College Library, as the gift of 'his Most Serene Majesty Charles II'.

In later times the island was purchased by the Talbots. Lewis tells us that in 1837 (at the time of the Talbot ownership) part of its well-watered lands had been subjected to cultivation; that the rocky grounds surrounding it formed a plentiful lobster and crab fishery, much frequented by Lough Shinny fishermen, who here pursued a lucrative trade; that the island abounded with rabbits, sea parrots or puffins and Cornish choughs; and that the Castle erected by Chaloner survived and was sometimes occupied by Lord Talbot de Malahide. Lambay was acquired about fifty years ago by the Hon. Nigel Baring, afterwards Lord Revelstoke, who used it as a permanent country residence. He greatly increased the amenities of the island and modernised the Castle to the design of Sir Edwin Lutyens. His son is the present proprietor. Visits can be made only by permission.

Return to the main road can now be made by a straight road, which soon passes on the right Turvey House, originally built by Sir Chris Barnewall in 1565, partly from the ruins of the famous Augustinian nunnery of Grace Dieu. All other traces of the nunnery have now disappeared, and Turvey, which externally at least shows little sign of antiquity, is now occupied by E. A. Counihan Esq. The front shows that the old gables have been built up, and inside there is a Priest's Hole. (See Sadleir and Dickinson, *Georgian Mansions in Ireland*.) Turvey has the distinction of being the reputed birthplace of the semi-legendary architect, Goban Saor (see also Kilgobbin, Route 18). The legend is taken seriously by so great an antiquary as George Petrie.

Turvey House was a fine three-storey, late seventeenth-century improvement of a medieval tower, the top storey having an unusual three Diocletian windows. Its fate is a shameful episode in the conservation record of the local authority, and still a matter of some controversy. It was allowed to deteriorate in private ownership in the early 1970s and eventually it was demolished. In its place is a pink, post-modern building housing the Turvey Country Club.

Turvey House 1971

Entrance

Interior

In ½ mile, after the main road is rejoined at Turvey village, it forks; the left branch being the direct road to Balbriggan, and the right leading to Lusk and Skerries (GNR bus route). Lusk, which is reached without incident in 2½ miles from the fork, is an attractive village of whitewashed thatched cottages, spaced at leisurely intervals and possessing pretty gardens. The un-Irish appearance of Lusk is doubtless to be set down to the fact that it lies in the heart of Fingal, the district of north County Dublin and south County Meath seaboard which has been settled for longer than any other part of Ireland. Lusk is dominated by the Protestant church, which, though in itself a dull enough early nineteenth-century building, possesses a fine mediaeval Tower with four round corner turrets, of which one is the pre-existing Round Tower. The latter has lost its cap, and is now crowned with a flat cone, but is otherwise well-preserved. The Church Tower may be ascended, giving a near view of the top of the Round Tower, and a fine prospect of the surrounding country. Beneath the mediaeval tower is a vault, and in the bottom storey are some monuments, notably that of Sir Chris Barnewall of Turvey and his wife (d. 1575 and 1607 respectively).

From Lusk, a road leads to the right past Rush and Lusk Station and an old graveyard with a church gable, to Rush, near the seashore. Here is the well-wooded demesne of Kenure Park, once the residence of the Duke of Ormond (who built the pier), later of the Echlin family, and later still of Sir Roger Palmer, Bart. It is a large, square cut-stone house, enlarged about 1840, with a particularly magnificent portico. The Palmers embellished it with valuable paintings of old masters and vases from Pompeii. In Rush there is also the stump of a windmill.

From here, the road leads northwards, skirting the Kenure demesne (inset in which are another old church and graveyard) to Lough Shinny and Skerries. On a gentle eminence to the left is Baldungan Castle, which belonged to the Knights Templar and later to the de Berminghams and to the Howth family. A mile outside Skerries to the left is Hacketstown, formerly a seat of Lord Holmpatrick. On some old maps this district is marked Holm Patrick, which is the old parish name.

Skerries, which until recently was a fishing village, has become a popular seaside resort. The latest stage in its evolution, as such, has been the establishment of a holiday camp on Red Island, the nearest of the four islands which lie off the coast. Red Island has long been connected with the mainland; the others are Colt Island, St Patrick's Island (on which there is

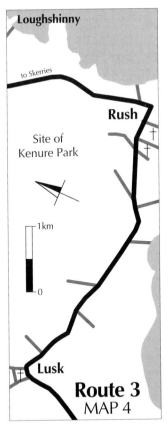

Loughshinny

to Skerries

Rush

Site of
Kenure Park

1km

0

Lusk

Route 3
MAP 4

The main road through **Lusk** loops around to follow the line of the ancient monastic boundary. Inside the old boundary, there is a medieval feel to the layout of tiny plots, cottages, sheds and fields, all apparently in different ownerships. Unfortunately there is only one thatched roof left in the village, where fifty years ago there were several dozen.

Only a fragment remains of the **old church** beyond Rush Station.

At the beginning of the main street of Rush the very impressive sweeping entrance gateway of the ill-fated **Kenure Park** can be seen. The old avenue is now a public park, at the end of which only the magnificent portico remains of the house, standing baldly in the middle of a 'green space', with a backdrop of palisade fencing and housing, an incongruous memorial to the lack of official concern about the county's heritage. No attempt has been made to create a suitably landscaped context for the soaring portico, and the eastern gate lodge and gates, intact up to recently, have now been allowed to fall into dereliction.

The **windmill stump** is still there, looking incongruous on a grassy mound.

Although the ruins of **Baldungan Castle** were cleared away in 1974, the more prominent ruins of the medieval **Baldungan church** are extant.

Hacketstown House is gone; only some dilapidated outbuildings and sheds remain.

Kenure Park c. 1930; see page 55 for its current state

a ruined church) and Shenick's Island, which, like Red Island, has a Martello tower. Skerries was returned in 1946 as having a population of well over 2,000. It shows a pleasant taste in colour-washed houses. In the old graveyard is the Tower of the old Protestant Church, with the modern church close by. The new Catholic church is a large basilican building. In or near the town are two windmills, one of them still retaining part of the wooden upperworks. In the main street is a monument to James Hans Hamilton of Abbotstown (see Route 7), one of the Holmpatrick family. Half a mile west of Skerries Railway Station are the remains of a fortified prehistoric camp, showing two rings of fortifications. Near here is Milverton Hall, the residence of Captain Woods.

A road may now be taken along the shore towards Balbriggan, skirting in two miles the wooded demesne of Ardgillan, the seat of the Taylor family. There is a pleasant bay here, with steep escarpments and a strand, and fine views of the Mourne range and Slieve Gullion can be seen. A plume of smoke from the Drogheda Cement Factory can usually be remarked in the distance. In 4½ miles, passing the gates of the abandoned demesne of Hampton (Baron Hamilton, see below), Balbriggan is reached.

Balbriggan may also be reached more directly by the main road from Swords, from which it is ten miles distant to the north. Nothing of note is encountered on this road till at eight miles the village of Balrothery is entered. The church here, like that of Lusk, was rebuilt by the Board of First Fruits, and, like that of Lusk, it has a mediaeval tower which appears to be the work of the same masons, and incorporates an imitation of the Lusk Round Tower. There is another old tower in the grounds of the Rectory.

Balbriggan, 21 miles north from the GPO, is best known for the woollen and hosiery industry carried on there. Its prosperity dates from a grant of the Irish Parliament obtained for it by Baron Hamilton of Hampton in 1761, when the present very attractive harbour was begun. It now contains about 2,500 inhabitants. But its history is much longer than this might suggest. It was the scene, on Whitsun-Eve 1329, of a battle between the de Berminghams and Talbots on one side, and the Verduns, Gernons and Savages on the other. On 20 September 1920, Balbriggan was again in the news. Twenty houses were destroyed and the smaller hosiery factory burned, by the British Auxiliaries claiming to avenge the death of a comrade—one of the most unpleasant episodes of that troubled period.

At present, as well as the hosiery manufactories of Messrs Smyth and Son and Messrs Stevenson, there are also saltworks at Balbriggan. A ruined

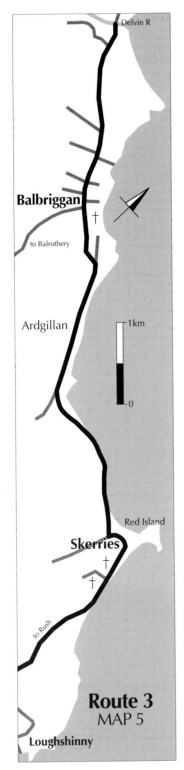

Balbriggan

to Balrothery

Delvin R

Ardgillan

1km

0

Red Island

Skerries

to Rush

Route 3
MAP 5

Loughshinny

Next to the **Catholic church** is the **Carnegie Library** of 1910 by Anthony Scott.

The two **Skerries windmills** were restored in the 1990s and are now open to the public.

Milverton Hall was demolished and replaced in the 1960s.

Ardgillan and its demesne and gardens are now open to the public.

Hampton, the principal seat in the Balbriggan area in the early nineteenth century, is still there. It is no longer a school, and at time of writing is being developed as apartments.

The village of **Balrothery**, scattered picturesquely across a hill and overlooked by the church and tower, has retained its scale and character.

The **Balbriggan** hosiery industry closed down in 1980.

The '**ruined church and a castle**' are to be found north of the town. Only a fragment remains of the church, said to be founded by St Molagga, the Bee-Man. He studied under St David in Wales, and brought back with him to Ireland a swarm of Welsh bees. Some fine stone carvings survive, one an arcade of four arches decorated with angels, the other, possibly a lintel, displays a figure and the paraphernalia of the Crucifixion with the date 1689. Only some ruined walls remained of **Bremore Castle** up to recently. It has now been reconstructed by Fingal County Council Parks Department and will shortly be open to the public. The reconstruction is based on the designs of David Newman Johnson, which in turn were based on historical records, particularly a sketch of the ruins of the castle as it was in 1787 by the antiquary Austin Cooper.

church and a castle are situated near the town; but apart from the harbour it presents few attractive features.

Four miles beyond Balbriggan, the road enters County Meath at Low-therstown, the mouth of the Delvin river.

Kenure portico; see page 51 for how the house looked in the 1930s

Santry Court before demolition

ROUTE 4

THE NAUL

	Miles from the GPO
Glasnevin	2½
Ballymun Charter School	3½
Forrest Great	5¾
Knocksedan	7½
Rathbeale	9
Ballyboghill	12
The Nag's Head	15
The Naul	17

This route leaves Dublin by Blessington Street, Berkeley Road, where there is a fine view down Eccles Street to St George's Protestant Church, between St Joseph's Catholic Church and the Mater Misericordiae Hospital (the largest hospital in Dublin), passing by a few yards of North Circular Road and Phibsborough Road. The Royal Canal is crossed by Cross Guns Bridge, and the road to the right (Botanic Road) is taken for Glasnevin village, but it can be by-passed by going down Mobhi Road which rejoins the main route later.

Glasnevin was, until recently, a village outside the city, and in the eighteenth century was perhaps the most fashionable place of residence in the neighbourhood. It is now best known for the Botanic Gardens, and for Prospect Cemetery which adjoins them, and is treated of in Route 5. The Botanical Gardens were founded by Dr Walter Wade, who in 1790 drew up and presented on behalf of the Dublin Society a petition to the Irish Parliament. Parliament gave two grants before the Union, and in 1877 the Gardens were taken over from the Royal Dublin Society by the Science and Art Department, and soon enlarged to 40 acres. The nucleus of the Gardens was the house and grounds occupied by the English poet, Thomas Tickell, who was Under-Secretary of State, and afterwards Secretary to the Lords Justice. His immediate superior was Joseph Addison, the essayist, and a yew-walk in the Gardens is still pointed out as Addison's Walk. Quite apart from the interest of the trees and other plants, and the glasshouses, the Gardens have great attractions owing to their being bounded on one side by the river Tolka.

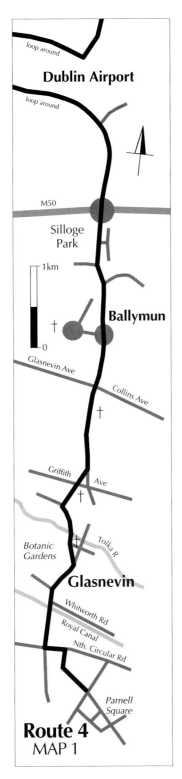

Dublin Airport

loop around

loop around

M50

Silloge
Park

1 km

Ballymun

0

Glasnevin Ave

Collins Ave

Griffith

Ave

Botanic
Gardens

Tolka R

Glasnevin

Whitworth Rd

Royal Canal

Nth. Circular Rd

*Parnell
Square*

Route 4
MAP 1

Glasnevin village is a cluster of small shops and terraces of houses threaded through by winding roads; adorned by the **Botanic Gardens** and the Tolka river, it still has the ambiance of a village in spite of the busy traffic. Our **Lady of Dolours Catholic Church** of the late 1960s, a pyramidic-roofed, steel-framed structure on the south bank of the Tolka, is one of the first modern churches to be built in Dublin incorporating the new liturgical policies of the Second Vatican Council.

In the Botanic Gardens the fine Fern House, erected in 1887 to replace an earlier timber building, was demolished and replaced in 1966 by an uninspiring building of that period. In the 1990s the surviving glass-houses, including one by William Turner, were carefully restored to their original condition.

Cactus House, Botanic Gardens c. 1940

In Glasnevin village itself, a number of small houses of the very early eighteenth century still survive. The 'Ink-Bottle School-House', which was until fifty years ago such a conspicuous oddity, has unfortunately perished. Just beyond the bridge, a gate at a crick in the road leads into Delville, the famous house built by Drs Delany and Helsham in about 1730, and originally called Heldelville which name was dropped for obvious reasons. Here the famous letter-writer, Mary Granville, Mrs Delany, lived and adorned the rooms with shell-work, and the gardens with grottoes, the remnants of which, one in particular which formerly contained a bust of Swift's Stella, still remain. Swift himself spent many hours here, and composed the inscription

FASTIGIA DESPICIT URBIS

which could, until recently, be seen on the fast-mouldering frieze of the Temple at the head of the grounds. The Temple has now (1948) been destroyed, but under it were vaults, which may still be traced in part; tradition has it—not improbably—that in these vaults were printed some of Swift's more dangerous broadsheets. A small hand-press was found here early in the nineteenth century. Delville was subsequently the home of Bishop Percy of the *Reliques*, when Bishop of Dromore, and later of the Geale family. In the mid-nineteenth century it belonged to Sir William Somerville, and was let to a Mr Mallett. It was for many years in the possession of the Lanigan O'Keeffes, and is now a home for elderly people, in the charge of the nuns of Bon Secours.

Immediately behind the Delville Temple is St Mobhi's Church (Protestant) which was built in 1707 and has a tower of an earlier date. Dr Robert Walsh, one of the historians of Dublin, was rector here in the early nineteenth century.

Continuing on past St Mobhi's Church, the direct road is rejoined at the Catholic church. A road to the right here leads to a house called Hampstead, which was the residence of Sir Richard Steele, the essayist, and in the later part of the century belonged to a gentleman called Davis. In 1837 it was occupied by B. O'Gorman Esq. At Stormanstown was born Miss Catherine McAuley, foundress of the Sisters of Mercy order.

At 3½ miles from the GPO, just after St Pappin's Catholic Church, is a crossroads, leading right to Santry village (see Route 3), and left to Poppintree (called after St Pappin of Santry), and ultimately to Dunsoghly (see Route 5). Just beyond the cross, on the left, is the old Charter School

Beyond the bridge and up Washerwoman's Hill, the 'crick in the road' has become the entrance to the **Bon Secours Hospital**. **Delville** continued in existence until 1951. On the completion of the new hospital, however, it was demolished, due, according to the nuns, to its poor state of repair.

At the top of the hill is the **Meteorological Office**, a truncated pyramid that was originally clad in limestone, completed in 1979, and designed by Liam McCormick.

Off Ballymun Road, down an old laneway called Church Avenue, **St Mobhi's Church** can be found.

In Mobhi Boithrin is **Balnagowan House**, one Dublin's earliest international style houses, built in 1930. It was designed by the English architect Harold Greenwood.

Hampstead Crescent (see page 65), a pleasant curved terrace of arts and crafts-type houses of about 1929, also designed by Harold Greenwood, leads to the considerable parkland demesnes of **Hampstead** and **Elmhurst**. Across an extensive stubble field surrounded by copses of beeches and scots pines the blue-grey undulations of the Dublin mountains line the horizon. The spires and towers of Dublin city seem to lie in a valley between. This is the site of **Hampstead Castle**, where later, in the house that took its place, Sir Richard Steele lived. Swift was entertained here, and wrote of the hospitality and pleasant surroundings. Elmhurst is a mid-nineteenth century house designed by Thomas Drew, but Hampstead is earlier; a private mental hospital is operated here, called locally **'Dr Eustace's'** after the three generations of doctors who ran the place in the late nineteenth and early twentieth centuries.

Hampstead

Stormanstown House was demolished in 1970.

What remained of the lands of University College Dublin's Agriculture and Horticulture Faculty after the development of the Ballymun housing scheme has become the campus of one of Ireland's newest third-level institutions, the **National Institute of Higher Education**.

of Ballymun, picturesquely situated among the trees. The fork left is taken here, and the Santry River is crossed. A mile and a half farther on is the hamlet of Coultry, where a road leads off on the left to St Margaret's (see Route 5). Three-quarters of a mile beyond Coultry is the Boot Inn, an ancient establishment which has been extensively modernised in recent years, and attracts a thriving trade from Dublin.

From this point on the road, a magnificent view is obtained of the west or departure front of Collinstown Airport (see Route 3), which is not visible to the general public from the airport grounds. The building is seen flanked by its ancillary buildings, the long convex front gleaming with steel and glass; and in the foreground are the concrete runways, usually alive with aeroplanes going to and fro about their business.

A little beyond the Boot Inn, on the opposite side of the road, is Pickardstown House, an attractive farmhouse, and half a mile on is Forrest Great, where a road leads to the right to Forrest Little (see Route 3) and on to the Airport and Swords.

At 7½ miles from the GPO is the picturesque Bridge of Knocksedan, over the Ward River. Just at the bridge there is a fine, circular flat-topped fort. To the right, before the bridge, is Brackenstown House, owned in the sixteenth century by the Burnell family, later by the Nugents, and in the reign of James I by Chief Baron Bysse, said to have been visited here by Cromwell. It then passed by marriage to Viscount Molesworth of Swords, who rebuilt the house.

Swift addressed one of the *Drapier's Letters* to the Lord Molesworth of the day at Brackenstown. It later belonged to the Manders family and to the O'Callaghans, and is now occupied by H. Ussher Esq., the well-known racehorse-owner.

At the crossroads, a road to the left leads to the old graveyard and ruined Church of Killeek or Killeigh. On the right may be seen the conspicuous ruin of Brazil or Brazeel House, built by Sir Richard Bolton, Lord Chancellor of Ireland in the reign of Charles I. He was impeached for having assisted Strafford's policy in Ireland, but lived to counsel Ormond in his negotiations with the Catholic Confederation in 1644. He also published the *Irish Statutes* in 1621. At Brazil, Owen Roe O'Neill encamped for a night after defeating a Parliamentary force and capturing Castleknock. Here also, in 1690, the Duke of Berwick made halt in the retreat from the Boyne.

Knocksedan is familiar to readers of O'Casey's *Shadow of a Gunman*, as

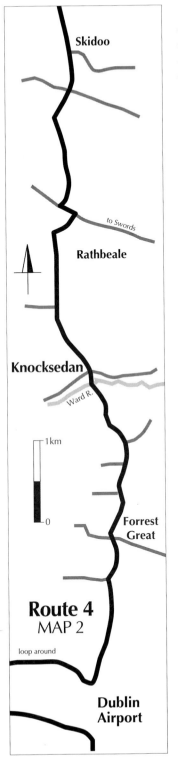

Skidoo

to Swords

Rathbeale

Knocksedan

Ward R.

1km

0

**Forrest
Great**

Route 4
MAP 2

loop around

**Dublin
Airport**

Ballymun is the site of Ireland's only serious attempt at high-rise housing. In 1949 it was a small village of a few cottages at the junction of Santry Avenue and Ballymun Road. During the housing crisis of the 1960s, in an effort to get the maximum 'units' for minimum expenditure, the infamous scheme of tower blocks was erected, increasing the population of the immediate area to 20,000. Now a major re-development scheme is under way which will involve the demolition of most of the high-rise blocks. North of Ballymun the old **Charter School** can be found; now called Santry Lodge, it is at present unoccupied and in need of restoration.

The sites of the hamlet of **Coultry** and the original **Boot Inn** are now covered by the runways of Dublin Airport.

Pickardstown House also disappeared in the expansion of the airport; **Forrest Great** is on Preservation List 2 of Fingal County Council and is, I believe, extant.

Brackenstown House is extant at the end of a kilometre-long avenue.

Killeigh is a featureless ruin in a raised, walled graveyard; from here Brackenstown House is visible.

The ruins of **Brazeel** were cleared about 1980 and have been replaced by acres of glasshouses.

the locality of an ambush during the War of Independence.

At 8¼ miles from the GPO is the Leas Cross, and at 9 miles is another crossroads (or, to be more exact, the route turns left for a few yards and then again right). On the right is Rathbeale Hall (see Route 3).

At 9¼ miles, the Meadow Water is crossed at Roganstown Bridge. Half a mile farther on, on the right, is Skidoo, which in 1786 was occupied by a family named McDermot. The road now begins to climb gradually, running across high ground, which gives a fine view of the rich plains of Meath to the westward.

The village of Ballyboghill is reached at 12 miles. The Ostman MacTurkil family were lords of all this part of Dublin for several generations before Strongbow. Ballyboghill derives its name from the Baculum Jesu, or Crozier of St Patrick, which belonged to Christ Church Cathedral in mediaeval times and was burnt by the Protestant Archbishop Browne in 1539. Strongbow and Fitzstephen took the place after a four-day battle, and then gave it to Holy Trinity (Christ Church) (Curtis: *Mediaeval Ireland*, 2nd ed. p. 75 & n).

The modern Catholic Church of Ballyboghill was built in the early nineteenth century, and enlarged in 1836. In the porch, an ancient font is used as a holy-water stoup. A little to the north of the village, on the left, is the old church of Ballyboghill, abandoned about the end of the eighteenth century. In it may be seen sedilia, an aumbry and, at the west end, an arcaded bell-cote surmounting the gable—a feature of the old churches of this district.

From Ballyboghill the road proceeds northwards without incident till, at 15 miles, it reaches the crossroads known as The Nag's Head, from an old inn which formerly stood here. A road to the right here leads to the Swords–Balbriggan road; and half a mile along it, in a hollow to the right, are another ruined church and graveyard. Very few features of the church survive, except an arcaded bell-cote as at Ballyboghill. Adjoining the churchyard is what seems to be an eighteenth-century ornamental grotto.

On the left, 1½ miles farther on, are the gates of Westown House, the seat in the eighteenth century of Lord Beaulieu. Until the early part of the present century, it was the residence of the family of Hussey, who kept hospitable house here. The estate has since been largely broken up. The village of Naul, which is reached at 17 miles from the GPO, is picturesquely situated on the Delvin River, which here forms the boundary with County Meath. Beside the Protestant church is a ruined church built by Col.

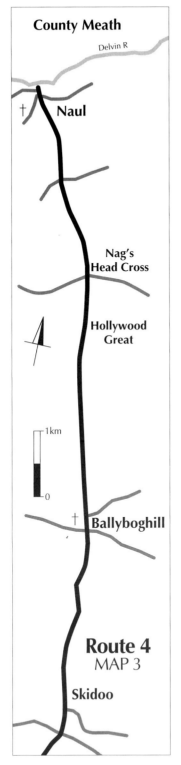

County Meath

Delvin R

† Naul

Nag's
Head Cross

Hollywood
Great

1km

0

† Ballyboghill

Route 4
MAP 3

Skidoo

For Rathbeale Hall, see page 35.

Skidoo is extant, at the centre of a well-known stud farm.

The Catholic church at **Ballyboghill** was re-roofed in the mid-twentieth century using exposed industrial angle-iron trusses which do no favours for the interior.

The old church with the arcaded bellcote has a fine sandstone Gothic east window.

To the right at the Nag's Head Cross, **Hollywood church** can be found down a narrow lane. It also has a tall arcaded bell-cote. From the graveyard there is a spectacular view southwards across the plains of north Dublin to the mountains—of Dublin city, hidden in the Liffey basin, only the airport, the Poolbeg chimneys and the Ballymun towers are visible.

The grotto mentioned is most likely the remains of a lime kiln.

Westown is long gone, as are its gates. The village of **Naul** is a neat place with a pub that bears no sign to advertise it. The Protestant church is gone, but the ruined church has some interesting surviving features such as a hooded ogee east window and a decoratively carved Gothic doorway.

Hussey of Westown in 1710; and overhanging the river is the picturesque ancient Castle.

'At Naul', says the *Post-Chaise Companion* (1786 edition), 'there is a most romantic glen, overhung with rocks, wherein are many caves.' But these we have not investigated.

Hampstead Crescent (see page 59)

ROUTE 5

THE WARD

	Miles from the GPO
Finglas	3¼
Dunsoghly	6¼
Ward	6¾
Six Mile House	7¾

This route follows Route 4 as far as the crossing of the Drumcondra and Galway railway lines, and the Royal Canal (1½ miles). Here the fork left is taken up the Cemetery road. The fork is named Cross Guns from an inn which formerly stood here. A modern inn of the same name occupies a site nearby. Prospect Cemetery, which now extends to left and right (the latter being the older and main portion) was founded in 1832 by O'Connell. The O'Connell Tower is a conspicuous object. The design was supplied by George Petrie in 1851, but many modifications and omissions were made in the actual building. O'Connell is buried in the crypt beneath. Others buried here include John Philpot Curran (the monument, a facsimile of the antique known as the tomb of Scipio Barbaticus, was designed by J. T. Papworth ARHA), James Clarence Mangan, Charles Stewart Parnell, Barry O'Sullivan the Tragedian, and Constance Gore-Booth (Countess Markievicz). The cemetery is surrounded by watchtowers, originally for protection against corpse-snatchers. A field now included in it is 'The Bloody Acre', a possible site of the Battle of the Wood of Tolka.

At Tolka Bridge the road crosses that river, which is to north Dublin what the Dodder is to the southern suburbs. Finglas village is entered at 3¼ miles. We are in the heart of the old 'land of the Norsemen', Fine Gall or Fingal, who even after the Battle of Clontarf retained a strong population of farmers and fishermen here. The name Finglas, however, means 'clear stream' (compare the suggested derivation of the Phoenix Park). From the Battle of Clontarf up to the Norman conquest, the Ó Cathasaigh ruled Fingal as overlords of the Norse occupiers, but a battle in 1171, when Strongbow defeated King Roderick O'Conor who was besieging the Normans in Dublin, put an end to their power. Some bones and armour have been found near Finglas Wood. It was an archiepiscopal residence in the thirteenth century. In 1649, the first Duke of Ormond camped here before his defeat by Cromwellians at the Battle of Rathmines. King James II

Kilsallaghan

Ward River

Newpark

1km

0

Ward

St Margarets

Dunsoghly Castle †

Dublin Airport

M50

Finglas

Tolka R

Prospect Cemetery

Royal Canal

Botanic Gds

Route 5

Prospect Rd

Glasnevin

Cemetery Road is now called Prospect Road.

Beyond **Prospect Cemetery** the road has been widened and the crossing of the Tolka can easily be missed.

The O'Connell Tower, Prospect Cemetery

is said to have slept here in Finglas Wood House in 1690, after the Boyne. The house, which belonged to the Seagraves, an old Fingallian family, was a substantial ruin in 1906, when Joyce illustrated it in his *Neighbourhood of Dublin*, but it has now completely disappeared. 'King William's Ramparts', however, which Joyce also illustrated, are still there, though their connection with King William is not proven. Two portions exist, one near the Rectory, and the other on a road leading southwards, from the road to Cappoge and Dunsink, very near the western edge of the village.

The Parish Church of Finglas (formerly Church of Ireland but now roofless and disused) is of great antiquity, but much altered in successive stages. In the churchyard is an ancient cross of simple type, which was buried by the villagers in 1649 to protect it from Cromwell. It was forgotten until 1816, when the Protestant curate, the Rev. Robert Walsh, recovered and re-erected it. A modern cross, with inscriptions in Latin and Irish, commemorates Dr John Lanigan, the historian, who was born in 1758, and was buried here in 1828. The church was abandoned in 1843, when the new church was erected and the monuments moved, including the large one of Captain Flower, now to be seen in the new church.

Finglas was celebrated until about a hundred years ago for its May-Day fair, and it possessed a maypole—one of the few in Ireland. In 1836, according to the *Dublin Penny Journal* of that date, there were at Finglas three lunatic asylums—Dr Harty's, Dr Gregory's and Dr Duncan's—and the paper accounted for them by the high reputation for salubrity which the place enjoyed. Finglas is still an attractive village, with a number of handsome houses of the early eighteenth century. Farnham House, which lies south-west of the old church, was the seat of Lord Farnham (Maxwell of County Cavan), subsequently a mental home, and now a nursing home. Among the Protestant incumbents of Finglas were 'Dilly' Ashe, punster, claret drinker and inconstant lover, and the poet Thomas Parnell, who held the living during the last few years of his life. Ussher lived here for a short time while Bishop of Meath.

The road from Finglas northwards crosses flat country, with occasional pleasant woods, but otherwise nothing of note, till it reaches, at 6 miles from the GPO, a crossroads (Kilshane Bridge). Dunsoghly Castle is visible some distance to the right. It is admirably described and illustrated in H. G. Leask's *Irish Castles*. Built in the fifteenth century by Thomas Plunkett, it is a tower 70 feet high with square turrets at the corners. It is a scheduled monument, and remains in excellent preservation. The most interesting

Finglas has suffered more from poorly planned development than most County Dublin villages. The dual-carriageway of the main Dublin-to-Derry road cuts a great swathe through the centre, leaving the ancient churchyard as an island in the midst of a litter-strewn confusion of buildings and roads.

A 15m long section of **King William's Ramparts**, a masonry wall with an arched niche, can still be seen near the new rectory. On the north side of the wall **St Patrick's Well** can be found, and although the superstructure is extant, the water is foul. The former rectory is now in private ownership. The other surviving section of the Ramparts, of earthen construction, is also extant although under threat.

Farnham House was demolished in 1954 to make way for the Convent of the Handmaidens of the Sacred Heart.

The only large house remaining in the village centre is **Rose Hill**, a tall, narrow house of the early eighteenth century, with an octagonal reception hall, a Gibbsian doorcase, and lunette attic windows. It has been suggested that it is the work of Sir Edward Lovett Pearce.

Dunsoghly Castle has been unoccupied for many years, and is now in the charge of Dúchas.

Dunsoghly Castle

69

features are the original oak roof timbers, still in position, and the small detached chapel to the south, with a carved panel depicting the instruments of the passion, and a well-preserved west window. It bears the date 1573, and the initials of Sir John Plunkett and his wife Genet Sarsfield. It was occupied as a dwelling house until fairly recent times, and many of the original windows have been replaced with large sash-windows. Close by is a circular fort.

Half a mile to the east of Dunsoghly is the village of St Margaret's, with closely adjoining it the old graveyard and the remains of the church. Here there is a fifteenth-century chapel founded by the Plunkett family, on the doorway of which is an interesting drip-stone in the form of a head, its companion being lost. There is also a mausoleum of the Morgan family, Catholic merchants of Dublin in the early eighteenth century, bearing a Latin inscription commemorating Andrew Morgan, who died in 1743, and another tablet of the same family from near the close of the century.

From St Margaret's, roads lead northwards to Skephubble and Chapelmidway, and eastwards to Knocksedan and Swords, or to Forrest Great and Cloghran, any of which are pleasant walks (for the last two, see Route 3).

Continuing in a straight line, the road reaches the village of Ward, named from the Ward river which also gives its name to the well-known Ward Union Hunt. A mile to the right here, on the road leading to Chapelmidway and Skephubble, is New Park, the seat in 1703 of Sir Robert Rochfort, whose son 'Nim' Rochfort was a friend of Swift. To the left are the scant remains of the Chapel of St Brigid. Almost two miles farther on, the road, which is the old coach-road to Derry and goes remarkably straight as far as Slane, enters the County Meath and at 13 miles reaches Ashbourne.

At 8¾ miles, however, a road forking right continues within the County Dublin for 2½ miles. It passes close to Kilsallaghan (reached by turning right again) where the castle, now ruined, was held by Hugh Phelim O'Byrne and a force of Irish Royalists against a large Parliamentarian force under Sir Charles Coote, in 1641. Near the county boundary, about a mile to the north, is another Mote.

St Margaret's is a scattered but pleasant hamlet showing no outward signs of its proximity to Dublin. **St Brigid's Well**, the size of a small swimming pool with steps down into it, can be found to the west of the modern church. It is known as the 'tepid well', because it never freezes over. The nearby church hall has some signs of being of eighteenth-century date.

To the north are the ruins of the pre-penal church, which has a good but damaged Gothic west doorway. The **Morgan mausoleum** and the **Plunkett chapel** have some good limestone and marble decorative work which is sorely in need of conservation and protection. One of the tombstones, dated 1728, is decorated with the paraphernalia of the Crucifixion, the northernmost example of this type I have seen.

The Morgan Mausoleum and the Plunkett Chapel in the old church yard, St Margaret's

There is little left of the old village of **Ward**.

New Park is ruinous and overgrown, its roof in a state of collapse.

The graveyard of **St Brigid's chapel** is still in use, although there is nothing left of the original chapel above ground.

At **Kilsallaghan** only fragments of the castle remain, south of a neat and tiny Church of Ireland church, rebuilt in 1812, with a gallery and a good east window installed in 1917.

ROUTE 6

KILBRIDE (CO. MEATH)

	Miles from the GPO
Cabra	2¼
— Dunsink Observatory	4¼
Cappoge	5
Holywoodrath	9½
County Boundary	11
Kilbride	12¼

Route 4 is followed as far as the North Circular Road, and the turn left is taken along it. At a fork in the road is the very large and conspicuous Catholic Church of St Peter, Phibsborough. This church succeeds an earlier and smaller building, illustrated in Wright's *Ireland Illustrated*, 1831. It was rebuilt later in the century, and the tower and nave of this rebuilding still remain. A third rebuilding had proceeded as far as the chancel and Central Tower, when, in 1868, there was a lawsuit about the strength of the Tower. The trial lasted thirty-eight days, and ended with the jury disagreeing. The upper part of the Tower was later removed. Goldie was the architect of the third rebuilding.

The left arm of the fork is the Circular Road continued; the right, which is Cabra Road, is the direction taken. Nothing of note is encountered until, at 2¼ miles from the GPO, the old Cabra Road from Blackhall Place (see Route 7) is joined. The turn to the right, however, is taken immediately, leading through a modern housing estate, and past the site of the now-demolished Cabra House (see Route 7).

In a little over ¼ mile is, on the left, the Dominican Convent of Cabra, which inhabits, among other buildings, Much Cabra House, an eighteenth-century building of red brick. It was the house of the Arthur family. The nuns came here in 1819 from Clontarf, but for a century previously they had had a convent in Channel Row (North Brunswick Street).

The Royal Canal is crossed at the eighth lock (H. S. Reilly Bridge, called after an early director of the canal), and, at 3½ miles from the GPO, is Cardiffsbridge, over the Tolka river. Here, in the early nineteenth century, there was a small iron-foundry. Cardiffsbridge House, originally belonging to the Seagraves, but then the residence of J. Newman, is picturesquely

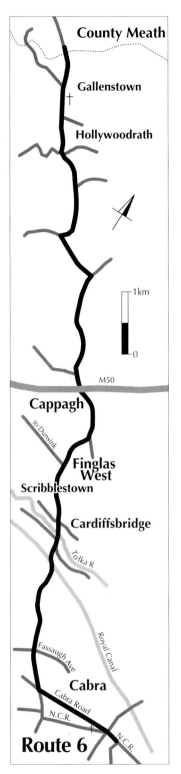

Although the Dominicans sold land for housing in the 1980s, the convent they founded in 1819 still occupies a considerable tract of land between the Ratoath Road and the Navan Road, and they are still involved in the education of girls with impaired hearing. **Much Cabra House**, however, has sadly been reduced to a single storey; only the ionic columned doorcase and the curved wings suggest its former quality.

The Tolka is crossed by a new bridge, and the original **Cardiffsbridge** stands like a monument in an adjacent field; the village that was gathered around it, together with **Cardiffsbridge House** and the **Jolly Toper** public house have been obliterated. **Rosemount** is also gone, replaced by a grassed 'open space'.

Cardiffsbridge House

situated, whitewashed with very boldly overhanging eaves. Behind it, on a road leading to Finglas, is Rosemount, occupied in 1836 by M. Rooney. On the left is a road leading to Scribblestown House and Scribblestown Park. The latter was formerly known as Scripplestown.

Detour: Dunsink Observatory

Half a mile from Cardiffsbridge, the road forks, the turn to the left leading in ¾ mile to Dunsink Observatory, and ultimately to Blanchardstown (see Route 7). The Observatory was founded as the Observatory of Trinity College by Provost Andrews, who died in 1774. The building was erected in about 1782, designed by Graham Myers. The first Professor of Astronomy was Dr Henry Ussher, who was succeeded in 1792 by Dr Brinkley, author of astronomical works and later Bishop of Cloyne. In 1791 the Professor was for the time being appointed the Astronomer Royal of Ireland, and regulations were introduced to ensure the astronomer's constant residence. In 1827 Sir William Rowan Hamilton, the celebrated mathematician, was appointed at the age of twenty-two, and remained here for thirty-eight years. A later holder of the office was Sir Robert Ball, the well-known popular astronomer, who later became Professor at Cambridge.

The office of Astronomer Royal lapsed in the 1920s, and the Observatory was for many years closed. It has recently been reopened in connection with the newly founded School of Cosmic Physics, under an arrangement whereby it shares with Armagh Observatory and Harvard University the ownership of a large telescope in South Africa. The building is a handsome one, surmounted by the dome of the original telescope. In the grounds stands a larger dome, which houses the photographic telescope presented in about 1880 by Sir Isaac Roberts, FRS. The present Head of the Observatory is Dr Bruck from Cambridge.

Return to main route

Half a mile beyond Dunsink, the route turns to the left at a T-junction. In a short distance is, on the left, St Mary's Cappagh, formerly Cappoge House. It has been much added to and is now an orthopaedic hospital. The turn right is taken at the next fork, and, at 6 miles from the GPO, the route forks left, reaching in a few yards the old graveyard of Ballycoolen (on the left). The remains of the church are very scanty, and few of the gravestones are old. Almost opposite the graveyard the route turns to the right, and in one mile reaches the crossroads of Hollywoodrath. On the right, just

With the exception of the litter that is a consequence of the nearby Dunsink Tiphead, the rural character of the narrow, linear oasis of the Tolka Valley is still intact. It is to be hoped that it will be properly preserved and protected. Most of the older houses along the valley, including **Scribblestown House** (now divided into two residences), Pelletstown and Dunsinea are extant, but **Scribblestown Park**, then the home of Lady Eva Forbes, was destroyed by fire in the mid-1970s.

Scribblestown Park, after the fire

Looming over the road to Dunsink is **Dunsink Tiphead**, a great hill of Dublin's garbage partly entombed in a grassy skin. The south side of the road is one long Travellers' encampment, lined with caravans, wrecked cars and litter.

The buildings that comprise **Dunsink Observatory** are extant, but they and their grounds look rather forlorn and neglected; the proximity of the tiphead seems to have the same effect on everything in the area.

In the midst of a run-down parkland setting **Cappoge House** still survives at the heart of **St Mary's Hospital, Cappagh**; it is a modest five-bay house with a porch supported on twin ionic columns.

The road takes you over the M50 and winds through a landscape of earthworks that will transform the countryside here into a network of new roads.

The old graveyard at **Ballycoolen** occupies a bramble-tangled mound, an incongruous patch of rural decay in the midst of the precision-machined buildings of the North West Business Park.

beyond the cross, is the house itself, of mid-nineteenth-century date, with a handsome loggia. It is now the Oliver Plunkett Colony of the Brothers of John of God. During the eighteenth century, Holywoodrath was the residence of Mr Serjeant Wood. About half a mile beyond the house, on the right-hand side of the road, is the Church of Ireland church at Gallenstown, also of mid-to-late nineteenth-century erection.

At 10½ miles, a fork to the left leads past Belgree House, and rejoins the main route a mile farther on. About a third of a mile beyond this fork, the road enters County Meath, and, after crossing Den Bridge (11¾ miles from the GPO), arrives at Kilbride, an undistinguished village with a conspicuous new Catholic church.

Bearing to the right at the church takes you in ⅓ mile to a laneway on the left; a short distance up this lane, the old Kilbride Church and graveyard can be found. The church is evidently of medieval date, but robbed of all its cut stone. By continuing along this road or bearing right, return may be made by the Ashbourne Road (Route 5).

The St John of God brothers sold **Hollywoodrath House** in 1958 and since then it has had several private owners. It is a great pile of a house, with bows at either end and the entrance loggia supported by four pairs of Corinthian columns. The present owner is a Mr Mulcahy.

The little church of **St Thomas, Mulhuddart**, is still there, clothed in trees.

St Thomas's church, Mulhuddart

Belgree House, which was a farmhouse of part mud-walled and part stone construction, was demolished and replaced in the 1970s.

The ruins of old **Kilbride church** and graveyard are extant.

ROUTE 7

CLONEE

	Miles from the GPO
King's Hospital	1½
Cabra	2¾
Ashtown	4
Blanchardstown	5½
Mulhuddart	7
Clonee	9¼

Leaving by the northern quays, the route passes successively the Metal Bridge (1816), Grattan (formerly Essex) Bridge (rebuilt 1874), and Richmond Bridge (1813–16); between Richmond and Whitworth Bridges (the latter 1816–18) are the Four Courts, on Inns Quay. The building occupies the site of the old King's Inns, which in mediaeval times was the Dominican Priory of St Saviour. The old Four Courts were closely adjoining Christ Church Cathedral, in what is now the churchyard. The west wing of the present building, which formerly housed the Public Record Office, was begun by Thomas Cooley in 1776; after Cooley's death in 1784, James Gandon was commissioned to re-house the courts. The foundation stone for the main block was laid by the Duke of Rutland in 1786, and the courts opened in 1796, but the building was not completed until 1802. It was much extended to the rear during the nineteenth century, and the original plan of storing the public records in the great space under the outer dome was never carried out. During Easter Week 1916, it was held by National forces, but escaped serious damage. During the last weeks of June 1922, it was again occupied by Irregulars under Rory O'Connor. It was shelled by light artillery from the quays, and, before it was finally evacuated, a number of internal mines were exploded. The destruction of the Record Office was equalled by the damage which the building itself suffered. It was restored and reopened for business in 1932. Unfortunately, the original design was not reproduced in the external appearance of the damaged parts. The great merits that the building still possesses are due to the massiveness of the central block, which enabled it to resist the explosions, and to the accident that so much external detail escaped damage.

Whitworth Bridge, immediately above the Four Courts, is on the site of

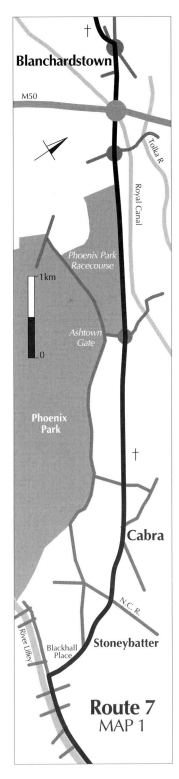

Owing to the one-way system on the quays it is no longer possible to drive westwards on the north quays; instead, the south quays have to be followed to Kingsbridge and crossed to the north quays.

Upstream of the **Metal Bridge** (still known as the Halfpenny Bridge) a slender new foot bridge designed by Howley Harrington Partners and known as the **Millennium Bridge** was erected in 2000 to give additional access to Temple Bar. Farther upstream an additional road bridge, **Frank Sherwin Bridge**, was erected in 1982, running across the Liffey from Watling Street.

The Millennium Bridge

While much of the **Four Courts** was not restored in accordance with Gandon's original design, in the 1960s the dies on the blocking courses on the fronts of the wings, left out in the post-1923 reconstruction, were fortunately replaced.

'The Bridge', for long the only bridge, which was rebuilt by the Dominicans in 1428. The next bridge, Queen's Bridge, replaced Arran Bridge (1683), which was swept away by a flood. It was designed by General Vallancey, the antiquary, and was finished in 1768. It is, perhaps, the most beautiful of the existing bridges.

The route now turns right up Blackhall Place. In Hendrick Street, on the right, there are a number of old gabled houses. On the left is the King's Hospital School (The Bluecoat School), founded in 1670 by Charles II. The original building was somewhat eastward of the present, and was used by Parliament while the building in College Green was in process. In 1773 it was rebuilt on the present site (part of Oxmantown Green). The architect was Thomas Ivory of Cork. As usual in Dublin, the architect's designs were not fully carried out. The central dome was intended to be much higher, and for many years remained unfinished. The present dome was substituted in 1894.

Blackhall Place becomes Stoneybatter, an old name of which half has been translated into English while the other half (*bóthar*—road) remains in Irish. The upper end of it is now called Manor Street. It now forks, and the left branch leads into Blackhorse Lane, and along the Phoenix Park wall. It rejoins the present route beyond Castleknock, and may be taken as an alternative. The right branch contains some old houses, and represents the village of Oxmantown, the town of the Ostmen or Scandinavians. The City Arms Hotel on the left, a fine Georgian building, is the social centre of the cattle-market, and was formerly the town house of the Jameson family, of Bow Street Distillery. After 2 miles, the North Circular Road is crossed.

The road now changes its name to Old Cabra Road and then to Windy Harbour. Cabra House, the site of which is on the right, was lived in by John Toler, Lord Norbury, Chief Justice of the Common Pleas. He was a self-made man, a notorious duellist, unlearned in the law, and finally removed when he had fallen asleep during a murder case. Lord Clare suggested that he should have been made a bishop. The house, called Little Cabragh by Elrington Ball, was inhabited in 1619 by the Seagraves, a Catholic family who were forced to leave in Cromwellian times, when it came into the hands of Col. Sir Hierome Sankey. Sankey was successively an Anglican, a Presbyterian, an Independent, and an Anabaptist, a divinity student, soldier, college don, officer, legislator and landowner.

On the corner between the road and Little Cabra is St Joseph's Institution for the Deaf and Dumb. At 3¾ miles is the old Workhouse, now

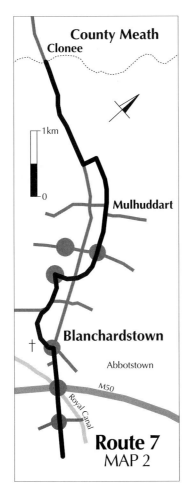

County Meath
Clonee

1km

0

Mulhuddart

Blanchardstown

Abbotstown

M50

Royal Canal

Route 7
MAP 2

There are no old gabled houses remaining in **Hendrick Street**, which, being on the fringe of the major Smithfield urban development works, is at time of writing undergoing renewal.

Gable-fronted houses on Hendrick Street c. 1950

The **Bluecoat School** is now the headquarters of the Incorporated Law Society.

The winding main street of **Stoneybatter** still has the feel of an urban village: it has not yet been seen as necessary to modernise the name of the tall brick and limestone public house called 'The Glimmer-Man' (see page 133).

Blackhorse Lane is today called Blackhorse Avenue.

The **City Arms Hotel**, although the façade has been altered on a number of occasions, is extant, with its short sweeps, lanterns and great stable gateway. Some of the old windows, almost flush with the external wall face, still remain. The building is currently occupied by the Free University of Ireland.

Opposite O'Hanlon's public house at the North Circular Road the cattle market was built over in 1979 with rather dull local authority housing.

Much extended, **St Joseph's Institution** today occupies a large campus. **St Vincent's Orphanage** is still there, sad and dreary and little altered.

St Vincent's Orphanage. A short road to the left leads to the Ashtown Gate of the Phoenix Park, where the attempted assassination of Lord French took place, on 20 December 1919.

Here there is a detour to Blanchardstown by a road to the right along the Tolka river, a distance of about 1½ miles.

From Ashtown, the road runs along the edge of the Phoenix Park Racecourse. On the right is the factory of the Ashtown Tin Box Company. At 5 miles on the right are Morgan's and Mercer's Schools, for boys and girls respectively, both founded early in the nineteenth century. The Royal Canal is crossed at Talbot Bridge (5½ miles) where the tall chimney of the old Blanchardstown Mills (now a margarine factory) is conspicuous. Talbot Bridge, like Granard Bridge immediately above it, and Ranelagh Bridge immediately below, is named for a director of the Royal Canal Company. The company was founded in 1789 by a retired shoemaker who had been a director of the Grand Canal. The first 22 miles cost £315,204. In 1818, control was vested in the board with the Lord Lieutenant as chairman, and in 1846 the canal was sold to the Midland Great Western Railway, whose line keeps it company as far as Mullingar. The graceful canal bridges are a very attractive feature. The Canal enters the Shannon at Cloondara near Longford, 40 miles north of Shannon Harbour on the Grand Canal. The Royal has never been commercially profitable.

The wooden spire of Blanchardstown Catholic Church is now visible on the left, covered with coloured shingles. On the right is Abbotstown, the seat of Lord Holmpatrick. The demesne contains what remains of the Great Wood of Blanchardstown, which once belonged to the Luttrell family. A distant view is obtained of the dome of Dunsink Observatory (see Route 6) on the ridge above the Tolka. In the Abbotstown demesne is a ruined church.

The road now follows the valley of the Tolka, and at 7 miles reaches the village of Mulhuddart. Half a mile to the right over the bridge is Our Lady's Well, covered with a white dome-like structure. A little farther along the same road is the ruined church. Here the soldiers of a Williamite force under Colonel Foulkes were all killed while sheltering on their way to Dublin in September 1690.

At 8½ miles is Damastown House, which was inherited in 1687 by the Rev. Charles Proby of Castleknock, who eloped with the niece and ward of Primate Narcissus Marsh 'and, as is reported, was married that night in a tavern'. Just before entering Clonee (9¼ miles) the county boundary is crossed. Clonee is of no particular note.

The **Phoenix Park Racecourse** is no longer in use and is awaiting redevelopment. The **Ashtown Tin Box Company** is no longer there, and **Morgan's** and **Mercer's schools** were swept away in road widening. The place where the Royal Canal was crossed by Talbot Bridge has become a Dublin spaghetti junction: the canal, railway line, M50 motorway, the Navan Road and the Blanchardstown Bypass all come together here in an intricate complex of concrete bridge structures. The old **Blanchardstown Mills** were cleared to make way for the Blanchardstown Bypass.

Blanchardstown church is still in use; built in 1836, it remained an unfinished shell until 1856, when the ceiling and gallery were constructed, and the walls dashed. Soon after, the tower was erected with a spire of an unusual monocoque construction.

The southern part of the **Abbotstown demesne**, although still retaining fragments of the Great Wood, is occupied by the James Connolly Memorial Hospital, built in the early 1950s as a TB sanatorium. It is a vast and depressing campus, a wide scatter of flat-roofed blocks separated by deserts of grass.

Abbotstown House is the headquarters of the Abbotstown Veterinary Research Laboratories, and at time of writing that part of the demesne not occupied by the hospital has been identified as the site for the controversial proposed National Sports Campus.

The ruined church in the Abbotstown demesne is extant.

Beyond Blanchardstown village is the **Blanchardstown Centre**, a large shopping complex built in the 1990s. Of **Mulhuddart** village not much remains except the public house.

Our Lady's Well, of very ancient origin, is still to be found in a little dip in the ground to the left of the road north of the Tolka, covered by a curious vaulted structure with a cross and a little plinth incised with devotional texts. It is, however, neglected now, coated with mud thrown up by passing cars, and the well water is foul. The vaulted roof may date from early in the eighteenth century. The shrine retained its popularity through the period of the Penal Laws, attracting on Lady Day (8 September), throughout the eighteenth and nineteenth centuries, large concourses of people.

The remains of the church, a few walls and part of a tower with a vaulted first floor, still stand at the highest point of the hill, overlooking a graveyard.

Damastown House was demolished to make way for an extensive industrial estate, part of which bears the name.

ROUTE 8

CASTLEKNOCK, LUTTRELLSTOWN AND CLONSILLA

	Miles from the GPO
Ashtown Gate	3¾
Castleknock	5
Luttrellstown	8
Clonsilla	9

Route 7 is followed as far as the end of Stoneybatter, where Aughrim Street forks to the left at 1⅓ miles. On the right of Aughrim Street (named after the Battle of Aughrim, County Galway, in 1691) is the Roman Catholic Parish Church of the Holy Family. The North Circular Road is now crossed, and at 2 miles is McKee (formerly Marlborough) Barracks, built by Lord Wolseley. From the Circular Road onwards the road is called Blackhorse Lane. On the right, at 2½ miles, is the Military Cemetery, and soon after, the Poor Man's Well is passed. The road skirts the Phoenix Park wall very closely, passing a number of turnstiles, rivals for the title of 'Hole in the Wall'. Though much built over in recent years, this part still retains some of the village character which formerly marked it.

Ashtown Gate, reached at 3¾ miles, was the scene, on 20 December 1919, of an attempt upon the life of Lord French, who was Viceroy at the time. This point is very near the Navan Road, which may be reached by the turn to the right. Between Blackhorse Lane and the Navan Road is the Phoenix Park Racecourse, the nearest racecourse to the city. It was opened during the latter half of the nineteenth century, on the site of a house called Ashfield, and, between 1900 and the present day, it has more than doubled its extent.

Castleknock, which is reached in 5 miles from the GPO, was granted by Strongbow to Hugh Tyrrel in the twelfth century. The Castle, which still survives though much ruined, was built by Hugh de Tyrrel, who was styled Baron of Castleknock, and in the thirteenth century a Richard Tyrrel founded here an Augustinian Abbey dedicated to St Brigid. During the Bruce's campaign of 1317, the Scottish army camped at Castleknock, with the intention of besieging Dublin, but abandoned the project and attacked

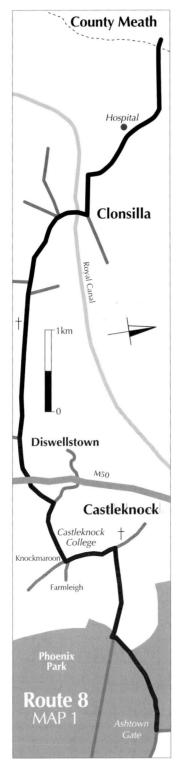

County Meta

Hospital

Clonsilla

Royal Canal

1 km

0

Diswellstown

M50

Castleknock

Castleknock
College

Knockmaroon

Farmleigh

Phoenix
Park

Route 8
MAP 1

Ashtown
Gate

The buildings of **McKee Barracks** are a blend of French Château, Elizabethan, Queen Anne and Tudor styles, and of such a large scale they cannot but be impressive with their red brick and terracotta turrets, mansards and steep roofs. McKee houses Army Headquarters, and is also the home of the Army Equitation School.

McKee Barracks

The **Military Cemetery**, established in the early twentieth century for British Army personnel, is extant and open to the public. The last burial was that of a Mrs Farrelly, who died in 2000 at the age of 104, and was buried beside her husband, who was interred in 1950.

I could find no trace of the **Poor Man's Well**.

Phoenix Park Racecourse is now disused, and awaiting redevelopment. Unfortunately, the late-nineteenth-century mock Tudor ticket offices opposite the Ashtown Gate are falling into disrepair; it is a pity to see such derelic-tion in such a prominent place.

Limerick instead. The Castle was captured by the Cromwellian General Monk in 1642, and recaptured by Owen Roe O'Neill in 1647. Lead-mines were worked here in the middle of the eighteenth century. but have long since been abandoned. The Protestant Parish Church, the most conspicuous object in the village, is modern but not ungraceful at a distance. It replaced the church of 1669, which Swift immortalised in his poem 'The Little House'.

The turn left in the village is taken, and, after about half a mile, the turn right at the crossroads. Here are the gates of Knockmaroon, the seat of the second Lord Moyne. The first Baron (The Hon. Walter Guinness) was one of the three sons of the first Earl of Iveagh (Edward Cecil Guinness), to each of whom Lord Iveagh gave a house in this district, so that the three houses (Knockmaroon, Farmleigh and Glenmaroon), with their grounds, form an almost continuous belt westward of the Phoenix Park. Walter Guinness had a distinguished political career, as well as being author of several travel books and a keen amateur of marine biology, a taste which his wealth enabled him to gratify. He was Minister of Agriculture in the British Government, and, during the Second World War, was British Minister-Resident in the Middle East, in which capacity he was assassinated by terrorists in Alexandria in 1944. His son, the present Lord Moyne, is also known as the poet and novelist Bryan Guinness.

A little beyond the gates of Knockmaroon, on the right is Castleknock College, a large school in charge of the Vincentian order, and incorporating an older house of the Warren family. The college was founded in 1833 at Ussher's Quay in Dublin, and in the following year the demesne at Castleknock was acquired. Its alumni have included Lord Russell of Killowen, the first Catholic Lord Chief Justice of England since the Reformation, Admiral Kane, hero of the Calliope escape, and Professor O'Reilly, who aided Newman in the establishment of the Catholic University. The buildings and playing fields are very extensive. In the latter is the Castle already mentioned, a particularly interesting example of a polygonal keep forming part of the outer defences (Leask: *Irish Castles*). It suffered extensive destruction, being used probably as a quarry, during the eighteenth century. The courtyard of the Castle is now used as a cemetery by the Vincentian Fathers. Also in the college grounds is a smaller castle-like building, said to have been originally a private observatory.

The road forks in less than half a mile, and the branch left is taken, passing Diswellstown (Kennan family in 1783, now Miss Laidlaw) and

The **Protestant church** with its pinnacled tower built from granite of many hues, remains a significant landmark in the village of Castleknock.

Knockmaroon is still there in its great sylvan demesne.

Castleknock College has been much extended over the last half-century, but at time of writing the Vincentians are making arrangements to close the boarding school after 130 years of operation. The day school, opened in 1987, will remain.

Castleknock College

Diswellstown House is extant, and opposite the Catholic St Mochta's church with its slender belfry, **Annfield**, which appears to have been re-roofed in recent years, is also still there.

Annfield, and, after the Catholic church, skirting the demesne of Luttrell-stown House on the left. Luttrellstown is, of all the seats in County Dublin, one of those to be identified longest with a single family. Unfortunately, such celebrity as the Luttrells can boast of is of an unenviable kind. Sir Geoffrey Luttrell, a favourite of King John, came over in 1204. Robert Luttrell was Treasurer of St Patrick's and Chancellor of Ireland in the thirteenth century. Sir Thomas Luttrell was Chief Justice of the Common Pleas in Ireland from 1534 till 1554. He obtained substantial grants of monastic lands, and sent a rare goshawk as a present to Thomas Cromwell. Nonetheless, at his death he left money 'for the salvation of the souls of himself and his brother Simon'. His second son, James, seems to have been a good landlord. Thomas Luttrell, Sir Thomas's grandson, was a leader of the Catholic party in the Irish Parliament of James I, and died in 1634. During the Commonwealth, the Luttrells were dispossessed in favour of Cromwellian Colonel John Hewson, who let it to Sir William Bury. Thomas Luttrell was restored by the Commissioners of Settlement in 1663, and was succeeded by his son Colonel Simon Luttrell in 1673. The family at this time was still Catholic, and Simon was a supporter of James II. His brother, Henry, who succeeded on his death in 1698, deserted to King William after the Siege of Limerick. He defrauded his brother's widow of her jointure, and was killed by an unknown assassin near his house in Stafford Street, Dublin, in 1717. It was popularly believed that he was in league with the devil, and the Devil's Mills or 'Black Mills' (now the Anna Liffey Mills on the Strawberry Beds Road) commemorate this. His son, the first Earl of Carhampton, lived mainly in England: *his* son, the second Earl, was the opponent of Wilkes at the famous Westminster Election of 1769, when the following observations were made of him by 'Junius':

> There is in this young man's conduct a strain of prostitution, which for its singularity I cannot but admire. He has discovered a new line in the human character. He has disgraced even the name of Luttrell.

He was involved in a most unpleasant scandal in Dublin (see the autobiography of Hamilton Rowan), and, as Commander-in-Chief, took a prominent role in putting down the '98 Rising. He sold Luttrellstown soon afterwards, and Mr Luke White, a rich printer and bookseller, ancestor of Lord Annaly, who bought it, found it advisable to change the name to Woodlands, which name it still bears on the Ordnance Maps, though a city bus now runs to 'Luttrellstown'.

Luttrellstown remained in Irish hands until bought by a Swiss-based company in 1983. It is now called Luttrellstown Castle and is a luxury hotel; an 18-hole golf course and country club has been developed in the eastern part of the 550 acre demesne. The rest of the grounds have survived with little change since they were first laid out in the eighteenth century, but at time of writing this contextual setting, almost unique at such a scale in Ireland, is under threat; planning applications have recently been made for a large development which will include conference rooms, two hotels, an equestrian centre, another golf club and over 100 dwellings.

Luttrellstown Castle

The house was entirely rebuilt during the nineteenth century, and was visited on three occasions by Queen Victoria, in 1849, 1853 and 1861. An obelisk in the grounds celebrates one of these visits. The Queen greatly admired the trees in the demesne. During the war of 1939–45 it was let to Signor Berardis, Italian Minister to Ireland. It is now the residence of Mr Brinsley Plunkett.

At 7½ miles from the GPO the road forks again, the right branch leading to Clonsilla Railway Station and village. Clonsilla is chiefly remarkable for the long cutting which the Royal Canal occupies between here and Blanchardstown. The towpath is continuous, and a pleasant walk may be taken by it, towards either Blanchardstown or Lucan. The bridges, which are fairly frequent, are very graceful. Just beyond Clonsilla Station, the Navan branch of the MGWR (CIÉ) leaves the main line, and there is a main road to the interesting old town of Trim in County Meath.

The county boundary is here at its nearest point to the city, being less than 8½ miles from the GPO, as the crow flies. At 1½ miles west of Clonsilla is the point where the counties of Dublin, Meath and Kildare meet. In the present Protestant Church of Clonsilla there hangs a bell from St Werburgh's in Dublin, cast in 1747 and brought here in 1855. Another bell of similar origin hangs in Castleknock Church. At Clonsilla House lives the Hon. W. E. Wylie, KC, well-known for his philanthropic enterprises and interest in horses.

Clonsilla is equidistant (2 miles) from Clonee (Route 7) and from Lucan (Route 9), by either of which return may be made.

Clonsilla railway station waiting room has a new curved-steel roof, but the older buildings seem neglected.

Clonsilla House was destroyed by fire *c.* 1980, and subsequently demolished, its demesne developed for a private housing scheme called **Porter's Gate**. Some of the fine trees of the old gardens were retained, including a great copper beech, which stands close to where the house was.

Gateway to Military Cemetery, Blackhorse Avenue (see pages 84 & 85)

ROUTE 9

LEIXLIP VIA THE PHOENIX PARK AND
STRAWBERRY BEDS

	Miles from the GPO
Parkgate	1¾
St Mobhi's College	3½
Knockmaroon Gate	4
Astagob	6
Broomfield	7
Lucan	8½

Leaving O'Connell Street by Bachelor's Walk and the northern quays, the Route passes, at 1½ miles, on the right, Collins Barracks, formerly the Royal Barracks, and often known as Arbour Hill Barracks. These buildings, which were built at various times from 1706 onwards, were, in their day, among the largest of their kind. Within the precincts may be seen the graves of the executed leaders of 1916, brought here from Kilmainham. A ceremony is held here annually, at Easter.

On the other side of the river, just beyond the busy wharves of Guinness's Brewery, is the fine east front of Kingsbridge Station, the terminus of the Great Southern and Western line to Cork. The building was designed by Sancton Wood and built in 1849.

Just inside the Phoenix Park, which is now entered through the main 'gate' (a misnomer since there is no longer a gate here) is the old Military Infirmary, designed by James Gandon in 1786. The architect presented the design gratis, but the cupola as erected is not as he designed it, and the centre has been altered. Many years later, Gandon had a scheme for the erection of a great triumphal arch at the Park Gate, instead of the Wellington Testimonial obelisk, the largest obelisk in Europe, designed by Sir Robert Smirke, architect of the British Museum.

The Phoenix Park, the greatest public park in these islands (Windsor Park, being a royal park, is, of course, in a different category, and is larger), and in proportion to Dublin almost without parallel anywhere, has a long history. The nucleus consisted of the lands granted by the Tyrrells of Castleknock to the Priory of St John at Kilmainham. At the Dissolution,

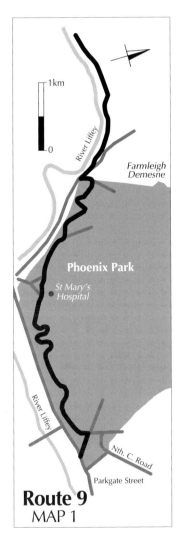

Route 9
MAP 1

Collins Barracks was restored and extended in the 1990s and now houses part of the National Museum.

Guinness is no longer shipped downriver by barge, but the north bank of the Liffey, opposite Kingsbridge Station (now called Heuston Station), has been densely developed with apartment blocks.

The main gate piers to the Phoenix Park were reinstated in the late 1990s.

The old **Military Infirmary**, which is noticed by few passersby because it is obscured by the trees of the People's Gardens, was renovated in recent years, and is now the **Army General Headquarters**.

The **Wellington monument** is still a major landmark; the only significant monumental addition to the park since 1949 is the 35 m high **Papal Cross**, erected for the visit of Pope John Paul II in 1979.

Army General Headquarters, Phoenix Park

these lands passed to the Crown, who used the Priory as a Viceregal residence. Later, a house named 'The Phoenix', on the site of the present Magazine Fort, was used for this purpose.

The original intention of Ormonde in laying out the park in 1662 was to provide a royal deer park. The cost was not less than £40,000, involving the purchase of large tracts of land, and the building of the wall. The park, which at that time included the Kilmainham lands south of the river, was well over 2,000 acres in extent, even larger than it is at present. The name 'Phoenix' is usually explained as the corruption of 'Fionn-Uisge' meaning clear water; and there seems no reason to doubt this. During the early Hanoverian period, many persons were allowed to erect lodges in the Park, which in later times were regularised as the Viceregal Lodge, the Chief Secretary's Lodge, Mountjoy Barracks, etc. Later still, these were adapted as Áras an Uachtaráin, the Papal Nunciature, the United States Legation, etc. The greatest single benefactor of the Park since Ormonde's time was Lord Chesterfield, Viceroy from 1745 to 1747; but of his improvements only the graceful Phoenix Column and, perhaps, a few trees, survive. During the last years of the British regime the upkeep of the Park cost over £8,000 per annum. Doubtless, it is now much more.

The People's Gardens are on the right after the Park is entered. At the statue of General Gough by Foley (recently decapitated, but now restored), a turn to the right leads to the Zoological Gardens. On the left is the Wellington Testimonial, erected in 1817 and adorned with bronze plaques cast from cannon captured by Irish regiments. It is 205 feet high, but, despite its great scale, it cannot be ascended.

The central road (Chesterfield Road) of the Park continues straight on from here, emerging at Castleknock Gate, and may be used as an alternative to Route 8, as far as Castleknock. After the Gough statue, there is a polo ground to the right and, on the left, are various playing fields for hurling, football and cricket.

Notice among the playing fields the Phoenix Cricket Club, founded in 1832. It is the oldest cricket club in Ireland. The first cricket match ever played in Ireland (reported in the *Freeman's Journal* at the date) was in the Phoenix Park, August 1792, when the Military Garrison played all Ireland, captained by Major Hobart, Secretary at War. The Duke of Wellington (then Captain Wellesley) played for the Garrison, and his side had the best of it; hence, no doubt, his later observation that the Battle of Waterloo was won in the Phoenix Park.

The fine equestrian statue of **General Gough**, by the sculptor J. H. Foley, was damaged again in 1956, and completely blown down in an explosion in 1957.

General Gough statue

On the right is the former Viceregal Lodge, now the residence of His Excellency S. T. O'Kelly, President of Ireland. It has a solitary air. In its original form, it was built in 1751 for the Rt Hon. Nathaniel Clements, then the Park Ranger, and was bought in 1782 as a residence for the Viceroys, for £10,000. A few years later, it was proposed by the Government to present the Lodge and grounds to Henry Grattan, as the house was in a bad state of repair. The patriot party, however, detected the ulterior motive, and the offer was declined. The Lodge was much enlarged by Francis Johnston, who gave it its present Old Colonial aspect, and it remained the Viceregal residence throughout the period of the Union (1800–1922), and, when the Irish Free State was set up, it became the residence of T. M. Healy, the first Governor General.

After the accession to power of the first Fianna Fáil administration in 1932, the house remained unoccupied for some time, but after the adoption of the new Constitution in 1938, it became the residence of the first President of Ireland, Dr Douglas Hyde, founder of the Gaelic League. In front of the ha-ha is the spot where on 6 May 1882 Lord Frederick Cavendish and Mr Burke were assassinated by the Invincibles.

A little farther on is the Phoenix Column, which formerly occupied the centre of the road, but was moved in about 1930 to its present position a little to one side, because it was an obstruction to motor-racing. It shows, as does the personification of the female head 'Anna Liffey' on the Custom House and O'Connell Bridge, the superimposition of a classical concept upon the corruption of a misunderstood Irish name. It is an extremely graceful Corinthian shaft, with a Phoenix rising in flames from the abacus. On the pedestal are the Stanhope arms and two elegant Latin inscriptions, forming a worthy memorial to the best of the eighteenth-century Viceroys.

To the left, the former Chief Secretary's Lodge may now be seen. It is approximately the same date as the Viceregal, and is now the United States Legation.

The Private Secretary's Lodge, near the Cabra Gate, has been re-named Ratra, and has, since his retirement from office in 1945, been the residence of Dr Douglas Hyde. West of this, towards the Ashtown Gate, is the old Under-Secretary's Lodge, now the Apostolic Nunciature.

Farther on, to the left of the main road, near White's Gate, is the Ordnance Survey Office, formerly Lord Mountjoy's Lodge, but for many years devoted to its present purpose.

At the Gough statue, the turn left is taken, passing Islandbridge Gate,

The portico of **Áras an Uachtaráin**, formerly the Vice-Regal Lodge, can be glimpsed from the main road through the park.

The **Phoenix Column** was moved in the 1930s to facilitate motor racing in the park, but has recently been reinstated in the centre of the crossroads.

The **United States Legation** has become the United States Embassy.

The **Papal Nunciature** was demolished in the late 1970s, liberating the sixteenth-century tower-house which it contained. An architectural competition was held for the design of a State residence for the Taoiseach on the site, but the idea was subsequently abandoned. What were formerly stables for the residence now house the **Phoenix Park Visitors' Centre**.

Ratra, where Winston Churchill lived for a time as a child, is still there, and in use as the Civil Defence Headquarters.

The **Ordnance Survey Office** still occupies the complex near White's Gate. It is no longer an establishment of the Army, but is operated as a semi-state company.

Papal Nunciature 1977

The tower-house revealed when the nunciature was demolished

and approaching the Magazine Fort. It occupies the site of the old Phoenix House, and was built in 1734. Its erection 'evoked the last satiric spark emitted by Swift's expiring intellect' (C. L. Falkiner: *Illustrations of Irish History*), when the Dean produced the impromptu quatrain:

> *Behold a proof of Irish sense,*
> *Here Irish Wit is seen;*
> *Where nothing's left that's worth defence*
> *They build—a magazine!*

The Magazine Fort was captured on Easter Monday 1916 by a party of Republicans who gained entrance by pretending to chase an errant football. It was again raided in 1941 by an illegal organisation which abstracted large quantities of ammunition therefrom.

The fork left is here taken, and the road soon doubles around the grounds of another lodge. It next approaches St Mobhi's College near Chapelizod Gate. This building was first erected as the Hibernian Military School, in 1767, and was greatly enlarged by Francis Johnston in 1808. It was subsequently used as a military hospital, but was reopened in recent years as St Mobhi's Gaelic Training College for (Protestant) Church of Ireland teachers. It is now (1948) to be turned into a Tuberculosis Sanatorium. Just outside the grounds to the west is a cromlech. On the right is the so-called Fifteen Acres where so many duels were fought in former days. The record, says Francis Gerard (*Picturesque Dublin*), equals that of the German duellists, and ended only in the 1850s.

The road now climbs, and, forking left, enters the Furry Glen, a picturesque and little-known amenity, containing an attractive artificial lake. Exit from the Park is made by the Knockmaroon Gate (which is nearer Glenmaroon House than it is to Knockmaroon House).

The Phoenix Park has always appealed to the imagination of Dubliners and visitors. As long ago as 1717 James Ward wrote of it:

> *Oft thro' thy cool retreats I silent stray,*
> *And lost in thought neglect my heedless way;*
> *Intent on nature's works my wondring mind*
> *Shakes off the busy town she left behind,*
> *Her wings she plumes anew, expatiates free,*
> *And quits the world for solitude and thee.*

In the mid-nineteenth century, it inspired William Wilkins to a remark-

The **Magazine Fort** is still there, much overgrown and dilapidated.

The park lodges are well-maintained and used as residences by park staff.

St Mobhi's College is today **St Mary's Hospital**, a conglomeration of buildings of many periods, including the long flat-roofed TB pavilions dating from 1948. The **Hibernian Military Academy** was established for the maintenance and education of the orphans and children of soldiers in Ireland. At the back of the complex is a fine chapel by Thomas Cooley, dating from 1771; it was a custom for the Vice-Regal family to attend Sunday service here late in the eighteenth century. In the graveyard, besides the graves of former masters and officials of the Academy, are rows of tiny crosses marking the burials of nearly one hundred child cadets who died here between 1865 and 1910.

The western part of St Mary's is now a Cheshire Home.

As part of the policy of reducing car access to parts of the park, the road through the Furry Glen is closed to vehicular traffic.

St Mobhi's College chapel

ably good poem on the Magazine Fort:

> *Round the staff the yellow leopards of England, weary of wars,*
> *curl and uncurl...*

The Park has also many associations with great gatherings of people; none perhaps more noteworthy than the celebrations held here in 1929 and 1932, the Centenary of Catholic Emancipation, and the Eucharistic Congress.

Though no public-houses are now permitted in the Park, there were several until comparatively recent times, notably Nancy Hand's, which had a sign depicting an old woman with a white cap, serving her customers.

Just outside the Knockmaroon Gate may be seen down to the left Glenmaroon House, the residence of the Hon. Ernest Guinness, which occupies both sides of the road and is connected by two bridges. Up to the right may be seen the lofty clock tower in the grounds of Farmleigh, the seat of the Earl of Iveagh. On the immediate right is Mount Sackville Convent School for Girls.

The fork to the left as one faces Farmleigh is taken, descending sharply into the valley of the Liffey, at 5 miles from the GPO. The road is very attractive, but there are few houses of note until, at 6½ miles, is Oaklands, the residence of John Nicholson Esq. and, at 7 miles, Somerton, that of Miss Laidlaw. At 7½ miles is 'The Wren's Nest' public-house, an attractive place set below the site of the old Strawberry Beds. During the last century, the Strawberry Beds were a very popular resort, and cars used to ply from Dublin in large numbers. There is now no bus on this road, and the place is no longer a resort on any scale.

The road, still following the Liffey, skirts the demesne of Luttrellstown, while on the left is Broomfield House, and across the river the woods of Hermitage, Woodville and St Edmundsbury (see Route 10). The Anna Liffey Mills (see Route 8) are also passed, and, at 8½ miles, Lucan is entered by crossing the Liffey. This route is perhaps best seen in autumn, when the colours of the old trees by the river are very beautiful indeed. For the continuation of the route, see Route 10.

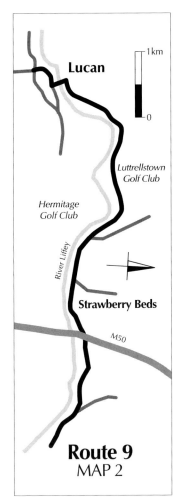

1km

0

Lucan

Luttrellstown Golf Club

Hermitage Golf Club

River Liffey

Strawberry Beds

M50

Route 9
MAP 2

Glenmaroon House is an exuberant example of mock Tudor. It has been occupied by the Daughters of Charity of St Vincent de Paul since 1949, when the last private owner, Arthur Ernest Guinness, died. In 1955 the Department of Health built a special school for the mentally handicapped in the grounds, and the complex is mainly occupied now by the Eastern Region Health Board.

The clocktower in the grounds of **Farmleigh** is still visible from the gates of Glenmaroon House. Bought by the state for £23 million in 1999, Farmleigh was extensively refurbished at a cost of £15 million and reopened in 2001 as a venue for state occasions and to accommodate guests of the state.

Mount Sackville, since 1864 a convent school of the Sisters of St Joseph of Cluny, is still there; it has been extensively, and not too sensitively, extended and added to over the years.

The old winding road westwards along the bottom of the Liffey valley, passing a scattering of picturesque little cottages, is a most pleasant rural route.

Oaklands is just visible between the trees before the road passes under the high M50 bridge; the bridge itself is the best vantage-point from which to see **Somerton**, (also called Summerton) which appears today in need of restoration. The owner in 1911, Mr T. K. Laidlaw, was the last High Sheriff of County Dublin appointed by the British government.

The Wren's Nest is still open for business, and **Broomfield House** is extant. The **Anna Liffey Mill** buildings now house a number of small industries.

ROUTE 10

LEIXLIP VIA CHAPELIZOD AND LUCAN

	Miles from the GPO
Chapelizod	3
Palmerstown	4½
Lucan	7½

Leaving by the north quays, the route passes the Parkgate entrance of the Phoenix Park (see Route 9) on the right, and runs along Conyngham Road, skirting the southern wall of the Park, with the Liffey below on the left. One of the houses on the river is named the Salmon Pool, and it was from this point that Oliver Gogarty, Senator and Poet, captured by enemies during the Civil War, made his celebrated Liffey swim to safety. At the Islandbridge Gate of the Phoenix Park there is a bridge over the Liffey, built in 1794, and named Sarah Bridge after the Duchess of Westmoreland. It is a very graceful single arch of stone, and retains its original iron railings.

It leads to Islandbridge Barracks, the Gate of the Royal Hospital (originally erected on Ussher's Quay and removed here in 1846), Kilmainham Gaol and Courthouse, and (on the right) to the entrance to the War Memorial Park, opened in 1938—a garden of remembrance of those Irishmen fallen in the war of 1914–1918, with terraces, fountains and a great stone cross, to the design of Sir Edwin Lutyens.

Passing the Chapelizod Gate, the road comes to the Roman Catholic Church of Chapelizod, which occupies a site very near that of the King's House, at first a residence of Sir Maurice Eustace, and, after 1665, a Viceregal residence until the death of Lord Capel there in 1701, when it was temporarily abandoned. It was again used as such during the second quarter of the eighteenth century, but was turned into a barracks in 1760, and sold in 1832. It has now perished, though a pigeon-house of the 1720s was visible until thirty years ago, and may be there still.

At Chapelizod, the road unites beyond the bridge with the road from Kilmainham. These have always been the two main avenues issuing from the city towards the West of Ireland: Athlone, Tuam, Galway and other places beyond the Shannon.

Chapelizod, 3 miles west from the GPO, derives its name from Iseult or Isolde, the tragic princess of the legend, who was shipped from Ireland to

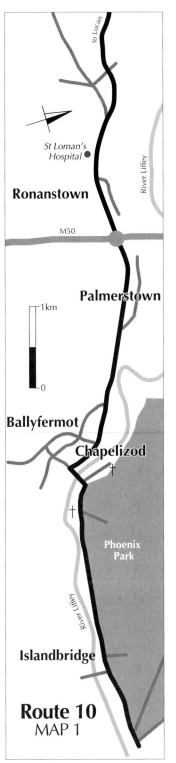

Route 10
MAP 1

The **Salmon Pool** was demolished and its beautiful riverside site developed for apartments in 2000.

The **Islandbridge Barracks** is still there, though it may soon be sold for development.

For **Kilmainham Gaol** see page 115.

Kilmainham Courthouse, next to the gaol, is still in use.

Kilmainham Courthouse

The **War Memorial Park** was refurbished in the late 1980s.

The site of the **King's House** and old pigeon house has been built over with apartments. Secluded **Chapelizod village**, however, still resists many of the pressures of contemporary development. At the beginning of the twentieth century, Weston St John Joyce wrote that it possessed 'some traces of old world respectability'. A hundred years later it still does; tiny laneways lead off the main street, many of the buildings date back to the early nineteenth and eighteenth centuries, and you may hear, as I did, the sound of a cock crowing somewhere in the back lanes.

marry King Mark. Her father had a chapel here.

Frisch weht der Wind
Der Heimat zu
Mein Irisch Kind
Wo weilest du?
Tristan und Isolde: Act I

The lands belonging to Chapelizod were granted by Hugh de Lacy in 1173 to Hugh Tyrrell, which grant was afterwards confirmed by Henry II. In 1176, they were given by the Tyrrells to the Hospital of the Knights Templars and, after the suppression of the Templars, remained in the hands of the Knights Hospitallers till the dissolution of the monasteries under Henry VIII. In 1665, the Duke of Ormond purchased the entire manor with the mansion from Sir Maurice Eustace, for the purpose of enclosing the Phoenix Park. In 1671, Colonel Lawrence, author of the pamphlet *The Interest of Ireland in its Trade and Wealth*, founded manufactories in this place, inviting over families from Brabant and Rochelle who were skilled in the manufacture of linens, diapers etc., and later on woollen manufacture was extensively carried on. Towards the middle of the last century, the chief industry of Chapelizod was a flax mill on a very large scale, erected by the firm of Leland and Thomas Crostwait, which employed 600 people. The population in 1837 was 2,181. The Phoenix Distillery Company was more recently situated at Chapelizod.

Besides the King's House already mentioned, other buildings of note in Chapelizod are the Church of Ireland church (reached by going straight ahead instead of crossing the bridge, and built in the time of Queen Anne) and an old and gloomy dwelling-house, known in Joseph Sheridan Le Fanu's novel as *The House by the Churchyard*.

Chapelizod has literary associations with James Joyce, who placed here the scene of one of the early stories in *Dubliners*, and also the location of *Finnegans Wake*.

A road to the left at Chapelizod leads past Ballyfermot across the railway and Grand Canal to the Dublin–Naas road. Ballyfermot Castle, an ancient building occupied in the last century, has disappeared. A school was kept there in the eighteenth century. Ballyfermot House is the seat of James Fottrell Esq. At Killeen, on the same road, an extensive paper-manufactory was carried on in the middle of the nineteenth century by John MacDonnell, the first Catholic Governor of the Bank of Ireland; the

No trace now remains of **Ballyfermot House** other than a corrugated iron-roofed shed which may have been one of the outhouses. The site of **Ballyfermot Castle** can be identified as a significant grassy mound behind **Le Fanu House**.

The **Clondalkin Paper Mills** at Killeen closed in the 1970s, shortly before an industrial boom that saw much new development in the area, which still continues.

Chapelizod village

principal kinds made were banknote paper for the Bank of Ireland and paper for the Dublin newspapers. In the enclosure of the establishment, which resembled a small town, were dwelling-houses for the workmen and their families; the house of the proprietor was situated in ornamental grounds nearby.

Among the residences in the immediate vicinity of Chapelizod are St Lawrence's (Captain C. B. Harty); Mulberry Hill, formerly seat of Leland Crostwait of the flax mills, later an institute for orphan daughters of soldiers; and Glenaulin, a large, red house, built by the late T. M. Healy, the Nationalist politician who became first Governor General of the Irish Free State and died in 1932. It is now occupied by Mr Healy's son.

About half a mile from Chapelizod on the right is Palmerston House, built by John Hely Hutchinson, Secretary of State for Ireland who became Provost of Trinity College in 1774, and occupied by his descendants, Lords Donoughmore. Palmerston House is now an asylum for the middle classes.

Just before Palmerstown is a road to the left leading to Clondalkin.

Palmerstown, 1½ miles from Chapelizod, is a small village near the Liffey. There was formerly here a hospital for lepers.

The place gave its name to the Viscounts Palmerston, of the family of Temple, whose property stretched from here to Chapelizod. The Temples removed to Ireland about 1601, and were enobled in 1721, when Henry Temple received the title of Viscount Palmerston. The second Viscount was father of the famous English Prime Minister Lord Palmerston, with whom the title died in 1865. Sir William Temple, the writer and patron of Swift, was of this family. The Catholic church here is one of the oldest in the Diocese of Dublin, and is now being replaced by a new building designed by Messrs Robinson and Keeffe.

A mile beyond Palmerstown, to the right, is Brooklawn, where lives Dr L. E. Somerville-Large, the oculist; and 1½ miles beyond Palmerstown, also on the right, is Hermitage, formerly the seat of Lord Luttrell, and now a golf club.

Half a mile farther on, the turn to the left leads to Esker, where are a number of attractive houses, and an old graveyard.

As Lucan village is entered, another road comes in from Esker, down a steep hill to the right. At the top of this hill, very near Lucan, is Canonbrook, the house built for himself by James Gandon the architect, after his retirement in 1805. Here he died in 1823. The house has been much altered, and is now the residence of Mrs W. E. Shackleton. Esker House is

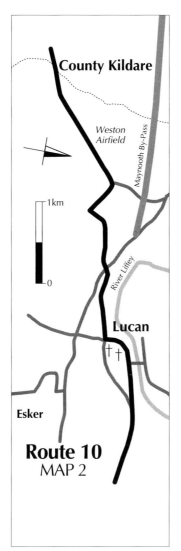

Route 10
MAP 2

St Lawrence's was demolished and replaced in the 1970s by the **West County Hotel**.

I could find no trace of **Mulberry Hill**.

Glenaulin, a red brick house with two circular turrets, is now a nursing home; the gardens have been built over with a small housing scheme.

Palmerston House is now the **Stewart Institution**.

Palmerstown village survives in a narrow backwater between the N4 and the Liffey.

Brooklawn, a pleasant Georgian house with a fine doorcase and a comforting disregard for symmetry, now presides over the campus of the **King's Hospital School**. Its neighbour to the east, **Riversdale**, a pleasant late-Georgian farmhouse, is extant and in use as a nursing home. The gardens have been built over with a sensitive scheme of modern houses which respects the primacy of the older building, and retains some of the old trees.

Hermitage is now a well-known golf club.

Canonbrook is still there, perched on a wooded hill and surrounded by a scheme of modern semi-detached houses.

Woodville has been demolished.

St Edmundsbury continues to be part of St Patrick's Psychiatric Hospital.

the residence of E. Bellamy Esq., the well-known sporting figure.

At the descent into Lucan Village are forked roads; on the right are Woodville and St Edmundsbury.

Woodville was in 1786 the residence of the Rt Hon. T. Clements of the Revenue Board, and St Edmundsbury of the Rt Hon. Edmund Sexten Pery, of the famous Limerick family, and one time Speaker of the Irish Commons. Woodville is now occupied by the Misses Eva, Letitia and Constance Hamilton, and St Edmundsbury is a private mental hospital attached to St Patrick's (or Swift's) Hospital in Dublin.

Lucan, which is now entered, at 7½ miles from the GPO, is best known for its connection with Patrick Sarsfield, and for its Spa. The older part of the town is between the river and the main road. In the grounds of Lucan House is the ruined church, and the Protestant church was built in 1822. It took the place of a small church, the site of which is now occupied by the Petty Sessions Court. The handsome single-arch bridge was built in 1794.

Lucan Demesne has a long history. The lands were granted to Richard de Peche at the Anglo-Norman invasion, and in 1220 were owned by Waryn de Peche, who founded the monastery of St Catherine near Leixlip. In the sixteenth century it belonged to the Sarsfield family, of whom the famous Patrick Sarsfield, of the Siege of Limerick, was a member. He was created Earl of Lucan by James II after the latter's abdication. At his death on the field of Neerwinden in 1693, the estate passed to his brother, William, who had married an illegitimate daughter of Charles II. This gentleman's only daughter and heiress married Agmondisham Vesey.

The present Lucan House was designed by a later Agmondisham Vesey, a capable amateur of the art. It is distinguished by having no back, the offices being reached by an invisible tunnel. The interior is also very fine, and there are genuine panels by Angelica Kaufmann. Mr Agmondisham Vesey invented a new method of slating, which is mentioned by the architect Sir William Chambers. His wife, Mrs Vesey, was the blue-stocking maliciously portrayed by Fanny Burney in her *Diaries*.

From the Veseys the Lucan property descended to a brother of Sir George Colthurst of Blarney, who sold it about twenty years ago to Charles O'Conor, a brother of the O'Conor Don. It was for some time occupied by Mrs William Teeling, daughter of Charles O'Conor. It is now let to the Italian Minister, and the demesne is open to the public under the name of 'Sarsfield's Demesne'.

A little beyond Lucan House, on the left, is the Lucan Spa Hotel. The

Esker is no longer a little country village, but part of extensive low-density housing development that has been spreading through the countryside around Lucan for the last two decades. The **old church ruin** and the graveyard are still there, though under threat from vandalism.

I found references to no fewer than three **Esker Houses** in the area. One was demolished in recent times, the second, just south of the old church ruin, is derelict and threatened, and the third is a pleasant nineteenth-century farmhouse overlooking the Griffeen River, which nearby is spanned by the remains of an ancient packhorse bridge.

The Italian Embassy still occupies **Lucan House**, but the grounds are no longer open to the public.

The **Lucan Spa Hotel** is extant.

Lucan House

building is modern, but there was a fashionable medicinal establishment here, with a great ballroom decorated by Angelica Kaufmann in the eighteenth century, when the waters were found efficacious in scorbutic and rheumatic complaints.

To the left of the Spa is a road leading past Backweston and Weston Park House—where lives Mr Kennedy, the aviator—to Celbridge in County Kildare, where is Conolly's great mansion of Castletown and also Celbridge Abbey, the home of Swift's Vanessa. Before Celbridge is reached, a turn on the right leads very soon to the so-called Newbridge—until it was recently rebuilt, the oldest bridge in this part of Ireland, which has some arches built by John le Decer, Provost of Dublin in the year 1302.

Up to the time of Cromwell, Backweston and the surrounding lands were in the possession of Sir Bryan O'Neill of the Clandeboye family.

At a mile from Lucan, the road enters County Kildare.

Backweston

Weston Park House is still there, and Mr Kennedy, after a most distinguished aviation career, is still hale and hearty in his late eighties. The aerodrome he established beside Weston Park continues to thrive; it has been the location for many aviation films, including *The Blue Max* in the 1970s.

Backweston is also still there, beside the Department of Agriculture and Food National Crop Variety Testing Centre.

ROUTE 11

NEWCASTLE LYONS AND ATHGOE

	Miles from the GPO
Guinness's Brewery	1½
Royal Hospital Kilmainham	2
Golden Bridge	3
Clondalkin	6¾
Milltown	9
Newcastle to Celbridge via Lyons	11½–13½
Athgoe	13

Leaving Dublin by Dame Street and Thomas Street, at 1½ miles from the GPO, the Route passes through Guinness's Brewery, which lies on both sides of the street and almost completely surrounds the Protestant and Catholic churches of St James's. Taking the left at the open fork, we pass on the left the South Dublin Union, first the Foundling Hospital, now St Kevin's Hospital. The Roman Catholic chapel is an interesting work, adjoining the Great Hall by Francis Johnston. The Union was strongly defended by the Insurgent forces in 1916, but suffered no serious damage. Adjoining it is the old City Basin, now barely visible through a permanently shut wrought-iron gate, and the right arm of the fork leads in a few yards to St Patrick's Hospital, popularly called Swift's, founded posthumously by Jonathan Swift as the first humane madhouse in the Three Kingdoms.

At Mount Brown we catch a glimpse of the Royal Hospital, Kilmainham, the earliest and one of the largest and most beautiful of Dublin's secular public buildings. It was founded as an Old Soldiers' Home by Charles II in 1680, during the brilliant viceroyalty of the First Duke of Ormond, and was designed by Sir William Robinson, the Irish Surveyor General. The large internal courtyard, surrounded by a loggia, the Great Hall and the Chapel, with a plaster ceiling by unknown, but probably Irish, artists (C. P. Curran in *Royal Society of Antiquaries Journal*, March 1940), and fine woodcarving are points of particular interest. The building was the official residence of the Commander-in-Chief, Ireland, and is now the administrative head-quarters of the Garda Síochána. Permission to see it may be obtained by writing in advance. Otherwise, it is not easily visible from outside; perhaps the nearest view is from the high ground to the left of Mount Brown.

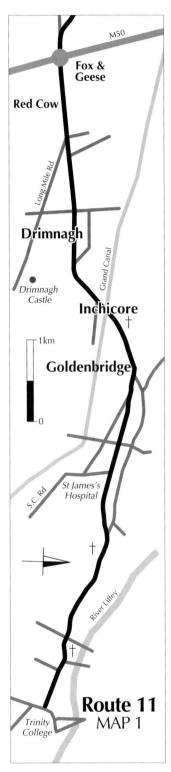

Guinness's Brewery has grown since 1947, and although its future has seemed at times in doubt, a major new visitors' centre was opened there at the end of 2000. The Catholic church of **St James's** is extant, but the Church of Ireland church is now a light fittings showroom. Around the brewery is an area of severe dereliction undergoing renewal, graffiti-daubed warehouses and boarded-up Corporation flats interspersed with recently developed private apartment blocks.

The former St James Church, James Street

St Kevin's Hospital grew to become **St James's Hospital**, a medical city of buildings of many periods; the splendid Hall of the **Foundling Hospital**, together with Francis Johnston's chapel, were demolished.

The **City Basin** has been filled in, but **St Patrick's Hospital** remains, now much extended.

The **Royal Hospital, Kilmainham**, was opened to the public in 1985 after extensive renovations. The following year it won the Europa Nostra Medal for architectural conservation. It houses the **Irish Museum of Modern Art**, and is also used for conferences and exhibitions.

Passing along Old Kilmainham, the road follows the bed of the Camac River, and to the right may be seen the grim rear view of Kilmainham Gaol, celebrated for having been the temporary residence of Parnell and others, and also as the place of execution of Pearse and other 1916 leaders. It is now deservedly disused, and the vegetation on the roof is rapidly turning it into a scenic feature.

At Goldenbridge, we turn left into Tyrconnell Road, and in half a mile cross the Grand Canal at the Third Lock. This great system, which links Dublin with the Shannon (to Limerick), and the Blackwater (to Waterford) with other branches, was begun in 1765 and completed by the end of the century. The Harbour, near Guinness's, and the Dock at Ringsend are both well worth visiting. The Grand is almost the only canal system in Ireland which is still a prosperous concern.

Three-quarters of a mile farther on, there is old Drimnagh Church with a graveyard, to the right, and a little later Drimnagh Castle is visible to the left. It was built soon after 1215 by the Barnewall family (Lords Trimleston and Kingsland), and held by them for upwards of 200 years. It was leased by the Loftus family (Earls of Ely, see Route 15) and came later into the possession of Lord Lansdowne. It is now occupied by Mr Hatch. Surrounded by a moat, it is one of the oldest domestic structures still inhabited in the country, and shows mediaeval work remodelled in Jacobean or somewhat later times. The result is both genuine and picturesque.

We now pass through the crossroads of Fox-and-Geese and Red Cow. At the former, a road leads on right to Ballyfermot and Chapelizod (see Route 9), and a little beyond the latter on the main road is an old toll house, of almost exactly the same pattern as another which still survives almost in the centre of Belfast. At Red Cow, we leave the main Naas Road, forking right for Clondalkin, which is reached in 1 mile by way of the Novitiate of the Little Sisters of the Assumption, formerly Mount St Joseph's Monastery. A few yards beyond the monastery, on the left, is an old tower.

Clondalkin, though a small place, displays a bewildering complexity of plan, which indicates great antiquity and former importance. Of this, the Round Tower, reached by turning left before Hart's public house, and thence bearing round to the right, survives as evidence. It is one of the smaller examples, built of rough masonry, but it retains its conical cap. The upper part, however, shows traces of having been rebuilt. The tower is remarkable for its high, battered base, but the present steps to the door are modern. The Abbey was founded in the seventh century by St Mochua, but

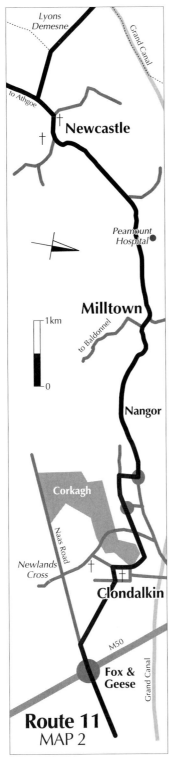

In 1960, under a Board of Trustees, the restoration of **Kilmainham Gaol** began, much of the work being carried out by volunteers and without grants. Funds were donated by the public, and earned by providing the gaol for the making of films, notable *The Quare Fellow* (1965) and *The Italian Job* (1969). In 1986 the buildings came into the care of the Office of Public Works, and are open to the public.

A few vestiges of the **old Drimnagh church** can be found down a lane opposite the entrance to Brooks Thomas.

The 1950s saw the development of many commercial and industrial concerns along the Naas Road, including the **Aspro head-quarters**, a good example of the international style designed by Alan Hope. It was demolished in the early 1980s.

Drimnagh Castle is no longer inhabited but was restored in the 1980s by a voluntary group and is now open to the public.

The road through **Fox and Geese** has become a six-lane highway through a vast industrial and commercial landscape.

The former **Mount St Joseph's Monastery** was demolished in the 1990s; only the graveyard and a few tall trees mark its location beside an estate of town houses and apartments. The bronze bell from the monastery is to be found today in St Thomas's church in Tallaght, while one of the statues from the grounds has been re-erected in the local national school.

The old tower is extant.

Beyond on the right is the **Carnegie Library**, a fine arts and crafts style building by T. J. Byrne, dating from 1912.

all other traces, save a rude granite Cross and a large stone trough in the churchyard across the road, have perished. The old church was ruinous at the end of the seventeenth century, and the present building was built soon after 1787, when the explosion of the neighbouring powder-mills had made its predecessor insecure. The foundation-stone of these powder-mills was laid by the Volunteer General, Lord Charlemont, with great ceremony, in 1782 (Ball's *History of County Dublin*, part IV). Clondalkin now boasts a large paper mill, seen on the right after taking the left turn which leads us out of the town.

In a little over a mile Deansrath, a handsome large farmhouse of the mid-eighteenth century (Mrs Mary Hughes), appears set back from the road on the right. Behind (i.e. to the north of) it is another of the innumerable castles of this very vulnerable corner of the Pale, and just behind that is the ruined church of Kilmahudrick. One-third of a mile beyond it is Nangor Castle, almost hidden by trees. It was built by John Falkiner, High Sheriff of County Dublin in the reign of Queen Anne, but from the road it appears as if it embodied earlier work, and had been again mediaevalised in the nineteenth century. It is now occupied by V. Hughes, Esq. Opposite it, on the left of the road, an avenue leads to Kilcarbery House, near which are Kilbride Castle and Church. The latter are more easily reached by turning to the left just before Milltown, which is reached in just under 1½ miles. From this stretch of the road, occasional views of the military aerodrome at Baldonnell, 1 mile to the south, may be obtained.

Milltown House, which stands in the village, is a handsome example of the medium-sized house of the mid-eighteenth century, a common type in County Dublin. A mile farther on, to the right, is Peamount Sanatorium, for the treatment of young consumptive patients. Most of the buildings are of wood, raised on stilts clear of the ground, and a National School for the patients is included among them. The road now proceeds without incident (save for a turning to the right which leads to Hazelhatch on the Grand Canal) to Newcastle, which is reached in 1½ miles.

Newcastle, known also as Newcastle Lyons or Newcastle juxta-Lyons, was formerly a place of importance. It lay in the territory of the Macgiolla-mocholmog sept (who are commemorated by a street in Dublin called St Michael's Lane). In the thirteenth century it had a Castellan, as befitted an important outpost of the Pale. It is said to have had, in the sixteenth century, six castles, of which perhaps three are now traceable. In 1613, it received a charter and returned two members to the Irish Parliament until

Clondalkin is now the bustling centre of a considerable extent of suburban sprawl. Fortunately, the modernisation of the village has not caused any significant alterations in the old medieval plan, or the destruction of many village buildings—for instance, the terrace of stone cottages opposite the round tower , erected in the 1870s, provide the tower and adjacent church with a good secular context. The paper mills, which were established in the early 1800s, ceased business in the 1980s, and the site is now occupied by Dunne's Stores.

Surrounded by houses built in the late 1990s, **Deansrath** is extant, although with aluminium windows and in commercial use. Behind the house a fragment of the old castle survives, caged in by a galvanised steel fence. Farther west is an 'open space', called Playing Fields on the OS map, but in reality a soulless desert of nitrogen-rich grass subdivided with the vestiges of old hedges festooned with plastic bags. In its midst, surrounded by a palisade fence, stands the ruin of **Kilmahudrick church** with a twin belfry.

The remains of **Nangor Castle** are extant, and under investigation by the archaeologists of Dúchas. South of the road, in the Grange Castle Golf Club grounds, **Kilcarbery House** can be found in good order; it is a simple late-Georgian farmhouse with an unusual, angular porch.

All that remains of **Kilbride Church** are some vestiges of bramble-covered walls, and the remains of **Kilbride Castle** are gone.

Milltown House is no more; of the old village only a terrace of ruined cottages and a much extended pub remain.

Peamount Hospital is still there, although I could only find one of the original timber buildings. **Peamount House** itself is a three-storey house with a simple door case, and an unusually proportioned central Venetian window, topped by a diocletian window divided in two by a large clock. It is probably of a late-eighteenth-century date; Sleator has a Mr Clinch living in it in 1806. It was acquired in 1912 for conversion into a sanatorium, but such was the fear of the local people of tuberculosis spreading into their community that the first timber pavilion ward was burnt down by an angry group of protestors, in spite of the foreman firing rifle shots over their heads. Two of the protestors spent 38 days in jail.

the Union. It was sacked and burned by the Duke of Ormond in 1641. It is now one of the most attractive villages in County Dublin.

As we enter, the Roman Catholic church is in front. The road to the left leads, in 2½ miles, to Rathcoole (see Route 12). On the right is the Old Rectory, a beautiful house of the early eighteenth century, now occupied by T. U. Sadleir Esq. In the grounds are the remains of a castle, and a yew-tree under which Swift is reported to have sat. Adjoining is the Church of St Finian, in front of which are some magnificent elms and the vestiges of a village green. A group of whitewashed thatched cottages completes the picturesque scene. The church is a remarkably large and fine mediaeval building, of which only the nave is at present roofed and in use as the Protestant church. It measures overall 111 feet in length. To the west is a massive mediaeval tower, containing two vaulted chambers with fireplaces and deep embrasures with stone seats. The nave was re-ceilinged in 1724, and some woodwork at the east end dates also from this time. The original east window has been re-erected in the old chancel arch, and contains some fine, flowing tracery. Eastwards of this is the now ruined chancel, with small windows of the fifteenth-century type, and a stepped gable. In the church-yard are an ancient rude cross, and a number of interesting monuments.

Immediately beside the church is a small, flat-topped mound, which seems to be constructed of some soft, slaty stone. Continuing on past the church, we see, on the left, the ruins of another castle. The second turn on the right leads past Newcastle House, skirting the demesne wall of Lyons.

Newcastle to Celbridge via Lyons

The Lyons wall is constructed of a curious reddish stone. The road here forms the Dublin–Kildare border, Lyons being in County Kildare. Lyons was built by Michael Aylmer in 1797, and the wings were added by the second Lord Cloncurry about 1810. The pillars of the portico have a strange history. Three of them had been taken by Raphael from the celebrated Golden House of Nero in Rome, and used in decorating the Palazzo Farnese. They were bought by the scientist Baron von Humboldt for the King of Prussia, together with a fourth pillar, apparently similar. This, however, had been painted red by Raphael to match the others, and Humboldt refused to accept them when he discovered this. But he sold them to Lord Cloncurry, who, a little later, discovered another pillar on his own account while excavating the Baths of Titus. This he had trimmed and polished to match the others. He relates that he got permission to remove

The whitewashed cottages have disappeared but Newcastle has retained most of the buildings mentioned, although it has become more difficult to gain access to them. The only remaining thatched building is McAvoy's pub.

The main entrance gateway of the Lyons demesne is impressive: it originally stood at Browne's Hill, County Carlow and was erected here when the whole Lyons demesne was owned by the UCD Faculty of Agriculture. The gate lodge opposite, although utilising old Portland stone doric columns, is a recent construction. **Lyons House** is now owned by Tony Ryan, founder of Ryanair.

Newcastle Glebe House

them from Rome only by threatening to cut them in pieces if permission were not given (*Personal Recollections* of Valentine Lord Cloncurry, Dublin 1860). Lyons is occupied by the Hon. Miss Lawless, daughter of the last Lord Cloncurry.

At 2 miles from Newcastle (continuing this road) is Aylmer Bridge (1782), which spans the Grand Canal, both sides of which are here planted with fine old trees, making a very attractive walk. The road then crosses the main line of the GSD & W Railway, and turns right. A little later, it forks, and both branches lead to Celbridge (see Route 10). That to the left is preferable, as it skirts some pleasant reaches of the Liffey. Three-quarters of a mile NNW of Newcastle is Colganstown, a handsome house of about 1770, possibly by Nathaniel Clements, with swept-back wings and a court-yard at the rere.

Newcastle to Athgoe

This road bears constantly left leaving Newcastle, and climbs steeply to a col between two hills. That to the left is in County Dublin; that to the right is the Hill of Lyons in County Kildare, and lies partly in the Lyons demesne. It was the scene of O'Connell's duel with d'Esterre in 1815, in which the latter was killed. From the top of the road, a superb panorama of the plain of Dublin, Kildare and Meath is visible. Conspicuous to the north is the huge mass of Castletown Conolly, 4 miles away. In front and slightly to the right of it, is a modern housing estate. At 1½ miles from Newcastle, the gates of Athgoe appear on the left. A castle of 1579 bears a much-worn contemporary tablet with the Catholic sign IHS interwoven with a cross, and the initials of William Locke and Katherine Allen, his wife. Below it is another tablet with the same legend, added perhaps in the eighteenth century. To the left is an eighteenth-century extension, with a fine, large fanlight, and, in the castle itself, a turret staircase leads to the roof, which is still intact. To the right and a little behind is Athgoe House, an elegant structure built some time before 1750, with plain pediments on east and west fronts, and some good plasterwork and joinery. It communicates with the old castle. The Lockes were a Catholic family, and tradition reports that Mass was said here in Penal times. They died out in 1833, and ownership passed to their O'Carroll cousins. In 1836, Mrs Skerrett lived here, and, more recently, a Mr Donnelly. Mr Kennedy Skipton, the present owner, is courteous to visitors and has saved the house from the decay that threatened it.

Colganstown House is extant.

Athgoe House and Castle are extant, nestling under the wooded hillside. The place is presently occupied by the Dennison family.

Athgoe House and Castle c.1950

The old drive is still traceable, and debouches on the Naas Road near Blackchurch Inn. At this end are the remains of Colmanstown Castle, near which is an arch of rough masonry covered with ivy, evidently erected in the eighteenth century as a 'picturesque' feature. Just across the field to the east (left) is an old graveyard, in which the site of a church can still be traced.

The County Kildare border crosses the Naas Road ¾ of a mile beyond this point.

The ruins of **Colmanstown Castle**, the original home of the Locke family before they moved into Athgoe Castle in 1579, are gone, and the nearby Gothic archway was demolished in the 1960s. The old graveyard with its ruin, thought to have been a medieval church dedicated to St Colman, is to be found two fields to the north from the Athgoe road close to where it meets the Naas Road.

The old **Blackchurch Inn**, a mud-walled, thatched public house that dated back to the eighteenth century, was closed in the late 1950s. It was owned by the Vicars family, who had in their possession accounts books going back two hundred years. It and the turnpike house opposite it were cleared away when the dual carriageway was being built in the 1960s.

Colmanstown Arch 1952

Blackchurch Inn 1964

Turnpike house 1964

ROUTE 12

BLACKCHURCH

	Miles from the GPO
Dolphin's Barn	1½
Crumlin	3
Drimnagh Castle	3½
Belgard (Newlands crossroads)	5½
Brownsbarn crossroads (for Saggart)	8¾
Rathcoole	10¾
Blackchurch Inn	13¼

Note: This route follows Route 11 for one mile between Drimnagh and Red Cow.

Proceeding by College Green and Dame Street, this Route turns off Christ Church Place, down Nicholas Street, so called from the old Protestant parish of St Nicholas Within. The remains of the church (1707) can be seen on the left, and to the right are seen the fine tower and cupola of St Nicholas of Myra, the Catholic Parish Church, built in the early nineteenth century. This was the old Bull Alley district, formerly a picturesque, if insanitary, warren, but almost entirely rebuilt by the Iveagh (Guinness) Trust in 1911 and onwards. At St Patrick's Cathedral, the right turn is taken down Dean Street, which in a few yards becomes the Coombe, the old quarter of the Huguenot weavers, whose Parish Church, St Luke's, is on the left, while the old Weaver's Hall is seen on the right. At the end of the Coombe there is a sharp turn left, and another sharp turn right into Cork Street, until recently noted for its old gabled houses. Though none of these remain in Cork Street itself, there are a few in the neighbouring streets. On the left is the Cork Street Fever Hospital, founded in 1802.

The Circular Road and the Grand Canal are now crossed at Dolphin's Barn. The road now traverses the new working-class suburb of Crumlin. A large area to the left is covered with roads called after the Dioceses of Ireland, or after famous ecclesiastical sites—Lismore, Durrow, Devenish, Monasterboice, Downpatrick, Ferns, Kilfenora, Clonard, etc. At 3 miles from the GPO there are, to the left, four churches in close proximity, the old Catholic church of Crumlin, a very attractive example of a fast-disappearing type, and, beside it, its large, new Romanesque successor.

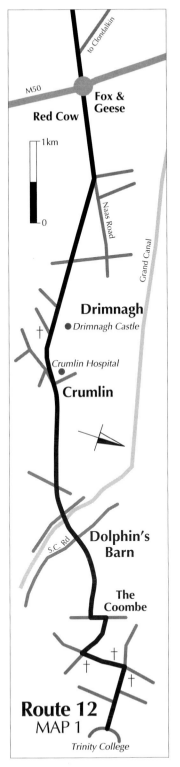

Route 12
MAP 1

Trinity College

St Nicholas's was unroofed in 1835, and shortened in 1911 when the road was widened. The adjoining **Iveagh Buildings**, built at the beginning of the twentieth century, were renovated and improved in the mid-1990s. The copper cupola of **St Nicholas of Myra** is partly hidden from view behind recent apartment buildings.

Dean Street and the **Coombe** are much changed since 1949, and none of the **old gabled houses** survive, although careful observation will turn up at least one Victorian house that echoes the tradition.

What remains of **St Luke's Church** can be seen behind Massey's premises; it is a roofless ruin, having been destroyed by fire in 1986.

The old **Weaver's Hall** was demolished in 1956, and the site is now built over with four-storey apartments. Some fragments, including the foundation stone and a doorcase, were salvaged and survive in private collections.

The **Coombe Lying-In Hospital** was demolished in 1974; looking somewhat incongruous, the elaborate columned entrance porch has been retained as a monument. The new **Coombe Maternity Hospital** was built at the south end of the Coombe in 1968.

The Cork Street **Fever Hospital**, which was opened in 1804, is extant, and is now occupied by the Eastern Region Health Board.

There is also the old Protestant Parish Church, and beside it a large new church in brick, designed by MacDonnell and Dixon. The principal residence was Crumlin House, a red-brick seventeenth-century house, of which the lower storey still stands, and which the connoisseur Hugh Lane wished to restore. A half mile farther on is Drimnagh Castle, described in Route 11.

At Fox and Geese, ¾ miles beyond Drimnagh Castle, the alternative route out of town (Route 11) is joined. The old Fox and Geese was on a slightly different site. Our route, however, continues straight on at Red Cow and, in one mile, reaches the crossroads at Newlands. This property was in the sixteenth century the seat of the Molyneux family, who bought it from the Stanihursts. It later belonged to the Coles, and in the eighteenth century was occupied by Arthur Wolfe, Viscount Kilwarden, the upright judge who was so unfortunately killed by Emmet's men in 1803. It was occupied by Lord O'Brien (Peter the Packer) in the later nineteenth century. It is now a golf club.

A little south of Newlands, on a road leading to Rathfarnham, are Belgard Castle and also Urney's chocolate factories. Belgard was formerly the seat of the Dillon family, later of the Talbots, and now of Major Hugh Maude. About seventy years ago, it was the residence of Dr Evory Kennedy, whose grandson, Page Dickinson, the architect and a prominent figure in the Georgian Society, was born here.

On a side-road close to Belgard there is a cross in memory of Katherine Tynan's father, who lived at a farm called Whitehall in the eighties and early nineties of the last century, and used to welcome Yeats, Æ, and the young poets and Parnellites to supper in all weathers.

At 1¼ miles beyond Newlands Cross, on the right is the gate of Corkagh. During the Commonwealth, Corkagh was occupied by a William Trundell, in the eighteenth century by a family named Findlay, later by W. Stockley Esq., and is now the residence of Mrs Colley. The family of Colley is connected with that of the Duke of Wellington, as well as with another general, Sir George Pomeroy Colley, killed at the British disaster of Majuba Hill; a Richard Colley who flourished circa 1730, changed his name to Wesley and became First Lord Mornington and grandfather of the Duke.

At 7¾ miles from the GPO, a road leads to the right towards Baldonnell and Kilbride Church. Baldonnell House was formerly the residence of the Carbery family, but the lands are now largely given over to the Military Aerodrome. The church is heavily ruined and very small, but contains

To find **Crumlin's churches**, detour left opposite the Crumlin Children's Hospital, along the old Crumlin road. On the left is the MacDonnell and Dixon church, a fine building, built with the last of the yellow bricks to be produced by the nearby Dolphin's Barn brickworks. It was completed in 1942, and received second place in the RIAI awards for that year, coming second to Desmond FitzGerald's Collinstown Airport.

Next to it is the old church, built in 1816 in what was a pre-Reformation grave-yard. It had become too small to cope with the increasing population; during the 1930s the number of parishioners grew from ninety to fifteen hundred. The old church is currently being renovated by FÁS for community purposes.

The modern Catholic church can be found half a mile to the left: the old church was demolished in recent years to make way for old folks' apartments.

Drimnagh Castle (see page 115) is passed, before the Long Mile Road takes you into one of the cauldrons of Dublin's industrial progress.

Urney's chocolate factory is gone, but **Newlands** is still a golf club, and **Belgard Castle** is the headquarters of Cement Ltd.

The cross commemmorating Andrew Cullen Tynan, who died in 1905, is a richly carved, limestone monument. Unfortunately **Whitehall**, where Tynan entertained young nationalists and literati, is in a very dilapidated condition and under threat. A small housing estate nearby is called **Tynan Hall**.

Nearby a new cemetery has been established, with buildings and landscaping designed by the Polish architect, Andrzej Wejchert.

Corkagh was sold to Sir John Galvin (see page 205) in the 1960s, but it was demolished soon afterwards, and the demesne was used for grazing cattle. The land was later taken over by Dublin County Council, and an extensive public park was laid out in 1986.

Little remains of **Kilbride church**.

There are two **Baldonnell Houses** extant. The older of the two is that opposite the Baldonnell aerodrome entrance, in the centre of a large apple orchard.

traces of a small cell in the north-west corner.

Brownsbarn crossroads, 1 mile farther on, has a road leading on the left to Saggart, a village lying half-way between this route and Route 13. It is best known for the Swiftbrook paper-mills, founded by the family of McDonnell. The 'swift brook' itself emerges from the Brittas reservoirs, flows through Clondalkin, and at Goldenbridge is known as the Camac River. It discharges into the Liffey under Kingsbridge Station. The Catholic Church of Saggart is of the early nineteenth century, and stands opposite the ancient churchyard. The ruins of a small castle may also be seen. From Saggart also, a choice of two roads leads up the Slade or Glen of Saggart, joining Route 13 between Crooksling and Brittas.

Two miles beyond Brownsbarn crossroads, and 10¾ miles from the GPO, the road enters Rathcoole, an attractive village strung out along the road, which is here very wide. It was a corporate town, ruled by a portreeve, and forming one of the southernmost outposts of the Pale. In 1642, an Irish force was defeated here by Sir Thomas Armstrong. In the following year it was the scene of a hideous massacre, when Sir Arthur Loftus, the Governor of Naas, set fire to a furze-covered hillside in which a large number of local men, women and children had taken refuge. Felix Rourke, the United Irishman, was born in Rathcoole in 1765, and hanged from the rafters of the Presbytery in 1803. The new Presbytery of Rathcoole is a handsome modern house (Brendan O'Connor, architect) embodying stonework from the derelict Munster Arms Inn.

Rathcoole House, on the left at the beginning of the village, is an old building, and on the right, near the other end, there is another handsome old house. At the end of the village, a turn to the left leads in 4½ miles to Kilteel in County Kildare.

Continuing on the main road, two miles beyond Rathcoole, on the right, is the road leading by Athgoe to Newcastle Lyons (see Route 11). Conspicuous to the left after leaving Rathcoole is the old windmill on the hill towards Kilteel.

Half a mile beyond the Athgoe road is the Blackchurch Inn, where the father of Felix Rourke, the United Irishman, kept a turnpike gate and a posting stage during the mid-eighteenth century. The turnpike house may still be seen opposite the inn. A road to the right, a few yards farther on, leads to Oughterard with its Round Tower (in County Kildare), and the main road itself enters County Kildare about ¼ mile beyond Blackchurch Inn.

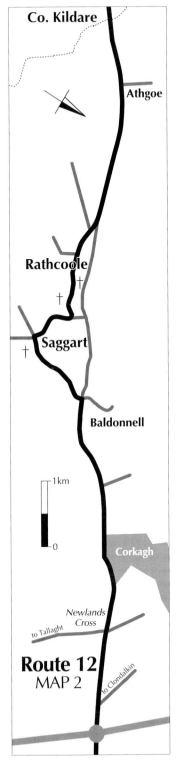

Co. Kildare

Athgoe

Rathcoole

Saggart

Baldonnell

1km

0

Corkagh

Newlands Cross

to Tallaght

Route 12
MAP 2

to Clondalkin

Swiftbrook Mills lie in overgrown ruins, awaiting the commencement of a development scheme for housing and offices.

In the grounds of **Saggart Catholic Church** is a fine modern sculpture of an angel by Sonia Caldwell. Carved from a dense opal stone from Zimbabwe, it was unveiled in 1999. As far as I could ascertain, **Saggart Castle** and its adjoining house were demolished in the 1960s.

Rathcoole village is, like most villages near Dublin, undergoing great expansion and change, and little evidence is visible of its important past. The **Church of Ireland Church** is a plain building currently under renovation. In the graveyard is the mausoleum of the Kennedy family, with a coat-of-arms finely cut in sandstone. They lived at **Johnstown Kennedy**, a mid-eighteenth-century house to the south east of the village.

The crosses on the gable of **Doon House** suggest that it was originally the presbytery designed by Brendan O'Connor.

Rathcoole House is derelict, standing starkly in a bare, grassy site; it and its grounds are in need of restoration.

The stump of the **old windmill** is extant; from here there are wonderful views that range from the Mournes to the Slieve Blooms.

The Dublin and Blessington Tramway ceased operations in December 1932; the last surviving railcar can be seen on display in the Belfast Transport Museum.

The nearest railway to this district is the Great Southern and Western line at Lucan, Hazelhatch and Straffan, several miles to the north. But in the mid-nineteenth century, a bill achieved its first reading in the British Parliament for the 'Rathmines, Rathgar, Roundtown and Rathcoole Railway', which was to start from the Coombe, passing through Harold's Cross and Terenure on its way towards Rathcoole. But it was never carried out, and the Dublin, Blessington and Poulaphouca Steam Tramway was built instead, starting from Terenure.

Old Crumlin Catholic Church

Old houses under Dolphin's Barn bridge (c. 1950)

ROUTE 13

BRITTAS VIA TEMPLEOGUE AND TALLAGHT

	Miles from the GPO
Harold's Cross	2
Terenure	3½
Templeogue	4½
Balrothery	5
Tallaght	7
Jobstown	9½
Crooksling	12
Brittas	14

The most direct route from the old centre of Dublin (Christ Church Place) is by Nicholas, Patrick and Clanbrassil Streets. This route is no longer from the GPO (via College Green and Dame Street) than by the alternative by South Great George's Street and Rathmines Road. It passes at 1 mile Christ Church Cathedral, and at 1½ miles St Patrick's Cathedral. The Grand Canal is crossed by Clanbrassil Bridge (now rebuilt as Emmet Bridge, formerly called after James Hamilton, Earl of Clanbrassil), at 1¾ miles. Just before the bridge, on the right, is an old public-house which until 1945 bore the name 'The Old Grinding Young', one of the few examples of an old inn-name in Dublin. At the beginning of Mount Drummond Avenue, on the left, is the large house in which Robert Emmet was captured by Major Sirr. It was then occupied by a family named Palmer.

In a few hundred yards is Harold's Cross Green, a long wedge-shaped park which perpetuates the village green of Harold's Cross, named after the Anglo-Irish family of the Harolds, who held dominion over this corner of the Pale. They were among the first Anglo-Normans to become Hibernicised, and in 1316 they were in confederacy with the O'Byrnes and the O'Tooles.

Harold's Cross still retains the character of a village, and some very attractive small houses stand around the green. On its western side is a building known as the 'Buggy Barracks', reputedly the scene of military torturings in 1798, and, until about 1943, another old building, distinguished externally by a gazebo which projected above the main roof. On the same side of the Green is Mount Jerome Cemetery.

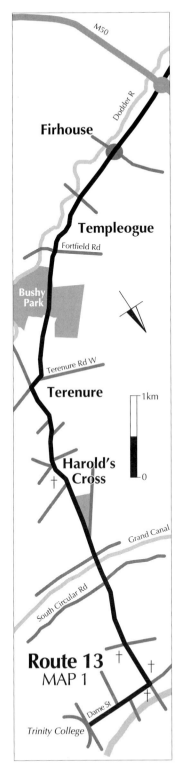

Route 13
MAP 1

Trinity College

The public house that was once '**The Old Grinding Young**' at Emmet Bridge is still there, next door to a smaller pub that up to recently was called 'The Glimmer-Man', a name familiar to those who lived during the 'Emergency' period.

Current thinking places the house where Robert Emmet was captured on the main road between Mount Drummond Avenue and the canal, on the site the red-brick artisan dwellings now occupy.

Harold's Cross park, which originally had a great rockery, a waterfall and a large pond, was designed by William Sheppard, who had worked with Ninian Niven. The park was opened in 1894.

Although the road frontage opposite the east side of Harold's Cross park has been considerably redeveloped over the last half-century, most of the houses on the west side of the park date from at least the nineteenth century; local people suggest that the **Buggy** or **Bogey Barracks** stood where Halls Electrical Wholesale premises is today.

Mount Jerome Cemetery is a grand example of a Victorian necropolis, densely packed with decaying granite and sandstone funerary monuments, some designed by distinguished architects of the day. The truncated remains of **Wilkinson's mansion**, (it was originally three storeys) with its elaborate window pediments, is still there, in use as a cemetery office. The elaborate Gothic entrance lodge to the cemetery, in an advanced state of decay, is in need of restoration.

In the middle of the eighteenth century, Mount Jerome was the property of Abraham Wilkinson, a rich merchant, who built a fine mansion (now the cemetery office) and embellished the grounds with lawns and shrubberies. It was sold by his son, an early Governor of the Bank of Ireland, to John Keogh, a leader of the Catholic Committee of 1792, whose descendants disposed of it to the Cemetery Company in 1835. The company had a capital of £12,000, and provision was made for the exemption of toll for all carriages passing to and from the cemetery. In the cemetery are buried Thomas Davis, the Young Ireland patriot; J. M. Synge; Edward Dowden; Æ (George Russell); George Petrie; Sir William Rowan Hamilton; Sarah Purser; and many other notable Irish men and women.

On the way to Terenure, the fine new Catholic Church of Our Lady of the Rosary is passed on the left. It is a large church of mountain granite, in the Renaissance manner, with a tall tower crowned with a stone cupola. No. 418 Harold's Cross Road, once lived in by John Butler Yeats during W. B. Yeats's childhood, is now occupied by H. G. Leask Esq., the architect and antiquary.

Terenure (3½ miles), formerly Roundtown, is now a suburb of Dublin, and terminus of the Rathmines and Rathgar tram. Until thirty years ago, it was a village of whitewashed houses, of which one remains a few yards up the Templeogue Road. These were arranged in a ring, which gave rise to the name. The modern name (borrowed from Terenure House) is explained as meaning the Land of the Yew-Trees. The present Bank of Ireland building occupies the site of the terminus of the old Dublin, Blessington and Poulaphouca Steam Tramway. The Bank of Ireland is passed on the left, and the turn on the right (Terenure Road West), which leads up to Crumlin, is not taken.

Half a mile up the straight road is, on the left, Bushy Park, formerly Bushe's House, the property of Sir Robert Shaw, a descendant of Robert Shaw, controller of the Post Office, whose eldest brother, William Shaw of the Sandpits, Kilkenny, was grandfather of the dramatist Bernard Shaw. Robert Shaw's son, the 1st Baronet, married the daughter and heir of the younger Abraham Wilkinson, mentioned above, who bought Bushy Park and other lands about Terenure and Templeogue, after moving from Mount Jerome.

Opposite Bushy Park are the large buildings and grounds of the Terenure Carmelite College. The house was built before 1783, in which year it was occupied by a family named Deane. It was later the seat of Robert Shaw

No. 418 Harold's Cross Road, a late Victorian terraced house, is now sub-divided into apartments.

Until the early 1990s two segments of the original **round houses** at Terenure still remained, but today only one short segment survives, rising out of the showrooms of Rathdown Motors, its Victorian rendering removed to fashionably expose the random stone walls and brick window linings.

The **Bank of Ireland** was designed by Millar and Symes and erected in 1932.

Lady Shaw died in 1946, and **Bushy Park** was taken over by the Religious of Christian Education nuns in 1953, who established a girls' school there. A number of additional buildings were added over the ensuing years, and the nuns now cater for 1,000 girls. The remainder of the demesne was built over with housing, playing fields and a public park, and the rich legacy of great specimen trees and what remains of the former ornamental gardens contribute greatly to the neighbourhood.

Bushy Park House

Terenure House is extant, a five-bay house between two generous bows with a pediment over the main entrance, hidden amongst the numerous extensions to **Terenure College** which have sprung up since the Carmelite Fathers took over the house and demesne. Unfortunately, the original entrance portico has been swallowed up by a large modern porch. The gardens of Terenure House were overseen in the early nineteenth century by James Fraser, who was to become one of the principal Victorian garden designers in Ireland.

(mentioned above) before his removal to Bushy Park. It was then deserted, until lived in by a wealthy Mr Taaffe. By 1836, it was in the hands of another wealthy man, Frederick Bourne. The original house has been much added to.

A little beyond it, Fortfield Drive leads off to the right, so named from Fortfield House (demolished about ten years ago), a very handsome Georgian mansion in which lived, from 1789 till 1805, Barry Yelverton, created Lord Avonmore in 1795. He was one of the leaders of the patriotic movement in 1782, was successively Attorney General and Chief Baron of the Exchequer. He was a famous wit, a convivial host, the friend of John Philpot Curran and founder of the 'Monks of the Screw', a pseudo-monastic drinking-club with many distinguished members. He supported the project of a separate Irish Navy in 1781, but, being heavily in debt, he voted for the Union in 1800.

The road now enters the village of Templeogue on the Dodder. According to Mason's *History of St Patrick's*, the church here superseded the mountain church of Kilnasantan after the Anglo-Irish Invasion. Nearly opposite the gate of Alberta, formerly Cypress Grove, is the graceful old Templeogue Bridge, over which passes the bus route to Firhouse, Old Bawn, Bohernabreena and Tallaght (see Route 14). At the end of the seventeenth century, the lands of Templeogue had passed from the Talbots, a Catholic family, into the possession of the Domvilles, who were also of Santry and Loughlinstown. The Domvilles built the original Templeogue House, incorporating part of the old castle; and a Sir Compton Domville, who was MP for the County of Dublin for forty years in the middle of the eighteenth century, decorated the grounds with great magnificence, laying out gardens, terrace walks, waterfalls, grottoes and temples. His heirs abandoned the place about 1780 and removed to Santry Court all the appurtenances, including the beautiful hexagonal temple which is still seen on the latter property (see Route 3). The original Templeogue House was subsequently pulled down, and a new house built, by a Mr Gogarty, in which remained a part of the walls of the Talbot castle. The story is told that during the Domville occupation, the prosecution for murder of Lord Santry (Sir C. Domville's nephew) was abandoned after the threat by the family that they would block up the City Watercourse which passed through the grounds and at that time constituted Dublin's water-supply.

Among the tenants of Templeogue House was Charles Lever, who lived here from about 1842 till 1844. The house was recently the residence of

Templeogue village is today a busy suburban centre; beyond, with the exception of a few good granite and brick council cottages on the left, all has changed. In the place of the gates and demesne of **Cypress Grove** are new roads and housing, although the house itself, with a particularly fine door case and fanlight, survives, in the ownership of a missionary order. Graceful **Templeogue Bridge**, which the poet Austin Clarke helped to preserve from the roads engineers, was demolished in 1976, two years after his death, and a wide concrete structure now replaces it. His home, **Bridge House**, was also demolished shortly after, and has been replaced by two mock-Tudor detached houses.

Templeogue House, after many restorations, is extant and in use as a Contract Bridge Centre. What remains of the gardens which adorned the house, mainly the great specimen trees, are still a major feature of the surroundings. The housing developers included lime trees in their landscaping, echoing the one standing beside the old house. (See Santry Court, page 32.)

Templeogue House in 1988

Henry White Esq., and, at the moment of writing, it is up for auction.

A little farther on the left is Cheeverstown House, now a children's hospital, and, on the right, where the road forks right to Crumlin and Kimmage, is the old church mentioned above. The City Watercourse is carried in a curve round under the wall of the old graveyard—an insanitary arrangement. The church itself is heavily ruined and of little interest, but there are some interesting tombstones.

At 4¾ miles, there comes into view on the left Spawell House (better seen, though from farther away, from the Firhouse Road). This building, now a farmhouse, was formerly the celebrated Templeogue Spa, from which the *Templeogue Intelligencer* was published. The large barn on the left of the house is said to have been the bath-house; it was partly taken down in 1946. The house itself has a most unusually shaped roof.

At Balrothery, 1¼ mile farther on, the road to the right leads to Tymon Castle and Greenhills (see Route 12), and that to the left leads to the footbridge below the City Weir near Firhouse. The weir was originally built to give a head to the City Watercourse (mentioned above), which begins here. When the Dodder is in flood, the volume of water cascading over the weir is an impressive sight. Beside the weir is a mound which looks man-made, but is more probably natural. Immediately below the weir, on the left bank, is Bella Vista, in the grounds of which is a building described on the Ordnance Survey as a church, but in reality is the engine-house of an old paper mill. The mistake is understandable, as the building has fine cut-stone pediments and tall arches at each end.

At 7 miles, Tallaght is entered. St Maelruan founded a monastery here in the eighth century, and the village, 'Tamlaght Maelruan', is named as 'the plague-burying-place of Maelruan'. The Rule of his house is extant in Old Irish. In the fourteenth century, the village became the country residence of the Archbishops of Dublin. Their castle, reputed to be of great magnificence, was used as a stronghold of the Pale against the raids of the O'Tooles and O'Byrnes from County Wicklow. At the Reformation, it passed into Protestant hands, and in 1729 John Hoadly, the Archbishop, pulled down nearly all of it. With the materials he built a new palace, which seems to have been a very piecemeal affair. In 1778, Archbishop Fowler used the ancient Cross of Tallaght when building a bathroom in the Palace. It was abandoned by the Archbishops in 1821, and bought by Major Palmer, who pulled it down and built a new house. It subsequently belonged to a Mr Lentaigne, who erected in the garden an arch made of the vertebrae of a

Cheeverstown House (formerly Kilvere) is extant, at the centre of an extensive modern development for the education of people with disabilities.

The **old Templeogue church** is also extant, sited in the midst of a green, over-looking a busy dual carriageway built about 1980 to deal with traffic to and from an expanding Tallaght.

Spawell House is still there, overlooking the only tract of undeveloped farmland in the area. It dates from 1703, and was originally an inn, called 'The Domville Arms and Three Tuns'.

Tymon Castle, a fifteenth-century towerhouse which was last occupied in 1779, was an imposing ruin until it was demolished in 1960.

West of Spawell, all has changed in the past thirty years. Beyond Spawell House many new roads converge on a major interchange of the M50. Although **Bella Vista** has been replaced, the **old paper mill engine-house** has been renovated and is in use as a dwelling. The **Firhouse weir** is still there, and a colourful new footbridge has been built to replace the old one.

At the next roundabout the sprawling conurbation of **Tallaght New Town** begins.

The late nineteenth-century main street of Tallaght has survived almost intact, owing in part to the shift of commercial emphasis a kilometre westwards to the new town centre developed around The Square in the 1980s and 90s.

In common with all religious orders, the numbers of student priests studying in the great **Dominican seminary** have reduced to a trickle: currently there are fifteen in all, and there are plans to move the seminary into the city. Much of **Lentaigne's gardens** still remain, an island of peace in the midst of the bustling new town. In the grounds is a walnut tree of great age called St Maelruan's Tree and which is said to date back to at least the Middle Ages; it is recorded that it was blown down in the 'Big Wind' of January 1839, but it has continued to grow and bear fruit. The Dominicans made a decision in the 1980s not to sell land for development other than for education purposes; they provided the land for Tallaght Institute of Technology.

whale from County Mayo, resting on mill-stones from the powder-mills at Corkagh, which blew up in 1787. In 1842, he sold or leased the place to the Dominican order, who possess it still. The roof-ridge of their church is a conspicuous landmark.

The Protestant church of Tallaght (at the south-western end of the village, on the road to Brittas) was built in 1829, not quite on the site of the old church. The tower, which still stands, adjoined the old church but is not connected with the new. The architect of the present church was Semple, who designed the 'Black Church' in Dublin, and Rathmines, Whitechurch and Monkstown Protestant churches. The view from the top of the old tower is worth the climb. In the church is a monument to Sir Timothy Allen of Allenton (see Route 14), who was Lord Mayor of Dublin in 1762, and died in 1771.

In 1867 took place the 'Battle of Tallaght', when a force of fourteen police took sixty-five Fenian prisoners, after a gun-battle in the main street. The main body of the Fenians was occupying Tallaght Hill, but dispersed after the battle, and the snowstorm which followed it.

Leaving Tallaght by the Protestant church, the road next reaches Jobstown (9½ miles). A point-to-point is annually held here. The road continues to climb up the foothills of the Dublin Mountains. At 10 miles there is a fork—the old road continuing straight up the mountain by Mount Seskin to Brittas, and the new bearing right. At 12 miles, the road runs under Verschoyle's Hill, parallel with the Slade of Saggart, a long and picturesque glen which debouches onto the Naas Road near Clondalkin (see Route 12). On a height to the left is Crooksling Sanatorium for consumptive patients. Shortly after this, the highest point in the road (797 feet) is reached, and the descent into Brittas passes a lake. This is of artificial origin, and originally served the paper mills at Saggart. It is now maintained by an anglers' association.

Brittas, at 14 miles, is of no particular interest. Here the road is joined by that from Bohernabreena over the Ballinascorney Gap (see Route 14). Beyond Brittas, the land to the left becomes flat and boggy, and fine distant views of the mountains appear. The county boundary into Wicklow is crossed at 14¾ miles.

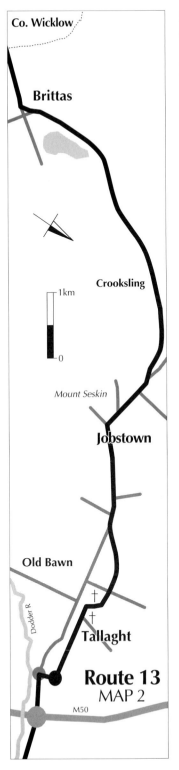

St Maelruan's Church of Ireland Church, designed by Semple, is still in use.

Jobstown is now at the centre of a large area of housing estates, and although the 'green spaces' are often grazed by piebald ponies belonging to Traveller families, the days of point-to-point racing are long gone. Just past the Jobstown Inn on the right is **Kiltalown House**, a simple granite-fronted building of about 1800, added to an earlier house which still survives at the back. It is one of the few smaller country houses around Tallaght to survive the sweeping developments of the 1970s and 1980s, and serves today as a community activity centre.

It is not until the Blessington road turns south under Verschoyle's Hill that the suburban spread of Tallaght housing peters out, and, except for the frequent bungalows, the road passes through countryside relatively unchanged since 1949.

Medieval tower at St Maelruan's church

Route 14

Brittas via Bohernabreena and Ballinascorney

	Miles from the GPO
Templeogue	4½
Firhouse	5¾
Old Bawn Cross	7¼
Bohernabreena Bridge	9
Ballinascorney House	11
Brittas	13½

This Route follows Route 13 as far as Templeogue village, 4½ miles from the GPO. Just beyond the village, the turn to the left is taken, over the bridge. In the Bridge House lives the poet and novelist Austin Clarke. A few yards farther on, Butterfield Avenue comes in from the left, leading to Rathfarnham (see Route 15). Very soon, a good view is obtained of Spawell House (see Route 13), with its steep truncated gable, masking the roofs. Until 1946 this house was washed a particularly pleasant orange colour, but it has now unfortunately been rough-cast in grey. Nonetheless, this road as far as Old Bawn is still noteworthy for the attractive aspect of the country, dotted with pastel-coloured houses, many with old walled gardens, against the gently sloping background of the mountains.

One mile on from Templeogue Bridge, just outside the village of Firhouse, is Delaford House, perhaps the most beautiful of the smaller houses in the Dublin neighbourhood. The part farthest from the road, two storeys high, is the older, and during the eighteenth century it was an inn. The road at this time ran much nearer the front than it does now. Towards the end of the eighteenth century, it was bought by Alderman Bermingham, who added the present front, of one storey only, with a front door adorned with a large fanlight, and semi-circular bows at either end. The original name of the house was Clandarrig, altered by Alderman Bermingham to Springfield, and by a later owner to Delaford. The house was occupied in 1913 by Dr Swan, and is now in the possession of John Murphy Esq. It is at present washed with a very beautiful shade of pink, and the joinery is painted white.

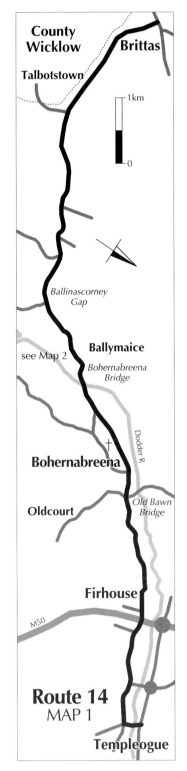

County
Wicklow · Brittas

Talbotstown

1km

0

Ballinascorney
Gap

see Map 2 · Ballymaice

Bohernabreena
Bridge

Bohernabreena

Dodder R

Oldcourt · Old Bawn
Bridge

Firhouse

M50

Route 14
MAP 1

Templeogue

For **Spawell House**, see page 139.

The road towards Firhouse no longer boasts attractive, pastel-coloured houses, since most, including **Cherryfield**, which retained its pink colour until the late 1970s, were demolished during the housing and road developments of the last three decades.

Delaford House became derelict after the sale of the surrounding lands for housing and, following a series of fires, it was demolished c. 1977.

In 2001 a new roadbridge was built connecting the Firhouse road to Templeogue at the old Dodder fording place. The old road from the ford to the Firhouse road, for two hundred years submerged by the growth of its two bounding hedges, will soon come back into use again as a pedestrian connection to a new riverside walk.

Delaford, west elevation 1959

Delaford, doorcase and fanlight

143

Firhouse, which is entered at 5¾ miles, is an attractive occurrence of cottages. The inhabitants were stigmatised by Handcock, the historian of Tallaght in 1877, as a 'wasteful, improvident lot, spending most of their earnings in drink' and in fighting—but this is no longer the case. A fork to the left here leads to Sally Park, Knocklyon Castle, Mount Prospect (all within ¼ mile) and ultimately to Ballycullen and Orlagh (see Route 15). Sally Park, on the right of this road, belonged originally to the Earls of Clanwilliam, and was bought by William Domville Handcock's grandfather in 1796. His grandson also lived here, and it is now occupied by Mr Cullen. There is a Carmelite Convent close by. Knocklyon or Knocklyon Castle is a small, square, three-storeyed building, with round towers at two opposite corners, much remodelled in the eighteenth century. It was once owned by the Ledwich family, and in Handcock's time had been held by the Magranes for fifty years and is still in their possession. Mount Prospect was during the early nineteenth century the residence of Dr MacDonnell, Provost of Trinity College, and is at present the residence of Mrs Gwynn, widow of a more recent holder of that office, and of her son-in-law, the artist Oisín Kelly. The remains of Dr MacDonnell's scenic waterworks may still be seen. At Beech Park, to the east of Prospect, lives the Rt Hon. W. T. Cosgrave, former Free State President.

In Firhouse itself, a footpath to the right leads to the Dodder weir and to Balrothery (see Route 13).

One mile beyond Firhouse there is, close to the road on the right, Sporting Hall, now Killininny, a fine early-eighteenth-century house, a farmhouse, with the remains of a walled garden at the rere. Half a mile farther on is the crossroads of Old Bawn. The road to the right leads to Tallaght (49 bus route); that to the left leads to Dollymount, Oldcourt, Orlagh and Mount Venus (see Route 15); while straight on (49A bus route) leads to Bohernabreena. Old Bawn House itself, or to speak strictly, what remains of it, is reached by going right over the bridge towards Tallaght, ignoring the turn to the right which goes up Tallaght Hill, and entering in at a gate of unpromising appearance a little farther on.

Old Bawn House was an almost unique Irish specimen of a Jacobean manor-house. It was first built in about 1635 by William Bulkeley, Archdeacon of Dublin, and shows in its plan traces of the Welsh origin of its builder. It was burned by the Wicklow clans in 1641, but apparently re-edified to the old model. Another member of the Bulkeley family, Sir Richard (1644–1710), was of some note in his day as a religious maniac and

The 'attractive' nineteenth-century cottages at Firhouse were unroofed in 2001. Nearby, the old stone wall to the north of the road bears the shapes of piers to former gateways, the ghosts of entrances to properties that no longer exist. The **Carmelite Convent of the Assumption** occupies a house originally built by the Fieragh family in the late eighteenth century. It was purchased by the nuns in 1827, who built a chapel and later a little Gothic-windowed schoolhouse in the grounds.

Opposite Morton's public house is **Sally Park**, formerly the home of William Domville Handcock, author in 1877 of *The History and Antiquities of Tallaght*, and subsequently of the architect T. J. Cullen. It is currently in use as a nursing home. To the west is an extensive area of 1970s and 80s private housing.

Knocklyon Castle is in excellent order but of **Mount Prospect**, only a pair of great gate-piers still showing the name remain at the entrance to a recently constructed housing estate. Beyond is an elegant suspension-structure foot-bridge spanning the M50 motorway.

Beech Park is extant and has recently changed hands. To the east of Beech Park, in a modest bungalow, lives the son of W. T. Cosgrave, Liam Cosgrave, former Taoiseach and former leader of the Fine Gael party.

Killininny House is gone, a modern house taking its place, but strangely, one of the original gate piers of the old house can still be seen behind the modern boundary wall.

The roofless remains of **Old Bawn House** survived until about 1975, with some of its outhouses serving as stores for the building contractors who developed the land to the west of Old Bawn Road. Then, in the next wave of development, the ruins and outhouses were swept away without trace.

Killininny House c. *1955*

pamphleteer, and a member of the Royal Society. The place passed by marriage in 1702 to the Tynte family, extensive landowners in south-eastern County Wicklow, who held it for about a century. About 1800, a paper mill was established here (it will be remarked that south-western County Dublin has always been the home of paper mills), and the house was apparently lived in by Mr McDonnell, the owner of the mills. Handcock (*History of Tallaght*, 1877, pp. 47–50) gives a very full description of the house and mills, which in his day supplied several of the Dublin daily papers. There is an architectural description of the house in Leask, *Irish Castles*, pp. 149–50, and a paper by the same author in the *JRSAI* for 1913. The mill was subsequently burnt, though relics of it may still be seen. In 1890, the house was still roofed, but by 1910 it had become very ruinous, and there is now little but the chimneys, some crumbling walls and the remains of one stucco fireplace to be seen. Around the building are traces of the water-filled moat which it once possessed as a concession to the claims of security; but this is difficult to disentangle from the mill-races, etc. The chief glory of Old Bawn was the stucco chimney-piece depicting Nehemiah building the walls of Jerusalem, which, together with part of the staircase, is now in the National Museum, Kildare Street. The chimney-piece bears the date 1635.

A few yards up the road to the left from Old Bawn cross (towards Mount Venus) is Allenton, a very fine house of circa 1730. It was perhaps built by Sir Timothy Allen, whose monument is in Tallaght Church (see Route 13). The back parts of the house, which are now rather ruinous, have the appearance of being older than the rest. There is in the back yard a square tower, which was probably a dovecote. It is now occupied by Mr Timothy Muldoon. At ¾ mile beyond Allenton on this road is Oldcourt House, now almost a ruin but possessing a long and continuous history. There are said to have been here a village and chapel, which have long since utterly vanished, their place being taken in recent years by a council housing estate nearby.

Opposite Oldcourt, a rough track leads up the mountain to Dollymount (see Route 15). Dollymount is seen to good advantage from this direction, as its enormous length appears fully extended.

Continuing on the road from Old Bawn cross, the route skirts the right banks of the Dodder for a mile, when there is a fork at the Catholic church and Bohernabreena House. A ¼ mile above Old Bawn Bridge is the spot on the bank where in 1816 took place the execution of the three Kearneys for the murder of John Kinlan, steward to Ponsonby Shaw of Friarstown.

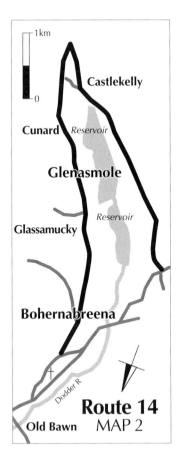

Route 14

Old Bawn   MAP 2

The road network in the area of **Old Bawn cross** has changed radically in the last decade or so, and Bridget Burke's tiny pub has been replaced by a massive, architectural Disneyland of a public house. The Oldcourt Road is reached in a roundabout way, where, in spite of being a listed building, **Allenton** was demolished in 1984. In the ensuing fifteen years, as the population of the surrounding area increased substantially, the outbuildings, including the square tower, have all but disappeared.

Oldcourt House was unroofed in 1950, and only a few of its ivy-covered walls now remain.

Little remains of **Dollymount House**, which is known locally as 'McCarthy's Castle', as the only recognisable element remaining is one of the towers that flanked the main house.

Bohernabreena House is still there, beside the church.

Allenton 1950

The trial was rather dubiously conducted and the prisoners protested their innocence. At the execution-place there were popular demonstrations in favour of the condemned men. It was for this execution that Lundy Foot of Orlagh (see Route 15) was afterwards assassinated.

The fork left at the Catholic church leads up over the mountain and ultimately joins the Military Road near Killakee (Route 15). Another branch of it leads up the eastern side of Glenasmole to Castlekelly and Glenasmole Lodge (see below) and also joins the Military Road.

On the main route, a few yards beyond the fork, on the left, is the gate of Friarstown House, the residence of Ponsonby Shaw, mentioned above, who spent large sums of money laying out grottoes, winding walks, waterfalls and an artificial lake, which were soon swept away by the sudden rains characteristic of granite mountain-valleys. The house was later tenanted by a Captain Bayley, and by a Scotsman named Watson. It is now in the occupation of J. Murphy Esq.

A ½ mile beyond the fork is Bohernabreena or Fort Bridge, built about 1837. Here is the beginning of the estate enclosing the Rathmines and Rathgar waterworks, which consists of two artificial lakes begun in 1880, occupying the northern half of the valley of Glenasmole. Admission for pedestrians is by permit obtainable at the City Hall, Dublin.

The road now passes through the townland of Ballymaice, in which are the remains of the deer park formerly belonging to Belgard Castle, Clondalkin (see Route 12). The road begins to climb steeply, and a fork left is passed, leading up the west side of Glenasmole to Glenasmole Lodge (see detour at end of this route). Glenasmole is left behind, and the bed of a small stream is followed. At 1¾ miles from Bohernabreena Bridge is the top of Ballinascorney Gap (approx. 1,000 feet). Here there is a granite cross, of no great antiquity and of unknown purpose, and a lonely road diverges to the left towards Kilbride, passing the mountain of Seahan or Seechon, on the top of which is a cairn containing a passage grave. This feature is found on many of the mountains in this vicinity.

Soon afterwards, the road passes on the left Ballinascorney House, formerly called Dillon's Lodge after the Dillons of Belgard, who built it as a shooting-box. For many years it was tenanted by the Bagenal family, and was captured in 1803 by Robert Emmet, who frightened the Misses Bagenal greatly, but 'did no more harm than consuming all the edibles in the house'. Dillon's Lodge was then tenanted by Gerald Tench, who from humble origins rose to the position of Equity Registrar in the Four Courts. Though

Friarstown demesne, its gardens and water features, disappeared under the garbage of the south suburbs of Dublin when the area became the Bohernabreena rubbish tiphead about 1970. **Friarstown House**, a modest, undistinguished three-bay building is extant, adjoining an extensive array of battlemented stables and barns, still in use, though in very poor condition.

The old barn at Friarstown House

The wooded demesne of the **Bohernabreena Reservoirs** has changed little in the ensuing years and it is still a place of resort for pedestrians and anglers.

The **granite cross** at the Ballinascorney Gap is extant, and is said locally to have been erected about 1880 in memory of a farmer who was killed here when his haycart overturned.

Ballinascorney House was abandoned about 1988, and subsequently subjected to vandalism and burning. The ruined walls still stand, overlooking what remains of an ornamental garden.

paralysed, he was a keen sportsman, and kept hospitable house here. The Lodge was later leased to Major Knox, founder and first proprietor of *The Irish Times*. Under his regime the tradition of hospitality flourished, and among other amenities he provided a brass band composed of printers' devils, which used to play on top of a horse-bus on the way to and fro. The property later belonged to Captain Hackett.

A mile farther on is Talbotstown House, where another side-road leads off to the left into County Wicklow towards Kilbride. A short distance along this road on the left is a stone cross bearing the inscription

I.N.R.I.

+

I.S.S.

I.B.

1804

which commemorates the death of a local resident called Bealis who, together with his horse, was overcome here during a snowstorm.

At 1½ miles beyond Talbotstown House, and 12½ from the GPO, the road joins the Blessington Road at Brittas Inn (see Route 13).

Detour from Bohernabreena Bridge to Glenasmole Lodge

The road which forks left at the Catholic church below Bohernabreena Bridge, runs in the rear of Friarstown House and forks again, when the right branch is taken. Farther on, the road is bounded on the left by the old wall of a deer park which belonged to Speaker Conolly of Castletown. Between Friarstown and Glassamucky National School there was, in about 1870, the 'Monastery' of St Ann's, which seems to have been a guest-house for quoit-players from Dublin.

> A few monks reside here, who hospitably entertain all who come, provided they bring their own provisions, or order them beforehand. Here, in the summer, and sometimes in the winter, a quoit club, so-called, meet occasionally, though several of the members are more famous for their musical, facetious, or gastronomic, than for their athletic achievements. The willing monks supply room, fuel and water, and many a pleasant evening is spent in the pure air of the mountain by its habitués.
>
> Handcock, *History of Tallaght*, 1877, p. 65

Talbotstown House is extant.

The ivy-covered remains of **St Ann's church** are extant, within an overgrown oval graveyard.

The famed thrushes of **Glenasmole** have been written about many times, including a poem of nine verses by Oliver St John Gogarty, which begins:

Do you remember that thrush at Glenasmole,
In the high lane on the west side when I made the engine stop.
When he perched across the roadway as if demanding toll:
So well within his rights was he, he would not even hop?

Talbotstown House

The name St Ann's is a corruption from Kilnasantan, which means 'the church of Santan', not of St Ann. The church is near the upper reservoir, on the right-hand side of the road. It has not been used for perhaps six hundred years, except for burials. There is also a holy well.

Glenasmole (the Glen of the Thrushes) figures prominently in the poems of the Fenian cycle. The old district of Uí Ceallaigh (O'Kelly) stretched south of Tallaght across the entrance to the valley. Until the beginning of the nineteenth century, the district was almost exclusively Irish-speaking, and was found particularly rich in folklore by Eugene O'Curry when he was working here for the Ordnance Survey in 1837. Three things for which, according to the old legends, the valley was chiefly remarkable were its large breed of thrushes, the great size of the ivy leaves found on the rocks, and the large berries of the mountain ash. The ash woods were destroyed about 1760 to make charcoal (see Petrie in the *Dublin Penny Journal*, 1835–36).

Half a mile beyond Kilnasantan is the hamlet of Cunard, and a ½ mile farther the village of Castlekelly, which now shows no sign of the building from which it is named. The route now approaches Glenasmole Lodge, built as Heathfield Lodge in the later eighteenth century, by George Grierson, the printer. Grierson, whose office as King's Printer in Ireland had almost become hereditary, was a very rich man and entertained sumptuously, but he died several thousand pounds in debt. His three daughters lived here for many years. Later, the house was occupied by a Mr Cobbe (the Cobbes of Newbridge, Donabate, had long been landlords) who rebuilt it. In more recent years, it was shared as a shooting lodge by the Dean of Christ Church and Sir John Maffey (now Lord Rugby), British Representative in Dublin. Close to the western boundary wall is a stone on which the Griersons placed an inscription, on 1 April 1844, relating to the exploits of Fionn with the stone, but this has now disappeared.

There is no passable thoroughfare beyond Glenasmole Lodge, but return may be made on the west side of the valley towards the Ballinascorney Gap. The round trip from Bohernabreena Bridge is about 6½ miles.

Glenasmole Lodge, dating from 1792, is extant, surrounded by 200 acres of gardens, pastures and moorland. It was extensively refurbished in 1964, incorporating interior features such as fireplaces, doors and architraves salvaged from a variety of Dublin properties. At the time of writing, the lodge is on the market for a sum of around £3 million.

Glenasmole Lodge in the early twentieth century

ROUTE 15

GLENCREE

	Miles from the GPO
Rathfarnham	3¼
Ballyboden	4½
Rockbrook	5
Mount Venus	5¾
Killakee House	6¾
Glencree	9

Rathfarnham, with a population of 9,000, 3¼ miles from the GPO, is usually reached from Terenure (see Route 13), from which it is about 1 mile distant. It is pleasantly situated on a gentle eminence, with various streams converging upon it. At the entrance to the village, on the right, is an old graveyard with the Protestant church adjoining. Opposite these is the main gateway to Rathfarnham Castle. Another entrance, facing the Dodder, is in the style of a Roman triumphal arch, and contains a gate-keeper's house.

The core of Rathfarnham Castle was built by Adam Loftus, Lord Chancellor and Archbishop of Dublin, in 1585. The property was inherited by the son-in-law of a later Adam Loftus, the Duke of Wharton, son of the profligate John Wharton and subject of Swift's most terrible invective (see 'A Brief Character' in *Swift's Works*, Vol. V, p. 27: Temple Scott edition). In 1723, it was sold to Speaker Conolly, whose nephew sold it in about 1741 to Hoadly, the latitudinarian Archbishop of Armagh, in whose family it remained until 1767, when the Second Earl of Ely (a Loftus and a direct descendant of the original builder) bought it. After 1798 it was abandoned, and then turned over to the military and to a grazier, who stabled his cattle in the banqueting hall decorated by Angelica Kaufmann. Towards the end of the nineteenth century, it was acquired by Lord Justice Blackburne, in whose family it remained until, in about 1910, it was bought by the Jesuit order. The order maintains a very fine library in the Castle, and a seismic observatory. The present Rector is Very Rev. Hugh Kelly, SJ.

In the middle of the village, is, on the right, a road leading towards Temple-ogue and Tallaght, by Butterfield Avenue, opposite which is a golf course, extending towards Bushy Park (see Route 13). The large house on the right at the entrance to Butterfield Avenue has associations with Robert Emmet.

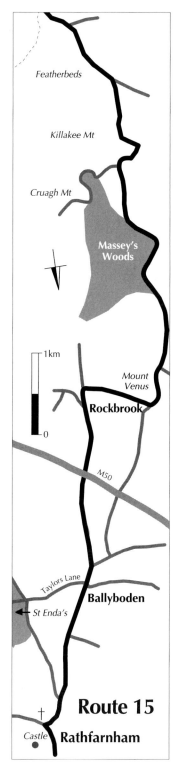

Featherbeds

Killakee Mt

Cruagh Mt

Massey's Woods

1km

Mount Venus

Rockbrook

M50

Taylors Lane

Ballyboden

St Enda's

Route 15

Castle **Rathfarnham**

The **Protestant graveyard** provides a little wilderness oasis in the midst of the dense development that now surrounds it.

Only one flank wall of the original gateway to **Rathfarnham Castle** remains; the rest was swept away during the construction in the 1980s of a new road bypassing the village. The castle, which was declared a National Monument in 1986, is now in state owner-ship and is undergoing long-term conserva-tion works. The seminary building that was attached to it, constructed in the 1940s by the Jesuits, was demolished in the early 1990s.

The north entrance to Rathfarnham Castle, a great **triumphal arch**, although now isolated from the original demesne by housing and roads, is extant, though unoccupied and poorly cared-for (see page 163 for picture).

Three eighteenth-century houses survive on **Butterfield Avenue**: **Butterfield House** (home in the eighteenth century of John Hely Hutchinson, Provost of Trinity College) on the right; **Old Orchard** on the left, and some distance farther west, at Washington Lane, will be found **Washington Lodge**. Under the assumed name of Robert Ellis, Robert Emmet leased a house on Butterfield Avenue in 1803 while making preparations for the insurrec-tion of that year. While it seems clear that it was one of the three named above, which house is a matter of conjecture.

Keeping to the right, the one irregular street, of which Rathfarnham consists, ends at the large Catholic church. Here, on the right, is the road leading past Ballyboden and Rockbrook. At a short distance from the church, on the left, is a fork leading to the gate of Grange Golf Club in about 1 mile, and thence to Whitechurch and Tibradden (see Route 15A).

Continuing towards Ballyboden (a bus route) is, on the right, Riversdale, a small country house which was W. B. Yeats's home during the last years of his life. About 1¼ miles from Rathfarnham is Ballyboden, a small village where is a turn to the left leading towards Grange Golf Club and Whitechurch (an alternative bus route to Rockbrook: see Route 15A).

Just beyond Ballyboden, on the right, is Billysbridge, on a road leading to Firhouse (see Route 13). At 5 miles from the GPO on the main road, Rockbrook is reached. It is a small village in the mountain parish of Cruagh. On the right is Rockbrook House, lately renovated by Lord Glenavy, Governor of the Bank of Ireland. It commands fine views of Dublin. Just beyond the village is Old Cruagh Churchyard, containing a ruined church and a later watch-tower, dating from the days of corpse-snatchers.

The road to the left at Rockbrook leads to Tibradden and St Columba's (Route 15B).

Shortly after Rockbrook (which is left by the road to the right before the churchyard) the ruins of Mount Venus come in sight. The cromlech in the grounds is one of the largest in Ireland.

> Only one end of the immense roofing stone is now raised from the ground, but two pillar stones lie beside it, and Mr Borlase in his important work on the Dolmens of Ireland says that if the roof-stone was ever raised on them, the cromlech must have been one of the most magnificent megalithic monuments in the world.... In a curious note in his sketch-book Gabriel Beranger puts forward a theory that this cromlech was overthrown by an earthquake which is recorded to have been felt in Dublin in 1690.
>
> Ball's *History of the County of Dublin*, Part iii, pp. 48–49

Mount Venus, which in 1790 was lived in by James Cullen, a 'distinguished amateur of the Fine Arts', and which 100 years ago was the residence of a family named Armstrong, has long been in ruins. In a passage of his Irish autobiography, *Ave*, in which he recalls a walk he took to the Dublin mountains as a young man, some time in the 1870s, George Moore

Riversdale is in need of restoration. In 2000 an application to demolish it was refused; it is hoped at time of writing that, although the grounds may be developed to provide apartments, the house may be refurbished.

Riversdale 1982

Rockbrook, a two-storey, five-bay Georgian house with a diocletian window at the centre, was the home of the 2nd Lord Glenavy, father of the late broadcaster Patrick Campbell. It is now a boys' private secondary school.

Mount Venus, admired by George Moore, is a ruin, but the tall and massive piers of its gates still stand, and the great collapsed dolmen remains, hidden in a grove of trees.

describes the place at the beginning of its decay:

> A gateway appeared—heavy wrought-iron gates hanging between great stone pillars, the drive ascending through lonely grass-lands with no house in view, for the house lay on the further side of the hill, a grove of beech-trees reserving it as a surprise for the visitor. A more beautiful grove I have never seen, some two hundred years old, and the house as old as it—a long house built with picturesque chimney-stacks, well placed at each end, a resolute house, emphatic as an oath, with great steps before the door, and each made out of a single stone… At the end of the great yew hedge, hundreds of years old, the comely outline of Howth floated between sea and sky, spiritual, it seemed, on that grey day, as a poem by Shelley. One thought, too, of certain early pictures by Corot. The line of the shore was certainly drawn as beautifully as if he had drawn it, and the plain about the sea, filled with Dublin City, appeared in the distance a mere murky mass, with here and there a building indicated, faintly, with Corot's beauty of touch. Nearer still the suburbs came trickling into the fields… A scheme for the restoration of Mount Venus started up in my mind; about two thousand pounds would have to be spent, but for that money I should live in the most beautiful place in the world.

Beyond the gate of Mount Venus is a road on the right, which rejoins Ballyboden at Billysbridge. A farther turn on the right leads to Tallaght (Route 13). At the corner here is the Augustinian monastery of Orlagh, built in 1790 by Lundy Foot, a member of the wealthy family of snuff-makers and tobacconists in Parliament Street, very prominent citizens in the late eighteenth and early nineteenth centuries. It was then known as Foot-mount.

Lundy Foot was the magistrate who brought the Kearney brothers to trial (see Route 14). He was twice attacked on his property in County Kilkenny, on the second occasion being stoned and hacked to pieces. He was buried at Rower Church, County Kilkenny, but some two years later his remains were removed to St Matthew's Church, Donnybrook, where a tombstone records his fate (Handcock's *History of Tallaght*). When he asked Curran to suggest a motto to go with his arms on the side of his carriage, Curran produced extempore 'Quid Rides'.

Orlagh was subsequently occupied by Carew O'Dwyer, an associate of O'Connell, and then by Nathaniel Callwell, Governor of the Bank of

Orlagh, with a wonderful view of Dublin city, Howth and Lambay, is still occupied by the Augustinian Order, but today it presents a bland, sad façade: a 'rationalised' entrance, Tyrolean render and plastic windows have largely taken away its character. It is, however, recoverable.

Orlagh in 1977

Ireland. The Augustinian Fathers have added a storey to the house, and the banqueting-hall, in which O'Dwyer used to entertain O'Connell, is now the chapel.

Near Orlagh, on the road leading to Old Bawn and Tallaght, is a laneway to the left leading up the mountain to Dollymount, sometimes called Montpelier House, or Ely's Folly.

This house, built by Henry Loftus, Earl of Ely, in 1763, has a frontage of enormous extent (about 360 feet), consisting of a central block with bowed projections, and long connecting ranges terminating in towers in the Gothic of the period. Large quantities of earth were transported up the mountainside by bullocks, to make the walled gardens which may still be seen in rear. These gardens contain some curious structures which appear to be cellars of some kind, and also circular, dome-shaped erections of masonry, laid out in rows, of which the purpose is obscure. The house was called Dollymount in honour of Lord Ely's niece, Dolly Monroe, a celebrated beauty. Though sumptuously adorned with stucco-work, it was not occupied for very long, and has remained derelict for upwards of a hundred years.

Dollymount can also be reached on foot via the so-called 'Hell-fire Club', a massive vaulted structure which crowns Montpelier Hill. This, like Dollymount, was built by the owner of Rathfarnham Castle, Speaker William Conolly of Castletown, County Kildare, in about 1725. A later Conolly, Squire Thomas, was indeed a member of the Hell-fire Club, but this is the only authentic connection.

Conolly's Folly (as it is best called) was largely built from the materials of a large prehistoric monument which till then occupied the site. It had first a slated roof, which was blown off in a storm. The present solid vault was then built; and the structure, though now denuded of all its cut stone and damaged by bonfires in honour of Queen Victoria's visit in 1849, remains extremely solid and likely to endure for some time to come. It is sometimes referred to as a 'shooting lodge'; and this is the only possible use to which it can have been put. But it is more probably a pure monument to the family's building zeal.

The road now winds southwards, and soon passes on the left Killakee House, the former seat of Lord Massey, now abandoned and in the course of demolition. It then joins the Military Road (the first part of which, starting near Cruagh Churchyard is no longer a public thoroughfare). This road was built after the 1798 Rising, and takes a course of 45 miles into County

For **Dollymount**, see page 147. The 'curious structures', possibly for grain storage, are extant.

Conolly's Folly, generally known now as the **Hellfire Club**, has been the site of many bonfires, celebrations and cider parties since it was damaged in 1849. Conservation work was carried out in the 1970s by the Office of Public Works, which included the installation of a concrete staircase, and in its present condition it must be practically indestructible. Traces still exist at the back of the building of the megalithic monument that once crowned the hilltop.

Killakee House, with its conservatory and fruit houses by Richard Turner, was demolished in the 1940s, but ghostly traces of the elaborate gardens designed by Ninian Niven, the remains of a circular pond, terraces and niches, can still be detected. In common with many other great houses that are no more, the fine little gate lodge, where the impecunious 8th Baron Massey died in 1958, survives.

Killakee House

Wicklow, through a district once deemed impassable. In about ½ mile, a turn to the left leads to the Pine Forest, a favourite excursion-place near Tibradden Mountain, on the Glencullen Road (see Route 16).

The road now passes over the Featherbed Mountain, a high plateau of bog, ordinarily a desert, but which in recent years has come into prominence as a source of private fuel for Dublin people. To the right, there are grand views across the valley of Glenasmole (Route 14) to high mountains. At 8 miles from the GPO, the road crosses into County Wicklow.

Thirty years ago it was common at a weekend to see as many as two hundred people on **Featherbed Mountain** cutting and stacking turf. At the time of writing, however, there are only about fifteen families regularly taking peat from the bog. Conscious of the need to preserve peatlands, the Wicklow National Park is not issuing any further turf-cutting licences.

Rathfarnham Castle north gate house

ROUTE 15A

RATHFARNHAM TO SANDYFORD

	Miles from the GPO
Rathfarnham	3¼
Loreto Convent	3½
St Enda's and the Priory	4
Marlay	4¼
Sandyford	8

The road from the Catholic church at Rathfarnham is to the left, but curves to the right at a short distance from the church. A little beyond the curve is the Loreto Convent, an extensive building, the central part of which was once the residence of George Grierson, King's Printer in the early eighteenth century. The house was later occupied by Dr Palliser and by Sir Dominic Corrigan, one of the first Catholics to attain medical eminence in Ireland since Catholic Emancipation. The property has been for more than a century in the possession of the nuns, who here and on the opposite side of the road, keep up a large school for young ladies. Many additions have been made to the original building.

The road ascends from the convent, half a mile distant from which, on the right, is the Hermitage, an eighteenth-century house, which was at one time the property of Edward Hudson, whose son, William Scott Hudson, did much to forward Irish studies. In the early part of this century, Patrick Pearse here set up a school, St Enda's, in which all the teaching was in Irish, and the heroic ideas of Irish nationality inculcated. Pearse was the most important of the young poets who were active in the reorganisation of the physical-force party, and he went forth from St Enda's with his brother, William, and his colleague Thomas MacDonagh to lead the Easter Week Rising of 1916. They were three of the sixteen executed men. The house, now occupied by Senator Miss Margaret Pearse, is, with its grounds, State property. In a corner of the place is a monument commemorating a horse which was killed at Waterloo.

Opposite St Enda's are the remains of another house of historic interest, the Priory. This was the country house of John Philpot Curran (1750–1817), the celebrated orator and wit.

Curran, born in County Cork, educated at Trinity College, Dublin,

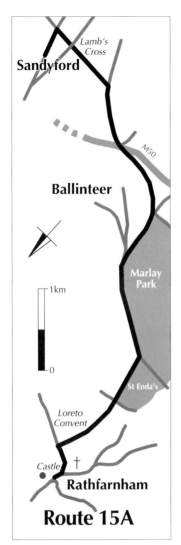

Route 15A

Nutgrove Avenue now connects Rathfarnham to Churchtown.

The **Loreto Abbey** buildings to the left on the Grange Road, and the lands around them, have recently been sold, and will be developed as apartments, with most of the existing buildings being preserved. The chapel, designed by Patrick Byrne with interior work by A. W. N. Pugin, was renovated in about 1980 with much timber replacement and the installation of steel hangers to support Pugin's lantern. St Joseph's wing, containing the concert hall, was probably designed by J. J. McCarthy.

St Enda's

When Margaret Pearse died in 1969, **St Enda's** was in a poor state of repair. It was renovated by the Office of Public Works and today houses the **Pearse Museum**, displaying artefacts and papers associated with the Pearse brothers. The grounds have been laid out as a fine public park, and you can still find many of the original follies and water features erected in the late eighteenth century by Edward Hudson, who was an eminent dentist.

The Priory, an undistinguished much-altered farmhouse, is now reduced to some fragments of walls shrouded in elder and snowberry shrubs, in the middle of a grassy 'open space' surrounded by modern houses. I could not find the stone slab marking the grave of Sarah Curran's sister.

spent two years at the Middle Temple in London, and was returned for the Irish Parliament in 1782 as a supporter of Grattan. In a large number of State Trials, from that of Rowan Hamilton in 1792 to that of Napper Tandy in 1800, he earned fame as an advocate of Irish patriots. In 1806, he was appointed Master of the Rolls. He died in London in 1817, and is buried in Glasnevin. His portrait by Lawrence is in the National Portrait Gallery.

At the Priory, the hospitable Curran gathered together a circle of friends, chiefly men younger than himself, upon whom he poured forth an incessant flow of comicalities, though in solitude or near-solitude he fell often into melancholy. The house has for us, as it had for him, the melancholy association of having been the scene of the last meeting between Curran's daughter, Sarah, and her lover, Robert Emmet, just before the latter's arrest as the instigator of the Rising of 1803. The broken-hearted Sarah died abroad some years later; as Tom Moore wrote:

> She is far from the land where her young hero sleeps,
>   And lovers are round her, sighing;
> But coldly she turns from their gaze, and weeps,
>   For her heart in his grave is lying.

Another of Curran's daughters is buried in the grounds of the Priory, where there is a monument to her. It is only a few years since the house, which is said to be haunted, has fallen into decay. The property belongs to the Loreto Convent. A quarter of a mile above the gate of St Enda's is a sharp turn to the right which leads to the gates of Grange Golf Club (see Route 15B) and Ballyboden (see Route 15).

Our Route continues left along Grange Road, past Eden, an old Cromwellian house modernised, and then passes on the right the gates of Marlay Grange and that of Marlay, the residence of Mr Love.

Marlay derives its name from George Marlay, Bishop of Dromore, whose daughter married the Rt Hon. David La Touche, grandson of a Huguenot who fought for William III at the Boyne and later made a fortune in Castle Street at worsted and banking. In the latter part of the eighteenth century, the La Touches were the wealthiest family in Dublin, and owned some of the finest houses in St Stephen's Green, as well as a country estate at Delgany. The Rt Hon. David La Touche, who became the first Governor of the Bank of Ireland in 1783, purchased the Whitechurch property, then called Grange, from Alderman Taylor in 1763. He was a man of marked artistic taste, who greatly embellished a demesne which contained about

Eden is now a public house.

Marlay Grange is extant.

Marlay House and the remaining 214 acres of the estate were purchased by Dublin County Council from the Love family in 1972, and the grounds were laid out as a public park. The house and out-offices, including what remains of the original Taylor house, have been undergoing restoration works over the last two decades. A craft centre was established in the stable buildings in the 1980s. There are two *cottages ornés* in the grounds. The smallest, at the eastern entrance, has been recently refurbished and extended, but the larger one, remodelled in Victorian times, is probably of an eighteenth-century date. It is in a poor state and urgently in need of restoration.

A cottage orné *in the Marlay Demesne*

400 Irish acres, and comprised what is now the golf course and Marlay Grange. Marlay is described by a writer in 1837 as enjoying 'all the advantages which fertility, high cultivation, variety of surface, copious supply of water, and varied planting and extent of prospect can bestow.' The present beautiful mansion was built in 1791, close to the old Taylor house, parts of which are still comprised in the buildings of the courtyard, a most striking feature. La Touche had many children, but, after their deaths, Marlay passed into the hands of the Tedcastles, coal merchants, in whose time Marlay Grange house was built on the property. The present owner of Marlay (the La Touche house) is an agriculturalist who has preserved the beauty of the place, the old walled garden, the artificial lake and the walks among the noble woods which surround the fields adjoining the mansion. In an outlying field, by the path to Whitechurch Parish Church, are extensive ranges of glass for tomato growing.

At a second entrance to Marlay, there is, on the left, a road to Ballinteer, an ex-servicemen's village, whence there is a descent to Dundrum on Route 17. Our Route continues for about ¼ mile, and turns to the left where a mountain road leads under Kilmashogue Hill (900 feet) to Lamb's Cross and Sandyford, a distance of 1½ miles. (For Sandyford, see Route 17.)

Marlay in 1958 (north elevation)

Marlay today (south elevation)

ROUTE 15B

RATHFARNHAM TO ST COLUMBA'S COLLEGE

	Miles from the GPO
Ballyboden	4½
Grange Golf Club	4¾
Whitechurch Church	5¾
St Columba's College	6¼

The road from Ballyboden (see Route 15) to Whitechurch passes a Carnegie Library and two very old houses, and turns sharply to the right at the gates of Grange Golf Club, where there are crossroads. The way straight on leads into the Grange Road (see Route 15A), the way to the left leads again to the Ballyboden Road, just beyond Rathfarnham. On it is situated Willbrook, the residence of Sir F. Moore, botanist and former Curator of the Glasnevin Gardens. The Grange Golf Club (18 holes) is, from a scenic point of view, the most attractive inland course in County Dublin. It was formerly part of the Marlay demesne, and, encircled by great woods, it has still the air of a country estate.

Our Route continues right in a gradual ascent past the village of Whitechurch. A well-kept Moravian cemetery is on the left, with closed gates and a high wall around it. The Irish associations of this religious body are chiefly in Ulster, but Dublin has long had a Moravian church (Kevin Street). The Pursers, formerly members of the firm of Guinness and more lately distinguished in scholarship and letters, were leading Moravians in Dublin.

At about ½ a mile from the Golf Club, on an eminence at the right, is the old Whitechurch Parish Church with a burial ground attached. The church is a picturesque ruin, with a late pointed doorway in the north wall of the nave. Adjoining it is Palmyra, the residence of Captain Sydney Perry. Facing Palmyra from the road is Whitechurch Lodge, recently renovated by E. Hughes Esq. Whitechurch Lodge was for many years the residence of William Swift (d. circa 1890) and his wife Elizabeth Kelly. Swift was descended from Godwin Swifte, Dean Swift's uncle. His wife having contested the validity of a marriage in the Papal States, he was the plaintiff in a complicated case for the restitution of conjugal rights, decided in his favour by the Privy Council in 1835. His mother was the Ianthe of Landor's

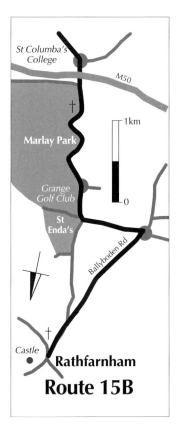

St Columba's
College

M50

1km

Marlay Park

0

Grange
Golf Club

St
Enda's

Ballyboden Rd

Castle

Rathfarnham

Route 15B

Of the '**two old houses**' near the Carnegie Library only one remains, **Newbrook**, a tiny early-nineteenth-century Gothic-style house of unusual plan, owned in the twentieth century by Sir John Irwin, who also owned an adjacent paper mill. The mill race still runs along the back of the house, and a water wheel existed there up to thirty years ago. The other 'old house' was **Kingston**, a mid-eighteenth century house where the architect T. J. Byrne, who designed the Carnegie Library, lived in the early part of the twentieth century. It was demolished about the early 1970s to provide access to a new local authority housing scheme. It is possible that Byrne also designed the two houses further along towards the Golf Club.

Willbrook, formerly the home of Sir Frederick Moore, curator of the Botanic Gardens until he retired in 1922, is a simple three-bay two-storey house of *c.* 1845. Lady Phyllis Moore, a keen gardener, laid out a fine garden at Willbrook, vestiges of which are maintained by the present owners, Mr and Mrs Hand.

The **Moravian cemetery**, up to recently quite well kept, is now becoming over-grown, and the path up the centre, dividing the buried males from the buried females, is covered in grass. The Dublin congregation died out in the 1980s. The Reverend John Berry was the last minister. The Moravian church in Kevin Street is now in commercial use.

The gable of old **Whitechurch** is daubed with graffiti, a victim of recently built housing in the area. The adjoining Harty family cemetery has been used as a paddock recently, and the tombstones are scattered and uncared-for.

Whitechurch Lodge and **Palmyra** are still in use, and at time of writing the latter is for sale.

poems, and in his youth he had known Goethe, at Weimar. A cripple in his old age, he had a lift made in this little house, and was killed in an accident in it. His story is told in his autobiography, *Wilhelm's Wanderings*.

A little beyond Whitechurch Lodge is the Protestant Parish Church, designed by John Semple, architect of the Black Church, and built in 1826. In the graveyard attached to it is the tomb of the La Touches of Marlay and the graves of several members of the Swift family, including Mrs William Swift. Another grave has the simple inscription: *My Son*.

Just beyond the church is a fork, with a road on the right leading past St Thomas, the residence of Miss May Guinness, to Rockbrook (see Route 15). A lane straight in front leads to Kelly's Glen, an attractive resort for pedestrians (to the right), and to the back of the Larch Hill Demesne, now occupied by the Boy Scouts of Ireland. In the demesne is a large crom-lech, supposed by Borlase to be unfinished, and probably the least known of the Dublin cromlechs. (See J. W. Poe: *The Cromlechs of County Dublin*, p. 25 ff.) It can also be reached from Rockbrook (see Route 15). Our route is to the left, and passes the two gates of St Columba's College, situated below Stagstown Hill, to join the road from Rathfarnham to Sandyford (see Route 15A).

St Columba's College, formerly Hollypark, was built about 1750 by Jeffrey Foot, brother of Lundy Foot of Orlagh (see Route 15). The house, which has been much added to, has beautiful stucco friezes in the Adam style.

The school was founded by Sewell, an Oxford clergyman, with the assistance of Lord Dunraven and Mr Monsell (both of whom subsequently became Roman Catholics) in 1843, the intention being to provide the sons of the Irish nobility and gentry with a system of education in conformity with the principles and formularies of the (then) united Church of England and Ireland, and with a course of instruction of the same nature as that of the great public schools of England, adding however to the curriculum the Irish language for the advantage of those boys who might later be landlords or clergy in Irish-speaking districts. The school was originally situated at Stackallen in County Meath, but was moved in 1845 to its present site. The Warden is the Rev. C. W. Sowby and there are about 150 pupils.

From the steps of the Warden's house (the original Hollypark) are grand views of Dublin and the Bay, and the very fine interior of the house contains tapestries and other treasures with which the school was endowed by Sewell, whose portrait hangs in the dining hall. The architect of the modern

Whitechurch parish church is an example of Semple's neo-Gothic at its slender best. The adjacent school has been sensitively renovated and extended as a parish centre. The surrounding graveyard is well worth exploration; of note are the finely decorated obelisk dedicated to John O'Neill, the La Touche family graves, and the grave of Sir Frederick Moore, a director of the Botanic Gardens, who lived in nearby Willbrook.

St Thomas narrowly escaped becoming a victim of the M50 motorway; while a number of modern houses west of St Columba's were cleared to make way for the road, it was spared and protected behind a great grassy mound of excavated material.

The gates of **St Columba's College** have been removed and re-erected up the hill on the western boundary of the college. The boarding school is still in operation, although the founder might be surprised to find that the establishment now accepts female students! The chapel, dating from the 1850s, is the work of William Butterfield, an English architect.

St Columba's College, formerly Hollypark, 1977

classrooms and dormitories was R. C. Orpen, a well-known antiquary and brother of William Orpen, RA, the celebrated artist. Names of many well-known Irish Protestant families, such as Parnell, Jebb, Gwynn, O'Brien and Hone, figure on its records. Stephen Gwynn, at present (1947) doyen of Irish Letters, was born here in 1864, while his father, the Rev. John Gwynn, was Warden.

Carnegie Library, Ballyboden

ROUTE 16

ROCKBROOK TO GLENCULLEN

	Miles from the GPO
Rockbrook	5
Glencullen	10
(for Rockbrook, see Route 15)	

The road from Rockbrook to Glencullen enters the wooded glen known as the Pine Forest, a favourite picnic resort on the estate of Owen Guinness Esq., Tibradden House. At 1½ miles from Rockbrook it passes Tibradden Hill (1,340 feet) on the left, and Cruagh (1,714 feet) on the right. Glendoo (1,919 feet) is a little farther on, also on the right. Here the descent begins, amid very beautiful scenery, to Glencullen (see also Route 17), passing on the way through the hamlets of Ballybrack and Brockey, and near that of Boranaraltry (i.e. 'The Road of the Harolds'), which lies to the right of the road on the other side of the Glencullen river.

This is the only part of south County Dublin where thatched cottages survive in any considerable numbers.

Near Brockey, on the left-hand side of the road, is a megalithic monument.

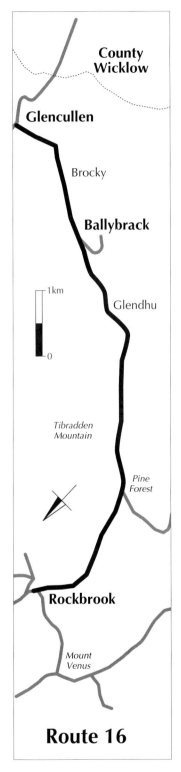

County
Wicklow

Glencullen

Brocky

Ballybrack

1km

Glendhu

0

Tibradden
Mountain

Pine
Forest

Rockbrook

Mount
Venus

Route 16

Tibradden House is extant in beautifully planted grounds, on the road going left at Rockbrook towards Larch Hill.

Cruagh Cemetery is on the right, a quarter of a mile from Rockbrook: the tower in the old cemetery dates back to the late eighteenth century when graves had to be guarded against grave robbers.

Old tower in Cruagh Cemetery

At the next junction the remains of a gateway are all that is left of **The Pine Forest Tearooms**, which provided refreshments for travellers in the hills up to the 1930s.

Beside the road below Tibradden Hill, an inscription on a boulder on the left commemorates one of Daniel O'Connell's great meetings, held here on 23 July 1823.

At Brocky are a number of relatively undisturbed ancient rundale fields, on the slopes down to the Glencullen river.

ROUTE 17

GLENCULLEN VIA BALLINTEER AND

BALLYEDMONDUFF

	Miles from the GPO
Dundrum	4
Ballinteer	5
Harold's Grange	6
Ballyedmonduff	9
Glencullen Village	10½
Glencullen Bridge and County Boundary	11¼

Route 18 is followed as far as Dundrum. In the village, the turn right is taken, down the hill over the bridge, to the left of which is the Pye Radio factory. The road then ascends, passing on the right Dundrum House and Wyckham, the latter of which is now a home for decayed merchants, formerly Simpson's Hospital in Bolton Street. On the left is Gortmore, a Carmelite House of Studies.

In 1 mile from Dundrum, the road on the right leads to Grange Road (see Route 15A). The angle between these two roads has recently been developed as a housing estate. Near the corner is Hilton, the seat of Geoffrey Taylor, Esq.

Continuing straight on, the road passes, on the left, Ludford Park, Dell Brook and Kingston, climbing steeply to arrive in 2 miles from Dundrum at the crossroads of Harold's Grange. The road straight ahead leads up Ticknock Mountain, and after passing a number of cottages, including some of the weekend type, peters out as a track. The road to the right also leads to St Columba's (see Route 15B), while our Route goes to the left and works round the mountainside, at a height of 500 feet, under Three Rock Mountain and above Stepaside, passing a ruined tower and other remains of the Grange of the Harolds (see Route 13).

At 4 miles from Dundrum, the road is joined by another coming up from Stepaside, and, after turning round a sharp bend, enters the district of Ballyedmonduff or Barnacullia, from which magnificent views towards the sea are obtained. Taylor's Folly is passed on the left, and Ballyedmonduff House on the right. About ½ mile from the road on the right beyond

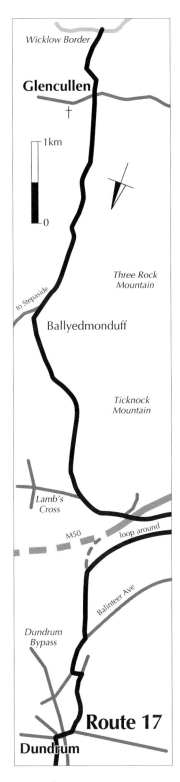

Wicklow Border

Glencullen

†

1km

0

Three Rock
Mountain

to Stepaside

Ballyedmonduff

Ticknock
Mountain

Lamb's
Cross

M50   loop around

Balinteer Ave

Dundrum
Bypass

Route 17

Dundrum

New road layouts have been imposed on the old road pattern, but it is still possible to follow most of this route.

The **Pye factory** has recently been demolished to make room for the Dundrum by-pass. **Dundrum House** has been replaced by housing. **Wyckham** is extant (see page 187). **Gortmore** became **Gort Mhuire** when it was taken over by the Carmelites in 1944; they have cared well for both the house and gardens over the years.

While much of the treed gardens of **Hilton** were absorbed by the road-widening of 1999, the house, a pleasant, rambling place where the painter Guggi lives and has his studio, has survived.

Beside the long, low and angular Wesley College, completed *c.* 1969, **Ludford Park** is extant, a modest late-Georgian house.

All that remains as evidence that **Dell Brook** existed are the tall, sparse scots pines around a small housing estate called Delbrook. Beyond, at time of writing, is the extensive site of the M50 extension, which has swept away **Kingston**.

The route as described cannot be followed directly because it is interrupted by the motorway: follow the road west and go left at Marlay Park to bring you back to the road past Lamb Doyles. Turn right at Lamb Doyles and follow the road, weaving its way between a scatter of homes which were once quarrymen's cottages: at the beginning of the twentieth century 42 out of the 45 families in **Barnacullia** were engaged in stone-cutting.

Taylor's Folly was in ruins by the mid-1950s and is no more. I could find no trace of the remains of **Harold's Grange**, and **Ballyedmonduff House** seems to have been supplanted by a modern house.

179

the latter, are prehistoric grave-sites which have been recently investigated by the National Museum.

At this point, the road, which has been climbing steeply all the way, is 1,064 feet above sea-level. It now descends steeply into Glencullen village, where it meets a road coming in on the left from Kiltiernan. In the village there is a Catholic church and a schoolhouse. Glencullen House, which faces south across the glen, was for many years the property of O'Connell FitzSimon, a kinsman of Daniel O'Connell, who used to visit here. In 1914, the poet Joseph Campbell was living at Glencullen House, and in the 1920s the novelist Francis Stuart and his wife, Iseult, the daughter of Madame Maud Gonne MacBride, stayed there.

The road descends out of the village, with a Pillar Stone on the left, and in ¾ mile reaches Glencullen Bridge, where it crosses the Glencullen river and the county boundary. The locality is known as the Devil's Elbow, and the pool below the bridge is much resorted to by bathers. Glencullen is commemorated by Synge in one of the most memorable of his short poems, in which he recalls boyhood days spent bird-nesting there.

At Glencullen, Johnny Fox's little pub has in the last two decades expanded greatly, and is a successful tourist attraction. The owner of the pub, a Mr MacMahon, also owns the nearby **Glencullen House**, which is exquisitely sited, nestling in a glen surrounded on three sides by beech trees, with a long view down the valley to the twin-peaked Little Sugarloaf. It has been unoccupied for the last few years, and could do with restoration.

Glencullen House 1977

ROUTE 18

STEPASIDE, GOLDEN BALL AND ENNISKERRY

	Miles from the GPO
Milltown	2½
Dundrum	4
Lamb's Cross and Kilgobbin	6½
Stepaside	7½
Kiltiernan	9

The road issues from Charlemont Street and crosses Charlemont Bridge on the Grand Canal (rebuilt 1946–47), to enter the suburb of Ranelagh. Mount Pleasant Square, the most attractive of the post-Georgian squares, is passed on the right, with the dome of Rathmines Catholic Church rising behind it. Sandford Church (Protestant), also on the right, was built by Lord Mount Sandford. Before Clonskeagh Bridge, at 2½ miles, our road turns right towards Milltown. On the right is Milltown Park, the Jesuit House of Spiritual Exercises, and on the left is Grove House, built in about 1760 and containing some fine plasterwork. On the right again is Rovers Football Club. Milltown village is at the bottom of a steep hill. Above it, on the right, are the large buildings of St Anne's Sisters of Charity, formerly Milltown House. After the crossing of the Dodder, on the left is Clonskeagh Castle, built by H. Jackson who took a prominent part in the Rising of 1798 and was obliged to emigrate to America. A road to the right along the left bank of the Dodder communicates with Rathmines.

Milltown, 2½ miles from the GPO, was in former times greatly esteemed by Dublin citizens, who used it as a place of recreation and amusement, and as a stage for refreshment on the excursion to Enniskerry. It was also a favourite resort for artists, the old bridge across the Dodder being considered exceedingly picturesque. Francis Danby, ARA, of Waterford (1793–1861), found inspiration on the banks of the stream up to its source in Glenasmole. The Dropping Well public-house on the road towards Rathmines has the distinction of being one of the few places in Dublin where customers may refresh themselves on an open-air terrace overlooking the river.

The road now crosses Milltown Bridge and ascends a slight incline, and, passing through a district known as Windy Arbour (compare Windy

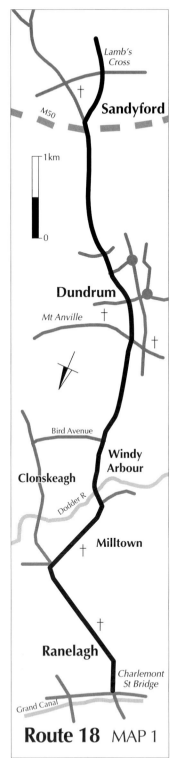

Route 18 MAP 1

Milltown Park is extant, but is much altered and sandwiched in the midst of a conglomeration of later buildings.

Just after turning right towards Milltown, there are, on the left, three large apartment blocks that are amongst the earliest such purpose-built buildings in the suburbs of Dublin. The third block, with a stepped south elevation, is built in what remains of the gardens of **Grove House**: the house itself is gone.

In the 1980s the profits from Irish League football could not compete with the real-estate value of the football pitch, and the **Shamrock Rovers** football grounds were sold for housing development.

Although considerable redevelopment of the **St Anne's Convent** campus is currently under way with the provision of apartments and commercial premises, the three-storey, five-bay **Milltown House** is extant, and being refurbished as offices. Opposite, a large old house called Geraldine House survived until the late 1980s.

Milltown village, a series of tiny cottages, a pub and a shop called Gormleys, were swept away in the road-widening of the early 1970s, and soon after **Alexandra College** was established nearby.

Clonskeagh Castle is extant.

The **old packhorse bridge** still serves as a pedestrian crossing of the Dodder, while beyond it to the west is a dense development of large apartment blocks built in the 1990s.

The **Dropping Well public house**, much extended, is still a popular venue.

Harbour in Route 7) leads towards Dundrum. To the left is Bird Avenue on which is situated a Marist House of Studies. The Avenue leads into the districts known as Goatstown and Roebuck, ordinarily reached by Clonskeagh Bridge (see above), near which are the extensive printing works of Messrs Browne and Nolan. The proprietors of this district were formerly the Barnewall family (Lord Trimlestown), and James II is said to have lodged at Roebuck Castle, built on the site of a very ancient building, when he encamped near Dublin. In the late eighteenth and early nineteenth centuries Roebuck became a favourite residence for Dublin merchants who built here many handsome villas and tastefully disposed grounds. One of these is now a Masonic Orphan School, and another the Mount Carmel Convent. Among the present residents of the district may be noted, at Roebuck House, Seán MacBride, TD, Minister for External Affairs, and his mother Madame Gonne MacBride (Maud Gonne, the Nationalist heroine whose beauty was described by Shaw as 'outrageous'). Near Roebuck House is the Sacred Heart Convent of Mount Anville, a large boarding school for girls, and farther, on the road between Dundrum and Stillorgan, is Farm-hill, at present occupied by Lord Rugby, the British Representative in Ireland. Mount Anville House was at one time the residence of William Dargan.

Dargan was the son of a tenant farmer in County Carlow, and his first large undertaking was the Dublin and Kingstown Railway. He amassed a great fortune which he laid out in promoting the growth of flax in the South of Ireland, and on the International Exhibition of 1853, and he was visited at Mount Anville by Queen Victoria and the Prince Consort, when they came to open the exhibition. The Queen offered him a baronetcy which he declined. He later lost his fortune in an attempt to improve Bray (see Route 19) and in investment in the Dublin, Wicklow and Wexford Railway. His statue by Jones stands in front of the National Gallery.

Beyond Bird Avenue, also on the left, are the high walls of the Central Criminal Lunatic Asylum. At the entrance to Dundrum, perched at the right above the railway station, is Taney Church (Protestant), the entrance to which is on a crossroads to Churchtown and Rathfarnham. In front of the railway station stands an old fountain very similar to that at St James's Gate. Taney Church deserves a visit. In the graveyard are the un-named resting places of the inmates of the Asylum, also the graves of William Halliday and his brother, David.

William Halliday was the most promising Irish Scholar of his time. He

The **Marist House of Studies** is based in the grounds of Casino, a long, low, pedimented house with a four-column portico entrance front to the south. The house was owned by the Emmet family in the late eighteenth century.

The **Masonic School** now houses the School of Architecture and Planning of University College Dublin, and **Roebuck Castle**, a great Victorian pile, houses the Faculty of Law. **Mount Carmel** is now a private hospital and **Roebuck House**, where the late Seán MacBride lived, is still there. **Mount Anville**, the work of architect James Skipton Mulvany, was visited by royalty again in 1985, this time Prince Akhito and Princess Michiko (later the emperor and empress) of Japan. The princess was a past-pupil of the Sacred Heart nuns in Japan.

Farmhill was demolished and the lands developed with private housing in the 1970s.

The **Central Criminal Asylum** is now called the Central Mental Hospital.

The modern **Taney church** (1818) is at the top of the hill to the east. Its belfry now houses the bells from St George's Church in Dublin (see page 37). The old **St Nathi's** (rebuilt 1760) is still in use. The entrance gate was erected by the parishioners in memory of the poet and writer Monk Gibbon (1896–1987) who was involved in the restoration of the church. Examples of Evie Hone's early stained-glass work may be seen in the church; she was born at Roebuck Grove. Also of curious interest is the font in the Baptistery: it was used in the baptism of the Duke of Wellington.

The '**old fountain**' still stands at the side of the main street below the station. It was erected in memory of Dr Isaac Usher, near where he was killed by a reversing car in 1917.

St Nathi's church, Dundrum

died at the age of twenty-four, in 1812. Daniel Halliday was a celebrated physician in Paris and the friend of Myles Byrne and other '98 men. The monument erected by their brother, Charles Halliday of Monkstown (see Route 20), is in the form of a broken column, and records of William Halliday that he had acquired, before his early death, an accurate knowledge of most of the European tongues, of Latin, Greek, Hebrew and Arabic, and of his own Hiberno-Celtic, 'so little an object of attainment and study to (Oh Shame!) the youth of this once lettered isle, he had fathomed all the depths, explored the beauties and unravelled the intricacies.'

Dundrum, 4 miles south of the GPO, is a station on the line from Harcourt Street. A considerable village, its prosperity dates from the early nineteenth century, when it began to be frequented by invalids, for the salubrity of the air and the great plenty of goats' whey, being especially recommended to sufferers from asthma. A number of the surrounding country seats and villas date from this time. The place is named from the Irish for 'fort of the ridge' and possesses the considerable vestiges of a castle, into the possession of which an officer of Cromwell's army entered in 1653. At the time of the Restoration, Dundrum was described as containing '14 persons of English and 33 of Irish extraction'. The Castle remained intact in 1802. At the end of the eighteenth century, the chief resident was the Hon. John Butler, MP for Newcastle Lyons, who lived at Wyckham. The same house was afterwards owned by the Huttons, the famous coachbuilders. It is now a home for decayed businessmen (see page 178).

A little beyond Dundrum, on the right, is an old country house called Dún Emer, which was for many years the site of the Dún Emer Guild, established by the late Evelyn Gleeson for the production of hand-woven carpets, embroideries and hand-printed books. She was assisted in this by the gifted sisters of W. B. Yeats, Lily and Elizabeth Yeats. Behind Moreen, another house on the right, is a ruined church.

The road now ascends past Ballawley nursery gardens (L. S. Smith, Esq.), and at 2 miles from Dundrum there is a fork. The left-hand branch leads through the old village of Sandyford and then to Kilgobbin and Stepaside; the right to Lamb's Cross and Stepaside passes Fernhill, the finely planted mountainside estate of Dr Joseph Walker.

Sandyford has been considerably built over in recent years. The motor bus having brought it within ½ hour of Dublin, it finds favour as a place of residence for office-workers in the city, who are here in full mountain air and have glorious views all around them.

The railway line originally crossed the main road into **Dundrum** village near the junction with Churchtown Road/Taney Road, to reach Dundrum station at the higher level. The main station building is extant, hidden behind some ugly 1960s' buildings. The Dundrum line is to be reopened as a modern high-speed urban transport system; construction works are under way at time of writing. In the days of the old railway, it used to take eight minutes to get to the terminus at the top of Harcourt Street; one wonders if this will be improved upon.

Dundrum is today a bustling town centre serving the surrounding housing areas.

Dundrum Castle, gaunt and windowless, hides in a grove of trees surrounded by modern apartment blocks. It is owned by archaeologist David Newman Johnson.

Wyckham, much extended, is still there, and is still a home for blind and infirm men. Much of the demesne has been developed for housing over the last forty years.

Dundrum Castle 1970

The road uphill from Dundrum is scattered with the vestiges of walls and gates to former demesnes. **Dún Emer** was demolished in the 1960s to make way for a housing estate called by the same name. **Moreen** has disappeared, to be replaced by the **National Mint**, in the grounds of which a few stones of the ruined Cross Church of Moreen are extant.

Fernhill is still there and its gardens are open to the public.

Moreen doorcase 1970

At Lamb's Cross is a turn to the right which leads to Rathfarnham and also to Rockbrook (see Route 15). The assembly of cottages seen from here on the mountainside is Barnacullia, an old settlement of stone workers.

Just beyond Fernhill is a turn to the right to Glencullen (see Route 16).

The lower road to Stepaside from Sandyford arrives there in 1½ miles. Beyond Sandyford, a left turn at the cross will take you towards Stillorgan. At Murphystown is Dún Gaoithe, the residence of Frank Aiken, a leading Cabinet Minister in Mr de Valera's Government. Just before the village of Kilgobbin is a road to the left to Carrickmines. On this road is situated the entrance to Glencairn, formerly the residence of Richard 'Boss' Croker, the Tammany Hall politician and Epsom Derby winner. The racing stables at this place are now owned by Mr Joseph McGrath.

Kilgobbin, 6½ miles from the GPO, named after St Gobban, is a small village agreeably situated among a number of small country houses with well-wooded grounds and pretty gardens. It was in the eighteenth century a famous resort of fox-hunters. The old inn in which they foregathered after the chase survives under the name of Oldtown House.

> To the right of the village is the old castle of Kilgobbin, and beyond it on a little mound are the picturesque ruins of Kilgobbin Church, with its graveyard. Of this church Mervyn Archdall, the celebrated antiquary, became rector in 1753, and carried out various researches from here. Near the church stands a fine and typical specimen of the High Cross—now defaced and crumbled by the weather. It is cut out of a piece of grey granite eight feet high, one foot four inches broad and eight inches thick. It was originally three feet eight inches across the arms, but the southern arm, with the segment of the nimbus on that side, is broken and lost. The cross had a small roll moulding round the edges, but not carried round the ring. On each face we can dimly see the figure of Our Lord in the long garment reaching to the ankles, which marks the early period of Irish Art, and with the excellent proportions of the cross suggests an age of nearly, if not over, a thousand years for the monument.
>
> Ball: op. cit. Part iii, pp. 70–71

The Church is said to owe its foundation to St Gobban, and the name of the Goban Saor is also traditionally associated with the building of Kilgobbin Castle. He was a mythical master-mason and gold-finder, and when the Castle was abandoned, searches for treasure at its foundations

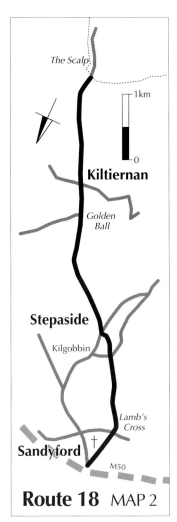

Route 18 MAP 2

The stone-workers' cottages on **Barnacullia** have become expensive and much-sought properties, with wonderful views across Dublin Bay.

Dún Gaoithe is still there, behind a screen of conifers. **Glencairn**, the British Ambassador's Residence, has been sold to a developer, and a new residence will be established near Marlay Park.

Oldtown House is still there, and opposite the entrance gates **Kilgobbin Castle** can be found.

Like many other villages of County Dublin, **Kilgobbin** seems to have vanished without trace. Turn to the right up Kilgobbin Lane after passing the castle to find Kilgobbin Church, which is sited on a long oval mound about ten metres above the surrounding land, overlooking the one-armed and very eroded high cross. From the church site good long views of the surrounding countryside can be had; while to the south the housing estates of **Stepaside** stretch into the distance; to the north and west is a remarkable extent of fields, hedges and trees.

Glencairn

undermined the walls and left it in a ruinous state. In the thirteenth century the Harolds were the owners, but a part of the lands of the parish, which include the Three and Two Rock Mountains, remained in the hands of the MacGiollamocholmogs, who had, exceptionally, entered the ranks of the Norman barons, and the wife of one of this family gave the lands near Kilgobbin and Ballyofryn to All Saints' Priory. Later on, Kilgobbin came into possession of a branch of the Walsh family. The Castle was seized by Talbot, an officer in the Irish Army during the rebellion of 1641, but his forces were driven out by General Monk. An interesting occupant of the Castle was Dr John Harding, one-time Vice-Provost of Trinity. Harding had been brought to Dublin from England to promote Laud's Anglican policy in the University, but he turned Puritan, and being degraded by the College, fought at Drogheda under Cromwell. He reappeared as a member of the Cromwellian committee for the restoration of the College in 1650, and henceforth resided at Kilgobbin, where he died in 1665. The modern Kilgobbin Castle is the seat of Mr Edward Lemass.

At Stepaside, where the Lamb's Cross and Kilgobbin roads meet, there is at the right another mountain road to Glencullen (see Route 16). On the left, beyond Stepaside, are the fields called St James's Park. Farther on, at Golden Ball, are the gates of the former Kiltiernan Abbey. A track to the right here leads to the Kiltiernan Cromlech, which, says Borlase, 'has the appearance of a sphinx-like monster, advancing out of the rocky hill on some half dozen short and rickety legs'. (See Poe, *The Cromlechs of County Dublin* p. 21 ff.) There were formerly round stones on each pillar of the gateway to the Abbey, but only one stone now remains. The last occupant of Kiltiernan Abbey was a rich, retired pawnbroker named Joyce; the house was destroyed by fire many years ago. The road presently passes the Protestant church, a neat edifice, which was built in 1826 of the local granite, to replace the church at Kilgobbin. Close by are the ruins of old St Tiernan's Church. To the left is a road leading to Loughlinstown and Shankill (Route 19) by the disused Ballycorus Lead Mines.

In pre-Norman times, Kiltiernan was portion of the MacGiollamocholmog territory, along with Glencullen, and the lands were retained by them after the conquest, and then devised by them to William de Carew, who handed them to the monks of St Mary's Abbey, Dublin, with the approval of John Dermot, nephew of MacGiollamocholmog. At the close of the thirteenth century the monks were accused by the King's Government of doing damage to the Royal Forest of Glencree (see Route 15) by introducing wild

At **Golden Ball** it is worth mentioning the **Semple church** with its slender Gothic spire, built in 1826. In the churchyard is the burial plot of the Jellett family.

The gates to the old **Kiltiernan Abbey** can be found to the left of Palmer's public house; the round stones have long gone. The Abbey and its boundary walls are in ruin.

The **cromlech** is only one of a number of megalithic monuments scattered on the hillsides around here. The **church**, which has a bullaun stone in the east window niche, has been partially submerged by the surrounding graveyard— only the top of the south door is visible. There are some good carved granite tombstones dating from the eighteenth century, including two with symbols of the Passion.

St Tiernan's church

beasts into it. After the dissolution of the monasteries, Kiltiernan was variously owned, at one time by the Fitzwilliams of Merrion (see Route 19), then by the Johnstons, and later by the Andersons. A noted eighteenth-century resident was Johnny Adair, a famous huntsman, a member of a family of wine merchants, of Hollybrook near Bray, now the seat of Sir Robert Adair Hodson.

The small village of Kiltiernan, 9 miles south-east from the GPO, is a post town at the junction of the four parishes of Kiltiernan, Tully, Rathmichael and Kilgobbin, and comprises the three hills of Kiltiernan, Glencullen and Newtown. On the last named of these, there is a cairn known as Ossian's grave. The land abounds in very fine granite which, in the early nineteenth century was much used for flagging and building in Dublin. Some sixty years ago was here situated the paper-manufactory of Messrs Hely and Co. of Dame Street. The owner, Mr Hely, invented and produced the gummed envelope.

Beyond Kiltiernan, on the left, is Kiltiernan Grange, the residence of the Misses Moore, and at the entrance to the Scalp, on the right, is St Bridget's, formerly residence of the family of Rafferty, the last representative of which devised the house and £40,000 to the order of the Sisters of Charity, which order she herself entered. The Sisters maintain it as a convalescent hospital.

At the Scalp, the road now enters County Wicklow. The name is derived from the word scallop. It is a deep chasm, at the very bottom of which ran the former road to Enniskerry. The modern road is cut out of a rampart of the defile, and is overhung with heaps of stones of enormous size, piled curiously upon each other. The sides of the chasm are not perpendicular, but slope considerably from the top. The Scalp was formed at the end of an Ice Age, when the waters imprisoned in frozen lakes in the County Wicklow highlands forced their way through the mountain barrier. There is a smaller replica of the Scalp, similarly formed, a short distance away in some fields near Ballycorus.

The Scalp is justly regarded as a remarkable natural curiosity; but its palmy days as a pleasure resort were in the thirties of the last century, and the lover of his kind who visits it today will find no sight to delight his eyes such as he would have found in that 'blessed primal time of innocence'.

For then (according to d'Alton's *History of County Dublin*, 1837), the philanthropist at the Scalp was frequently rewarded by witnessing 'groups of citizens, in their hours of recreation, chasing the goats from the lowlands, like chamois, to the topmost rocks, arranging themselves triumphantly

On the right beyond the gates to Kiltiernan Abbey is the unusual and pictur-esque light-blue-painted Our Lady of the Wayside Church, a steel-framed, timber-clad structure built in 1928, much in vogue for wedding photographs.

Kiltiernan village, with its terrace of granite-faced cottages, is one of the few such in the county to survive the second half of the twentieth century. At one end of the village is an early square-section elm water-pump. Subsequent pumps made in cast iron copied the square form (there is one at Kilmacanoge) until the more familiar round model was introduced late in the nineteenth century. Beyond, on the left, a modest granite-faced house fronts the older **Kiltiernan Grange**.

St Bridget's Nursing Home, much extended, is today the Dublin Sport Hotel, which, in addition to a fine golf course, provides for its guests and visitors Ireland's only artificial ski-run.

Kiltiernan village

through their aromatic pastures, and, at the approach of sunset, spreading on their tables of sparkling granite, viands of more than ordinary relish and enjoyment'.

At a turn of the ravine, the road descends towards Enniskerry, with fine views of Bray Head and the two Sugar Loafs and their rich, well-wooded valleys, and meets the Old Connaught road, which has ascended the hill from Little Bray, with the hill called Katty Gollagher on the right.

Geraldine House, Milltown 1983 (see page 183)

ROUTE 19

STILLORGAN ROAD TO BRAY

	Miles from the GPO
Donnybrook	2½
Mount Merrion	5
Stillorgan	5
Foxrock	6½
Cabinteely	8
Shankill	8¾
Little Bray	13
Bray	13

The road leading to Bray by Donnybrook issues by Leeson Street, called after the Leeson family, wealthy Dublin brewers and Earls of Milltown, whose family seat was at Russborough, near Blessington. After crossing the canal, it passes through some of Dublin's most attractive suburbs, presently becoming Morehampton Road (formerly Donnybrook Road). At the head of Morehampton Road is Bloomfield, a hospital for the insane, established by the Society of Friends.

Donnybrook (from the Irish *domhnach*, meaning a church), 2½ miles from the GPO, is situated on the Dodder, crossed by the handsome Anglesea Bridge (note the inscription on both sides). On the right, before the bridge, is the closed graveyard of the former St Mary's Church. Here are buried Archbishop King, politician and theological writer, and Sir Edward Lovett Pearce, architect of the Parliament House (now the Bank of Ireland), who died at his house in Stillorgan in 1733. On the left across the bridge, a turn leads to the Blackrock Road (see Route 20) through Simmonscourt where is the modern Protestant Church of St Mary's, designed by John Semple and built in 1827. The window in the south wall of the nave (in memory of Minnie, wife of Mr Justice Madden of Nutley) was designed by Burne-Jones. Simmonscourt House is the residence of Mr John McCann, chairman of the Grand Canal Company. A Poor Clare Celestine Convent is close by.

The large Catholic church of Donnybrook facing the bridge is also of the nineteenth century, and was built from a design of Pugin and Ashlin.

The village of Donnybrook was for many centuries remarkable for its

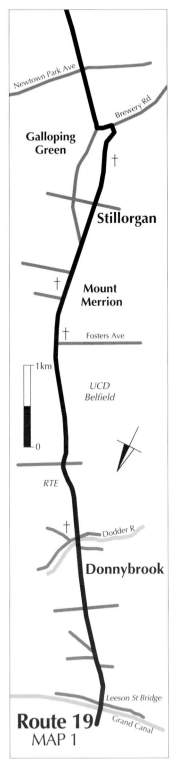

Route 19
MAP 1

Bloomfield is still there. The original house, which the Society of Friends bought in 1810, has been added to and now caters for 60 patients. Next door is the **Royal Hospital**, Donnybrook which was known, in times of less sensitivity about these matters, as the Hospital for Incurables. **Buckingham House**, the late-eighteenth-century house in which it was originally established, is extant.

St Mary's graveyard is very ancient; it first came into use about AD800, and the last burial took place in 1936. Also buried there is the writer Richard Madden (1798–1886) and the landscape painter William Ashford (1746–1824).

The **Protestant church of St Mary's**, not immediately recognisable as a Semple design, is, for most of the year, hidden by a thick screen of trees and shrubs. **Simmonscourt House** has been replaced by a series of mock Regency townhouses.

Interior, St Mary's Simmonscourt

The **Poor Clare Convent** is still there.

The **Catholic Church of Donnybrook**, dedicated to the Sacred Heart, has three intricately decorated stained-glass windows by Harry Clarke. One of the reasons listed for its erection in 1866 was that 'some expiatory monument was necessary in the neighbourhood to atone for the unholy orgies, intemperance, and riotousness, annually indulged in at Donnybrook Fair…'

fair, the patent of which was granted by King John, to continue for five days, commencing on the Monday before 26 August. Horses, cattle and sheep were sold, but the principal object subsequently became amusement and diversion. The fair continued into the nineteenth century, when it was suppressed as a scandal by the Corporation, who bought up from the holders the patent of King John. Donnybrook Castle, erected in Elizabeth's time by Sir William Ussher, was demolished in 1759. Swift's Stella used to visit at a large Jacobean house on the green owned by Alderman John Stoyt.

In the vicinity of Donnybrook, on the Stillorgan and Bray Road, are Shamrock Hill, the residence of the Hon. T. Sullivan; Montrose, of Major Vincent Kelly; and Ardmore, of F. H. Hall.

At about 1 mile from the church, on the left, is the Nutley housing estate. Nutley itself was built for George Roe, a wealthy distiller, in the early nineteenth century. It was later lived in by Judge Madden, the Shakespearean scholar (d. 1917).

The road from Donnybrook to Cabinteely was formerly noted for the number of fine and well-planted demesnes on either side of it. A writer in 1819 compared the district through which it passed to 'an immense forest, where the different mansions seem bursting through the green foliage of these umbrageous clusters'. Few if any of these mansions still remain in possession of the families of their original creators; some have been purchased by religious bodies, others have been divided into smaller properties. The number of big houses on extensive grounds still remaining in private hands is, however, notable, in view of the closeness of the metropolis.

At about ½ mile from Nutley, on the right, is Belfield, and a little farther, on the left, is St Helen's, built in 1754 for T. Cooley, MP for Duleek, later owned and enlarged by the Nuttings, who constructed an artificial lake beside the house.

About ¼ mile beyond St Helen's, on the right, is Merville, the seat of John Foster, later Lord Oriel, the last Speaker of the Irish House of Commons and a resolute opponent of the Union. Merville is now the residence of Colonel Joseph Dudgeon, the noted horseman, who has here a riding school.

At Merville, a turn to the right leads towards Mount Anville and Dundrum (see Route 18).

Beyond Merville is Mount Merrion, lately laid out as a large estate of suburban residences. Mount Merrion House was originally the property of Viscount Fitzwilliam, from whom it was inherited by the Earls of

Shamrock Hill has been replaced by a development of townhouses. **Montrose** is perhaps a surprise survival, surrounded as it is today by the broadcasting buildings of **Radio Telefís Eireann**, which include the Miesian television studios of 1960 designed by Michael Scott's office. **Ardmore** and **Merville** are extant and a part of the University College Dublin campus.

Nutley survives at the centre of **Elmpark Golf Club**.

Belfield, a good, compact house of the 1790s, is another of the old houses retained and refurbished by UCD when it developed its new campus on the surrounding lands in the mid-1960s.

St Helen's was sold in 1988 by the Christian Brothers, who had maintained a novitiate and provincial headquarters there. They received a figure in the region of £5 million for the house and 71 acres, and the property was sold on twice over the ensuing two years. It was declared a National Monument in 1994 and is now the **Radisson Hotel**; it has been extended considerably and quite successfully, with an understated modern design using Portland stone cladding. Some of its well-planted grounds, what remains of gardens designed by Ninian Niven, survive, but a large area of the site has been developed with apartment blocks.

Of the **Mount Merrion House**, built by the Fitzwilliams in the early eighteenth century, only a wing survives; **another Mount Merrion House**, a fine and imposing Victorian mansion which stood on the Stillorgan Road, was demolished to make way for the **Stillorgan Park Hotel**.

Mount Merrion House, Stillorgan Road c. 1987 before demolition

Pembroke, who had here their Irish seat up to about twenty years ago. In 1786 it was occupied by John Fitzgibbon, later Earl of Clare. Part of the house has now been adapted as a convent, and the old stables and part of the woods still remain.

Stillorgan, 5 miles south-east of the GPO, is a village standing on about six acres in the Barony of Rathdown. To the right of the village is a turn leading to Dundrum and Goatstown. At the end of the village, after a sharp descent, is a turn left, leading to Blackrock. This latter road leads through the district known as Stillorgan Park, on which formerly stood Stillorgan House, the seat of the Allen family. The obelisk here was erected to the design of Sir E. L. Pearce. The outlying portions of the property were sold at the end of the eighteenth century when Carysfort Avenue and Carysfort Park were built. The lawyer and orator Saurin lived at Carysfort Park.

About ¼ mile from the village, to the left, on extensive grounds, is a home for mentally afflicted gentlemen under the care of The Hospitaller Brothers of St John of God. This was formerly Stillorgan Castle. Opposite it is the eighteenth-century Protestant church, enlarged in 1812, and, a little beyond the church, on the left, is Brewery Road, so called from the ale and beer brewery which was carried on for many years by the Darley family. The Darleys are a very versatile race: one was Gandon's right-hand man in the building of the Custom House, a mason and a stone-cutter; another was an architect. The family also contributed to music and to poetry, and the poet George Darley (1795–1846) spent his boyhood at Springfield, Stillorgan. At the Grange, Stillorgan, lives the Dean of Christ Church, whose family is also connected with the Darleys.

The Brewery Road leads to Stillorgan Station on the Harcourt Street and Bray Railway, past the Stillorgan Reservoir, and on the far side of the station towards Sandyford are the Leopardstown Racecourse, the Children's Sunshine Home, and Burton Hall, the residence of Mrs Ryan, proprietor of the Monument Creamery.

The road to Bray ascends past the village called Galloping Green at the head of which there is a turn to the left leading directly by Newtown Park Avenue into Blackrock (see Route 20A). To the right is the Leopardstown road. The next feature on the way to Bray is the fine Catholic church of recent construction in the Lombardic style. The church stands at a turn leading to the village of Kill o' the Grange, where there is one of the largest cemeteries in Dublin, Dean's Grange (see Route 20A).

Beyond the turn to Kill, on the right is Westminster Road, on which is

The **obelisk** at the top of Carysfort Road is a dramatic fifty-foot high structure built upon a rustic grotto of boulders, best seen in winter when not hidden by the foliage of the surrounding trees. Designed by Sir Edward Lovett Pearce as a mausoleum for Lady Allen, wife of the Earl of Carysfort, who lived at Stillorgan House, it was built in the late 1720s.

Carysfort Park is used as part of the **Michael Smurfit Graduate School of Business**, associated with UCD, which bought the extensive buildings of Carysfort College in 1989; the matter was a subject of some political controversy at the time.

The Brothers of John of God are still involved in the treatment of mental disorders on their extensive campus, the nucleus of which was **Stillorgan Castle**, destroyed by fire in 1908.

The Grange was demolished in the 1960s and is now the site of the Esso (Ireland) headquarters.

The **Children's Sunshine Home** and **Burton Hall** survived major road-widening and the considerable commercial developments that have taken place to create the Sandyford industrial estate. Burton Hall is in the ownership of the Brothers of John of God.

The **Lombardic-style Catholic church** is still there, but its façade has been partially obscured by a new pedestrian bridge.

Burton Hall

situated Kilteragh, a mansion built in 1909 by Sir Horace Plunkett, founder of the Irish Co-Operative movement, who here offered a distinguished hospitality to friends and supporters of his movement from all over the world. The house, burned down during the Troubles of the year 1922, was rebuilt and is now arranged in a number of flats. Westminster Road leads into Foxrock, an area of about 500 acres, laid out in the past sixty years with detached villas, some of great elegance. It is one of the principal residential districts for well-to-do Dubliners.

At Cornelscourt is the turn to the right leading to Kiltiernan and the Enniskerry road (Route 18), and passing the venerable ruins of Tallagh or Tully Church, with sepulchral crosses in an ancient cemetery. It is said to have been dedicated to St Olaf, who had a church (St Tulloch's) in Dublin, and St Dolough's nearby, as well as St Olave's in Waterford.

Just before Cabinteely, on an eminence at the right, is Cabinteely House among fine plantations. Formerly called Clare Hill, the mansion was built by Robert Nugent, who became Earl Nugent in 1776, a grandfather of the Duke of Buckingham of Stowe in Bucks in England. Nugent was a relative of Robert Byrne, a descendant of the O'Byrne dynasty, who had been able to retain property in this vicinity, and had a seat at the then Cabinteely House, which was on the opposite side of the road from the present Cabinteely House. Nugent, who died in 1788, bequeathed Clare Hill, the present Cabinteely House, to the Byrnes, and three Misses Byrne were living there as late as 1837. House and demesne are now owned by Joseph McGrath, Esq., of the Hospital Sweepstakes, a racehorse owner and former Free State Minister. The original Cabinteely House was pulled down in 1794 and a house called Marlfield erected on its site by John Dwyer, a Dublin solicitor. For the past fifty years Marlfield was owned by the Hon. Judge Kenny and his descendants, who have now sold it.

At Cabinteely, a small village 8 miles south-south-east from the GPO, are turns to the left and right. The left turn leads into Rochestown Avenue, and on it is the entrance to Marlfield. The right turn leads to Tully Cross and Carrickmines and, at a short distance on the left, is Glendruid, built by a Quaker Barrington in 1808, and at present occupied by Mr Ross Williamson. In the grounds is one of the finest cromlechs in County Dublin. Opposite Glendruid is Knocknashane, formerly Brennanstown House, a seat of the Pim family, and now owned by Senator James Douglas.

At 1½ miles from Cabinteely, at Loughlinstown House, a road to the left leads to Ballybrack village and to Killiney (see Route 20). At this corner is

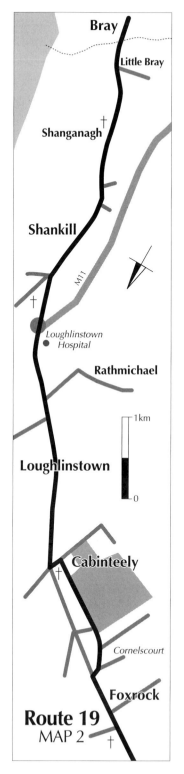

The picturesque ruins of **Tully Church** remain; I have some concerns, however, about the effects of erosion on the decorative stonework of its ancient crosses.

After the death of Joe McGrath in 1969, **Cabinteely House** and much of the demesne were taken over by Dublin County Council. A fine public park of rolling grassland and copses of trees, bisected by a stream, was opened there in 1988. Plans are well advanced to open the house to the public.

The gardens of **Marlfield** have recently been built over with a dense estate of detached houses, and the house is currently being converted into luxury apartments.

Marlfield House

Brennanstown Road still has stretches of rural brambly hedges between its high stone walls; **Glendruid** and **Knocknashane** (now called **Brennanstown House** again) are extant.

a big tree under which Wesley preached during a visit to Ireland. Loughlins-town House, of Jacobean date, is one of the oldest remaining country houses in Ireland; it is Domville property and is now occupied by Major the Hon. H. C. Alexander, brother of the well-known General, and of Lord Caledon.

On the right, after Loughlinstown House, is the site of an extensive encampment, held there in 1795 and for several years after the Rising of 1798. It was described as 'extremely well situated for the purpose; watered by a mountain river and a perpetual spring, capable of supplying an army of 20,000 men. It consisted of 125 houses built of wood, pitched and canvassed, covering an area of 120 acres.' (Ferrar, *View of Ancient and Modern Dublin*, 1796). There was also a ball-room and coffee-room supplied with Irish and foreign newspapers, and public breakfasts, patron-ised by the wives of the nobility and gentry.

Above this site is a large building, formerly the Rathdown Union Workhouse, now the County Hospital.

About a mile from Loughlinstown, the road reaches Shankill Railway Station, and is joined on the right by a road from Kiltiernan (Route 18) and on the left by a road from Ballybrack (Route 20). Shankill is situated in the ancient parish of Rathmichael, which lies between the sea and the parish of Kiltiernan. Before the Norman conquest, it was the northern boundary of the territories Obrun (Uí Brien Chulann) and Othec stretching south to Newcastle in County Wicklow.

> The Parish of Rathmichael possesses the finest prospect in the County of Dublin, a prospect which for combination of beautiful sea and mountain scenery has few rivals in the British Isles… Apart from its charm of situation the parish is interesting on account of its histori-cal associations. Many remains of past ages, marking the different periods into which Irish history may be divided, either exist or have been found within its limits. These include cromlechs at Carrick-gollon and Shankill; a rath or caher near Rathmichael; three churches of Celtic foundation—namely, those of Rathmichael, Shankill and Kilturk; the base of a round tower; and four castles dating from the time of the Pale—namely, those of Shankill, Shanganagh, Ballycorus and Rathmichael, the latter being commonly called Puck's Castle.
>
> Ball's *County Dublin*, part iii, pp. 79–80

Loughlinstown became the site of one of the first dual carriageway roads in Ireland in the 1960s, and is currently the scene of major commercial and housing development works.

Loughlinstown House, which can only be glimpsed in wintertime through the trees, is now the headquarters of the **European Foundation for the Improvement of Living and Working Conditions**. The previous owner was Sir John Galvin, who erected a fine swimming pool pavilion, designed by Alan Hope Associates, behind the house, around which he planted a million daffodil bulbs. The house and demesne were taken over by Dún Laoghaire Corporation in 1976; the lands were developed for housing, while the house and immediate surrounds were bought by the EU, who built a conference centre in the stable yard. The swimming pool was floored over and the pavilion converted into offices.

The **County Hospital** is now called **Loughlinstown Hospital**.

Loughlinstown House c. 1900

The ancient church of Rathmichael, near which the round-tower base can be seen, was formerly surrounded with a cashel wall, of which remains were visible in Petrie's time, a hundred years ago.

Rathmichael glebe house was lived in by Dr Lyon, Swift's guardian, and by the historian Leland; it is now the property of M. Bernard, Esq.

The remains of Puck's Castle and of Ballycorus Castle are on the road from Kiltiernan to Shankill; those of Shanganagh Castle are on the road between Ballybrack and Shankill. Shanganagh Castle, part of which was erected in 1408, by Thomas Lawless, later came into possession of the Walshes, who, with the Barnwalls, both Roman Catholics, were the principal landowners of Rathmichael parish before the Commonwealth. Ousted by the Puritans, they regained their properties at the Restoration, and the Walsh family remained in occupation of Shanganagh and also of Old Connaught parish nearer Bray, until the middle of the eighteenth century, when these lands passed into the possession of a Mr Lewis Roberts, who planted Old Connaught with 38,000 forest trees. Mr Roberts was a member of the Dublin Society and the son of a member of Parliament.

About ¾ mile from Shankill on the Bray road stands the modern Shanganagh Castle, the extensive grounds of which are bounded on the east by the sea. The house is a mansion, built by General Sir George Cockburn about the year 1797. It was added to and castellated by G. Morrison the architect. Cockburn stocked the house with a collection of marbles and paintings, gathered together in Italy, and a fine library. Being of progressive opinions, he celebrated the Reform Bill of 1832 by erecting a handsome column of Grecian marble in front of the house; but some years later he recorded his disillusionment by inscribing at the back of the column the words—

July
1838
Alas To this Date
A Hum Bug

In the grounds are traces of the old church of Kiltuck attributed by O'Curry to St Tucha. On Cockburn's death, Shanganagh passed into the ownership of Mrs Rowan Hamilton, who died there in 1920, having reached her hundreth year. The house has recently been in use as a hotel. The Grecian column was purchased after Mrs Hamilton's death by her grandson, Harold Nicolson, the broadcasting MP.

The ruins of the **old Rathmichael church** provide another picturesque rural scene, but again I would have concerns about the effects of erosion on the monuments there. The modern Rathmichael church is the work of Benjamin Woodward.

Rathmichael glebe House is extant, and called **The Old Glebe**.

Of **Puck's Castle** there is little remaining to usefully conserve; nothing remains of **Shankill Castle**.

Shanganagh Castle is today a prison.

Rathmichael Glebe House 1952

A little beyond the gate of Shanganagh, a narrower road to the right leads up to the old castle of Shankill, and to the road on which is situated the entrance to Old Conna Hill, a handsome stone mansion with grounds celebrated for their beauty. The original house was built by Mr John Roberts, son of the already-mentioned Lewis Roberts, who divided the rest of his estate into leases in perpetuity. Old Conna Hill is now the residence of the Rialls, formerly bankers in Clonmel, to whom it came by marriage into the Roberts family.

Farther on the Bray road, nearly opposite to the Church of Crinken, is an entrance to Old Connaught House, which was the residence of the orator Plunket, afterwards Lord Chancellor. Sir Walter Scott visited here during his tour of Ireland in 1825. It is now a religious institution. In the grounds are the ruins of an old church. Nearer to Bray, on the left, is Woodbrook, to which (in the years before the First World War) were attached a concert-hall and also the finest cricket-ground in Ireland. These attractions were provided by the owner Sir Stanley Cochrane, the son of the wealthy mineral-water manufacturer. A golf-course now occupies a large part of the grounds.

Adjoining Woodbrook is Solas Teoranta, the electric bulb and glass factory, occupying the site of a Celtic monastic establishment. The place was formerly called Corke Abbey and was the seat of the Verner family.

Overlooking Little Bray is a Loreto Convent, and on the right a road to Enniskerry by the Dargle River. Little Bray is a part of the township of Bray which lies in County Dublin. Father James Healy, the celebrated wit, who was born in 1824 and died in 1894, was Parish Priest of Little Bray from 1867 to 1893, when he went to Ballybrack. Beyond Little Bray, the road enters County Wicklow and the town of Bray.

Old Conna Hill was in use as a hotel between 1953 and 1963, and in 1984 it became a private preparatory school.

Old Connaught, a great granite pile, has been converted into apartments.

Woodbrook House is extant, overlooking an artificial lake.

The Victorian **Corke Abbey** was demolished in the 1950s.

The **Loreto Convent** is extant.

Rathmichael Church

ROUTE 20

THE COAST ROAD TO BRAY

	Miles from the GPO
Ballsbridge	2
Merrion	3
Blackrock	4½
Monkstown	5
Dunlaoghaire	6
Dalkey	8
Killiney and Ballybrack	9½
Bray	10

The road issues along Merrion Square North. No. 1 is the house in which Sir William Wilde lived during his son Oscar's boyhood. Behind it, in Lincoln Place, is the Turkish Bath in which Mr Bloom reclined; it is now owned by a firm of dry-cleaners. At the end is Holles Street Maternity Hospital. It was rebuilt on the site of Antrim House, the architect being Vincent Kelly. In its original form, when it occupied only the buildings behind Antrim House, it was the scene of the famous 'Oxen of the Sun' chapter in *Ulysses*.

At the end of Mount Street, the Dalkey tramline crosses the Canal and enters the Pembroke district at Mount Street Bridge, a scene of fighting in Easter Week 1916, which a monument commemorates.

On the Monday of Easter week, a body of veteran Loyalist Volunteers was ambushed by the National Forces while returning unarmed from a march in the Dublin hills, six being killed. On the Wednesday, while approaching the bridge, a detachment of Sherwood Foresters, just landed at Kingstown, was halted by republican forces who had posted themselves in twos and threes in the houses. The republicans, who were about 130 in all, finally retired into Bolands Mills at Ringsend, where Mr de Valera was in command. They lost only six men, but the Foresters before taking the position sustained very heavy casualties, four officers being killed, fourteen wounded and 216 soldiers killed or wounded.

Northumberland Road lies in the famous Pembroke Township (abolished in 1930), which took its name from the ground landlord, the Earl of Pembroke, and is the most attractive residential district on the outskirts of

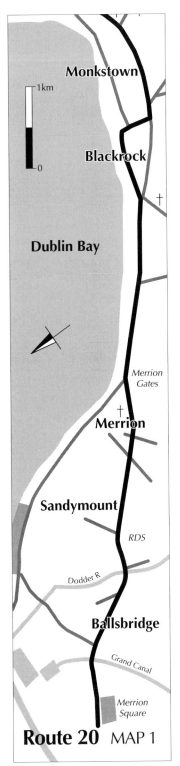

Route 20 MAP 1

No. 1 **Merrion Square** is now an American educational establishment.

The **Turkish Baths**, which were opposite the back gates to Trinity College were demolished in the late 1970s.

Holles Street Hospital is still there.

Many of the Georgian terraces of **Lower Mount Street** were demolished in the 1970s and replaced by the unsure and poorly built commercial architecture of the period.

Clanwilliam House, from where a Horatio-like defence of the canal bridge took place in Easter Week 1916, was demolished in the late 1970s and replaced by a brown brick-faced office block. Across the bridge is **St Stephen's Parochial School**, a brick building by Benjamin Woodward with steep roofs and tall chimneys, which was another strongpoint during that battle; it has been recently restored and converted into a hotel and restaurant.

No. 25 **Northumberland Road**, the house which saw the most fierce fighting during the Rebellion, is extant. It was garrisoned by just two men, Lieutenant Michael Malone, Eamon de Valera's aide-de-camp and Seamus Grace; Malone chivalrously but unwisely promised the owners of the house that he and Grace would not cause damage or break loopholes through the walls. They held up British reinforcements for the battle in the centre of Dublin, a force of 2,000 Sherwood Foresters, for five hours. Eventually Malone was killed, but his companion escaped: in this one engagement the British suffered 234 casualties, about half their total casualties during the course of the Rising.

Dublin. The estate includes Sandymount (to the left) and Donnybrook and Clonskeagh (to the right). The management has always been very particular in granting leases, exercising supervision over building, and enforcing proper upkeep.

At the top of Pembroke Road is Lansdowne Road; a turn to the left leads to Lansdowne Railway Station and to Lansdowne rugby football ground, where the international matches are played. Beside it are the Botanic Gardens of Trinity College, formed early in the nineteenth century. Botanic House was until lately the residence of Walter Starkie, Fellow of the College, musician and Spanish traveller.

At Ballsbridge, 2 miles from the GPO, the tramline crosses the Dodder. Ballsbridge, formerly a village in the parish of Donnybrook (see Route 19) towards which the road to the right leads, is now noted chiefly as the site of the Royal Dublin Society.

The Society originated in 1731 as the result of the effort of Thomas Prior, 'Premium' Madden and other scientific gentlemen, and was the first of its kind in Great Britain or Ireland. When incorporated by Charter in 1749, its object was stated to be the improvement of husbandry and other useful arts in Ireland. In 1821, it received the designation of 'Royal'. The Society held its meetings in Shaw's Court till 1767, when it moved to Grafton Street. Thence in 1796 it removed to Hawkins Street, where a house was built for the laboratory, library and galleries. In 1815, the Society purchased for £20,000 the great mansion of the Duke of Leinster in Kildare Street. Here, in addition to the library, museum and lecture-room, there were apartments for members. In 1877, the library formed the nucleus of the newly formed National Library, and has since been reformed again. Leinster House remained the headquarters of the Society until 1922, when it was taken over for the uses of the Legislature of the Irish Free State. Previous to 1922, for many years, the Society had held its Spring Show and the famous August Horse Show on extensive grounds acquired at Ballsbridge, and on these grounds were built in 1923 the present headquarters of the Society, with ample space for library, etc. The Society has a very large membership, and the annual subscription is as low as £2 2s. The management is vested in a Council. The former Drawing and Modelling School of the Society became the present National College of Art beside the National Library.

Our route now enters Merrion Road. To the right of the tramline are Shrewsbury and Ailesbury Roads. The Archbishop of Dublin's (Church of

The area of the old **Pembroke township** still contains the most attractive, and certainly most valuable residential property in Dublin. **Ballsbridge** is now a place of hotels, office blocks and luxurious apartments, referred to in a ballad some years ago as 'Lisneyland', a reference to the well-known auctioneering firm Lisney & Co.

The **Trinity Botanic Gardens** have disappeared, replaced by **Jurys Hotel** and the **Berkeley Court Hotel**.

The circular, precast concrete structured, **Embassy of the United States** (Johanson & Scott) now occupies the large acute-angled site between Pembroke Road and Elgin Road, where **Lea House**, the headquarters of the Irish Tourist Board, formerly stood.

The **Royal Dublin Society**, which celebrated its 250th anniversary in 1981, is still in existence. Although the Spring Show was discontinued in 1992, the Horse Show is still a major event for the Irish farming community; the annual subscription, however, is today a hundred times what it was in 1949.

Opposite the RDS is the headquarters of the **Allied Irish Banks**, completed in 1980, the most expensive building contract in Dublin up to that time. Beyond the RDS is the new **Four Seasons Hotel**; rarely does one see such an excellent example to illustrate a lecture on scale and sensitivity in urban design. Opposite it is another hotel, occupying the former **Masonic School** and retaining the red-brick façade and tower designed in the 1880s by McCurdy & Mitchell.

The comparative youth of the houses and the relative wealth of their owners has meant that almost every house on **Ailesbury Road** and **Shrewsbury Road** has survived intact since 1947. Little else has changed other than the fine rich mixture of trees that line the roads which are now wonderfully mature, and Ailesbury Road has become the 'embassy quarter' of Dublin, and is the location for five embassies and three ambassador's residences.

The Masonic School

Ireland) Palace, formerly in St Stephen's Green, is one of the many large villas on Shrewsbury Road. Ailesbury Road is a handsome, modern avenue with large houses, mostly built in the 1880s or 1890s, on either side. No. 73 was built and occupied by R. M. Butler, the late Professor of Architecture in University College. He furnished the house in large measure with chimney-pieces, door-cases, etc., rescued from Irish country and other houses, on which he was an eminent authority. Off Ailesbury Road, to the left, is Seaview Terrace, where at No. 6 lived Anthony Trollope during his employment in the Irish Post Office. Stephen McKenna, Greek and Gaelic scholar, translator of Plotinus, lived in the same house from 1908 to 1913, and a later tenant of the same house, also identified with the cultural and national movement, was Senator Colonel Maurice Moore, brother of George Moore, who died here in 1940. Near here, in the last century, remains of the Danish invasions were found—the bodies of 600 persons, one of whom was buried apart with a sword in his hand.

Close to Sandymount Station, on the left, Georgeville, the birthplace of W. B. Yeats (1865), stands in Sandymount Avenue.

At Merrion Gates, the Strand Road from Irishtown joins the tramline, which now comes out on the shore of Dublin Bay and gives a view from Howth to Dunlaoghaire Harbour. The strand here when the tide is out is very fine and broad, and is thronged in summer weather with men, women and children from the poorer parts of the city, bathers and picnickers. A Corporation scheme is afoot which will enable the strand to be used at all stages of the tide.

On the right of the tramline (see Route 19) between Merrion and Blackrock are a number of fine demesnes and parks, with residences built in the eighteenth century by noblemen and wealthy Dublin businessmen. Elm Park is now a golf club, and Merrion Castle, the successor to an old castle which was ruinous in 1779, is now St Mary's Asylum for the Female Blind. Part of the out-offices was the famous Coach and Horse Inn, which existed till about 1887, and in a wall of one of the outbuildings, visible from the top of the tram looking towards Dublin, is a sheela-na-gig. On Booterstown Avenue is a Sisters of Mercy Convent, formerly Collognes, once the residence of the d'Oliers, a Huguenot family, and named after the place in France from which they had come; also Booterstown House where lived F. Elrington Ball, the editor of Swift and historian of County Dublin. Beyond Booterstown Station, on the right, are the extensive grounds of Blackrock College, founded in 1859, a large school of the Holy Ghost

No. 6 Seaview Terrace, where Trollope lived for five years, is still there. It was here he completed *Barchester Towers* and wrote *Castle Richmond*.

Georgeville, at the western end of Sandymount Avenue, has a plaque commemorating Yeats's birth.

Continued reclamation of land at the Pigeon House has led to the further silting up of **Sandymount strand**, and today, although a popular place for walking, bathers and picnickers are rarely seen in numbers.

Although the land was bought for a new **St Vincent's Hospital** in 1934, it was not until 1970 that the new hospital was completed. The architects were Downes and Meehan, who had visited the Bergspital in Berne and incorporated many of its features in the new St Vincent's.

Elm Park has survived as a golf clubhouse.

St Mary's Asylum for the Female Blind is still there, albeit under the more contemporary title of **St Mary's Home and Rehabilitation Centre for the Blind**. The oldest buildings, the eighteenth-century **Merrion Castle** and late nineteenth-century nunnery buildings, are shuttered up and awaiting renewal work. North of these is a little village of modern terracotta tiled, red-brick chalets where the patients are looked after by the Sisters of Charity. A stone head and a plaque displaying the Fitzwilliam coat of arms are built into the wall of one of the new buildings, but of the old outbuildings or the sheela-na-gig, I could find no trace.

The pre-cast concrete headquarters of **Jacobs International** replaces one of the few fine international style commercial buildings that Dublin possessed—the **Imco Drycleaning and Dyeing Works** of 1939, designed by English architect O. P. Bernard; it was demolished in the mid-1970s.

Opposite, on Bellevue Avenue, is an ancient **graveyard** which was in use from the fourteenth century until 1866. Of note is the gravemarker commemorating those who died in the wrecking of the *Prince of Wales* packet on the nearby shore in November 1807; on the same night a troop transport called the *Rochdale* was also wrecked, and the total death toll in excess of 380 was one of the factors that led to a decision to build the 'haven' harbour at Dún Laoghaire.

Booterstown House, the home of the Ryan family can, but for its grand pilastered porch, be easily missed. An unusual feature are the first-floor windows in the wings, which are larger than those on the ground floor.

The **Sisters of Mercy Convent** was also an industrial school for orphaned girls. Some former inmates have spoken out recently about the cruelty that they experienced there as children.

Fathers, formerly a group of houses called Williamstown. Among the alumni is Mr de Valera. At the corner of Cross and Booterstown Avenues Kevin O'Higgins was assassinated on the morning of Sunday, 10 July 1927. Cross Avenue leads from Booterstown Avenue to Mount Merrion Avenue (see below). In a house on Cross Avenue lives Mr de Valera. He formerly occupied a smaller house slightly on the Dublin side of this, and later another between them on the other side of Cross Avenue.

On the right, before entering Blackrock, is Mount Merrion Avenue, which connects the tramline with the Stillorgan Road (see Route 18). Opposite is Lisaniskea, a fine large house. The oldest part (that next to the road) was built by the philanthropic Lady Arbella Denny about 1747. Later in the century, it was enlarged, and in 1783 was described by John Wesley as an 'earthly paradise'. Its present owner, Pierce Higgins, Esq., keeps the house and grounds in admirable order.

Near the entrance to Mount Merrion Avenue is Frascati, successor to a house said to have been erected by the mother of Lord Thomas Fitzgerald, known as 'Silken Thomas', in Henry VIII's reign. In 1790, William Ogilvie, the schoolmaster who married the Duchess of Leinster and became MP for Donegal, lived here, and later it was occupied by her son the United Irish leader Lord Edward Fitzgerald and his French wife, Pamela, and was then again a school for some years. The house was later divided into four separate dwelling-houses, in one of which is Lord Edward's private theatre. In another, Field Marshal Sir Henry Wilson passed his childhood.

Blackrock, reputed to be the healthiest district on the coast, has a population of about 9,000 people. At the end of the eighteenth century it was in great repute as a social centre, and its inns (of which one, The Three Tuns, survives) were famous for their claret. Blackrock possesses sea baths and a park of 14 acres with ornamental lakes and some small buildings which are the only relics of its eighteenth-century phase. An older relic is the fragment of the Cross preserved at the head of the street.

A little beyond this, to the left, is Maretimo, built by Sir Nicholas Lawless, the first Lord Cloncurry, who amassed a great fortune as a draper and banker at the end of the eighteenth century. He died here in 1799 just before the Union (for which he voted) was passed. The house was until recently the dower-house of the Cloncurry family, whose principal seat is Lyons, near Newcastle (see Route 11).

Valentine Browne Lawless, the Second Lord Cloncurry, was sworn a United Irishman in early life, and lay prisoner for a long time in the Tower

Lisaniskea has survived, but its neighbour across Mount Merrion Avenue, **Frascati**, became a *cause célèbre* during the prolonged but unsuccessful campaign by conservationists to save it. It was eventually demolished in 1983. Its destruction, however, and replacement by a supermarket and a carpark, and the demolition of a number of other significant Dublin buildings around the same time, had the result of focusing the attention of the general public and the local authorities on the value of conserving our scarce built heritage.

Maretimo was demolished *c.* 1970 and replaced by an apartment block. The elaborate bridge constructed by the Dublin and Kingstown Railway company to allow Lord Cloncurry access from the house to a bathing place on the shore is still there, however.

The staircase of Frascati House before demolition in 1983

of London. He later became one of the most distinguished figures in Irish public life, as a leader of Liberal peers and a patron of the arts.

Maretimo is now divided into flats, as is Blackrock House, an eighteenth-century brick mansion a little farther on. The housing estate here on the right was designed by the late Manning Robertson.

The tramline now passes Stradbrook Road on the right, opposite to which is Temple Hill House, formerly Neptune, the residence of John Scott, Lord Clonmell, whose town house was until recently the Municipal Gallery in Harcourt Street. He was an able but unscrupulous man, who rose to high judicial office and died on the eve of the 1798 Rising, observing in his last moments that he bitterly regretted the course of his career. He left a very revealing diary (privately printed). Lady Clonmell was a Miss Lawless, related to the Cloncurry family (see above). While Clonmell was living at Neptune, he fell foul of a patriotic printer named Magee, whom he persecuted. Magee's revenge was to invite a large number of friends to a 'Grand Olympic Pig Hunt' on lands adjoining the gardens of Neptune. The result was that the terrified animals, previously anointed with grease, made havoc with Clonmell's garden.

The Stradbrook turn on the right divides into three inland roads, the first of which leads through Newtown Park Avenue across the Stillorgan Road to Leopardstown; the second of which ultimately joins the Stillorgan Road at Cabinteely; and the third of which issues at Ballybrack by Rochestown Avenue. For a brief description of the last-named, see Route 20a.

Continuing along the coastal tramline, we pass through Monkstown; on the right are a number of old-fashioned villas situated in pretty grounds. On the left are roads leading to Seapoint and Salthill Railway Stations; at the head of Seapoint Avenue is Seapoint House, formerly residence of Martin Bourke, who founded the Shelbourne Hotel about 1825. Monkstown Church at the end of the Monkstown road will repay the attention of those interested in the curiosities of early nineteenth-century architecture. This considerable building designed by Semple has been described as something of a mule between the Gothic and Saracen. The Arabesque interior is made of plaster to represent great blocks of granite.

Among the interior monuments is one to William Digges La Touche, of Sans Souci on the Blackrock road. He was a member of the great Huguenot banking family, and in early life was British Representative at Bassorah. He contended against the slave trade and ransomed at his own expense the people of Zobeir when the town was captured by the Persians.

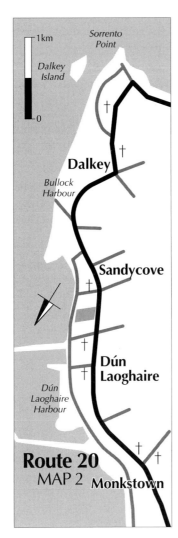

1km

Sorrento Point

Dalkey Island

†

Dalkey

Bullock Harbour

†

Sandycove

†

†

Dún Laoghaire

†

Dún Laoghaire Harbour

† †

Route 20
MAP 2 **Monkstown**

Blackrock House is extant, if becoming a little distressed. The two-storey entrance porch with Portland stone doorcase is probably a nineteenth-century addition. On the shore below the house is a ruined hexagonal brick teahouse with Gothic windows which could be contemporary with the porch.

Temple Hill House, called **Neptune** again, is extant, and is leased by Trinity College.

Opposite Temple Crescent is the entrance to an extensive campus owned by the Daughters of Charity of St Vincent de Paul, combining the grounds of two houses, **Craigmore**, a fine Victorian house designed by John McCurdy, and **Dunardagh**, a large Italianate house of similar age probably designed by E. H. Carson. Craigmore came into the possession of the nuns in 1926, and, now called **St Teresa's**, is a centre for Alzheimer sufferers and the handicapped. Dunardagh was taken over in 1939, and, now called **St Catherine's**, is a seminary for missionary nuns.

Neptune

To the right of Monkstown Church, past the old Friends' Meeting-House, is Monkstown Avenue, on which are Monkstown House and Monkstown Park. In the grounds of Monkstown Castle, once the seat of Charles O'Neill, MP for County Cork in the Irish Parliament, and now the residence of Dr De Courcy Wheeler, are two ancient castles. Monkstown House has been divided into flats, in one of which lives the architect Raymond McGrath. Monkstown Park, a large villa in the Italian style, was built in 1843 by Charles Halliday, on the site of an older house. Halliday, who died here in 1866 and was buried in the grounds, was a scholar and antiquarian, author of *The Scandinavian Kingdom of Dublin*, and also a leading figure in the commercial and financial life of Dublin. His valuable collection of Irish pamphlets, broadsheets, etc., is in the Royal Irish Academy (see also Route 18). The house is now a boys' school (headmaster, H. W. A. Evans).

On the left the tramline passes Monkstown Hospital and the old harbour and village of Dunleary, soon entering modern Dunlaoghaire (late Kingstown), 6 miles from the GPO.

The place takes its name (the Fort of Leary) from Leary, son of Niall of the Nine Hostages, who reigned from 429 to 458, and had his residence here. George IV embarked at Dunleary on 3 September 1821, after the first visit, other than wartime visits, ever paid to Ireland by a British monarch. In commemoration of the occasion, the name was changed to Kingstown, under which appellation it is still remembered and sometimes known. A monument was also erected, near Carlisle Pier.

In the eighteenth century, Dunleary was a fishing cove, with a packet-station. Arthur Young in his *Tour in Ireland* notes that there was a hotel and coffee house for the reception of visitors. The remains of this old building are above the gasworks.

Now one of the larger towns of southern Ireland, Dunlaoghaire dates its importance from the construction of the Harbour, which was begun in 1816, from the designs of the famous Rennie, and finished in 1859. In 1834, it was made the station for the royal mail packet to Holyhead, and it gradually became the chief place of embarkation and debarkation of passenger traffic to and from Dublin. The intercourse with Dublin was at the same time facilitated by the construction of the Dublin and Kingstown Railway, the second railway in the (then) United Kingdom. The contractor was William Dargan, son of a tenant farmer in County Carlow, who in this undertaking laid the foundation of a great fortune. The line of 5½ miles

Monkstown Church is still a major feature in the streetscape of Monkstown, and the **Friends Meeting House** is still to be found on Pakenham Road.

Monkstown House, with its great tower, has been a community centre since 1969. It houses a Montessori creche on the ground floor.

Monkstown Park houses a large school run by the Christian Brothers.

Monkstown Castle is still a single dwelling at the end of a shrub-lined avenue, but most of the grounds have been developed with housing. The **'two ancient castles'**, a bawn gate house and an adjacent towerhouse, have been tidied up and landscaped by the Board of Works.

Monkstown Hospital was closed in 1990 and demolished soon after. Apartments called **Monkstown Gate** have been built on the site.

Medieval castle at Monkstown 1977

was completed in 1834 at an expense of £200,000, and the original station buildings (as at Blackrock, Seapoint and Salthill) are still in use and worth inspection.

For many years the mail-boats to Holyhead were owned by the City of Dublin Steam Packet Company, an Irish company. After the war of 1914–18 the service was transferred to the London Midland and Scottish Railway Company, much to the disadvantage of the travelling public.

The town of Dunlaoghaire consists of one long, narrow street, of about a mile, chiefly of shops and business-houses, with smaller streets and avenues branching from it. It is well provided with hotels and boarding-houses, and there are three yacht clubs along the front of the Harbour—the Royal Irish, the Royal St George and the National—a public pleasure-ground, and a public baths. Dunlaoghaire is the home port of the Irish Lights vessels.

From Dunlaoghaire to Dalkey the tramline remains fairly close to the sea, which is seen at intervals down the streets to the left. The railway-line turns inland, following more or less the line of the old Atmospheric Railway, which was opened in 1843, and extended from Kingstown to Dalkey.

This railway, supported by Brunel and opposed by Stevenson, was operated by a stationary engine. (The engine-house stood on Atmospheric Road, Dalkey.) The engine worked a pump which exhausted the air from a tube 15 inches in diameter set in the ground between the rails. In the tube a piston or plug was drawn along by suction, and in turn drew the train after it. The connection was made through a slit in the top of the pipe, on either side of which were continuous leather flaps, coated with wax and tallow. Various mechanical contrivances were supposed to re-seal the slit after the passage of the train, but it became necessary to employ each train for this purpose.

The line continued in use for eleven years, and speeds of 30–40 miles per hour were quite usual. The principle was finally abandoned, however, owing to the difficulty of dealing with rats, who gnawed the leather flaps for the sake of the grease.

In more recent times, the Dunlaoghaire line has again been the scene of experimental traction, for it was here that the Drumm Battery locomotives were first put into service in 1931.

Continuing along the tramline, the route passes No. 29 Sandycove Road, Glasthule, where in 1864 Sir Roger Casement was born. A plaque on the

The three **yacht clubs** are still there.

St Michael's Catholic Church in George's Street burned down in 1966, and was replaced by a modern building, designed by Pearse McKenna & Partners. The old spire, a landmark in Dún Laoghaire, was retained.

The **Mariner's Church** now houses the **National Maritime Museum**.

No. 29 Sandycove Road is extant.

St Michael's Church, Dún Laoghaire before the fire

house records the fact. Visible to the left beyond Scotsman's Bay, on the point of land which projects and includes the 'Forty-Foot' bathing-place, is a Martello Tower, one of the many along this coast. Built during the early 1800s against the threat of French invasion, this particular tower has an even greater claim to fame, for it is the scene of the opening chapters of Joyce's *Ulysses*, and was occupied by Joyce, Dr Oliver Gogarty and Dermot Trench during the year 1904.

At 7½ miles is Bullock, formerly a little fortified town and now possessing a well-preserved castle with a commodious addition, above the modern granite harbour. The castle was built by the monks of St Mary's Abbey, Dublin. During the eighteenth century, Bullock was a stronghold of smugglers. There are roads on the right leading towards the Killiney Hills.

The road now rises and in ½ mile enters Dalkey. Dalkey is attractively situated on the southern shore of Dublin Bay, and beyond it the coastline turns sharply south. It had an ancient dignity as the port of Dublin from Anglo-Norman times until the seventeenth century, when it became a poor village. Scattered over it are various buildings called castles, which once served as defensive depots for the merchandise of the city of Dublin, which was embarked on Dalkey Sound, where the vessels lay, in consequence of the shallowness of the navigation of the Liffey. There are many entries on the Pipe Rolls of the embarkation of wine and provisions at Dalkey, to be sent to the army of King Edward I in Scotland.

All this country along the southern shore of the bay from Dunlaoghaire to Dalkey presented up to as late as 1800 an almost uniform character of wildness and solitude—heathy grounds, broken only by masses of granite rocks, and tufts of furze, and almost uninhabited except in the walled villages of Bullock and Dalkey. The district known as the Commons of Dalkey extended from the village to the eastern extremity of the bay, 'the Sound', a channel lying on its north-east, and the rocky hill of Dalkey on its south. Old writers speak of the picturesque beauty of these Commons, and in 1840 a contributor to the *Irish Penny Journal* declared that there was nothing to remind the spectator of what once had been. The rocks had been nearly all removed, or converted into building material 'for the assemblage of houses of the most fantastic construction'.

Modern Dalkey thus dates mainly from the early nineteenth century, and is remarkable for the number of very narrow lanes, with granite walls and miniature villas of the period. These are most often of one storey only, of granite, brick or stucco, painted in gay colours. Most of the Dalkey

The **Martello tower**, immortalised by its brief Joycean connection, now houses a museum commemorating the writer. Behind it is **Geragh**, an international-style house designed by Michael Scott and completed in 1938.

Bullock Castle is extant, and part of a large nursing home.

Geragh, Sandycove

foreshore, which is steep and rocky, is in private hands. Near the Loreto Convent School (a little east of the conspicuous nineteenth-century Protestant church) is a lane leading down to the sea. On the right, near the bottom, is a long underground tunnel, running for over 100 yards parallel to the coast. It is large, well ventilated and easily passable. Off it, to the right (inland) a branch leads to a well. It is said to have been built in order to satisfy a public right of way to the well without interrupting the lawn of the adjoining house, which descends smoothly to the shore.

Dalkey Harbour (otherwise Coliemore Harbour) is a small semi-natural cove on Dalkey Sound, facing Dalkey Island. Shortly before the building of Kingstown Harbour, various schemes were mooted for building break-waters across the Sound, but all were abandoned as too expensive and too exposed. The sound is never less than 8 fathoms at the lowest tide. At Victoria House, overlooking the Sound, lives Senator Seán McEllin.

The Island, uninhabited save by rats and goats, contains 18 acres and is fertile in grass. It has a Martello Tower and an old church dedicated to St Begnet or Benedict. In 1575, Dublin was visited by the plague, and a number of citizens sought refuge on Dalkey Island. During the eighteenth century, it was the annual practice to elect a 'king' of Dalkey, to the accom-paniment of much buffoonery. The practice was voluntarily discontinued in 1797, to avoid suppression by the Government on political grounds.

Dalkey is sometimes claimed to be the birthplace of John Dowland, the Elizabethan poet and magician. In the 1830s, it was the scene of a Gold Rush. The daughter of a Scottish workman employed on the Harbour works dreamed of gold being found at various places in Dalkey, and many plots of land changed hands at enhanced prices. Finally, some medical students let loose cats painted with phosphorous among the nocturnal diggers, who thereupon dispersed.

The tramline ends at Dalkey. The route then crosses the railway line at the station, and, keeping left, enters Sorrento Road, which runs above the line to Sorrento Point. The Knocknacrea road to the right ascends to Torca Hill, overlooking Killiney Bay; here among other villas is Torca Cottage where Bernard Shaw spent a part of his boyhood.

Conspicuous on Sorrento Point is Sorrento Terrace, a row of large mid-nineteenth-century houses. The Trinity College philosopher, Henry Moeran, lived at No. 2. The County Clare poet and philosopher, Francis MacNamara, died at No. 1 in 1946. Below, to the right (looking towards Bray Head), is Sorrento Cottage, where for many years lived the dramatist

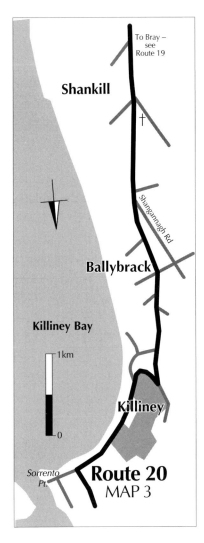

Route 20
MAP 3

The continuing general affluence of the area has ensured that most of the older houses of the Killiney area remain extant and in excellent order, although some gardens have been sold off and built over.

Victoria House is, at time of writing, on the market for a figure in excess of £7 million.

Torca Cottage, a simple house, is still there with a plaque at the gate commemorating Shaw, who commented 'I am a product of Dalkey's outlook'. He spent eight summers in Dalkey.

Sorrento Terrace is still a much-sought-after address; the novelist and film-maker Neil Jordan lives at No. 6.

The Four Winds on Torca Road, a fine example of the international style, is attributed to Eric Whyte, an English marine engineer; it was completed in 1952.

Sorrento Cottage is extant in the owner-ship of David Evans, better known as 'The Edge', a member of the rock group U2. At the time of writing the house is the subject of a controversial planning application.

Sorrento Terrace

Lennox Robinson, and before him Sir Francis Brady. The road, at the right, called Vico Road, ascends with villas on either side, and presently discloses the justly celebrated view of Killiney Bay, a long and lovely curve to which the Bay of Naples has frequently been compared. The road is cut near the base of the three hills named the Three Sisters, the first of which is crowned by a dismantled signal-tower, and beyond are Killiney Strand, the Vale of Shanganagh, Bray Head and the Sugar Loaf mountains.

A mile beyond Sorrento Park is Mount Eagle, the fine residence of Eoghan O'Brien Esq., with gardens overhanging the sea. Opposite Mount Eagle is one of the entrances to Killiney Park (formerly Victoria Park), which was opened to the public in 1887 on the occasion of the Irish visit of the Duke of Clarence. The Park comprises the second of the three hills already mentioned and was formerly a portion of the lands of Killiney Castle (see below). Lord Clonmell stocked it with deer in 1795. At the summit (474 feet) is a magnificent circular view of Howth, Dunlaoghaire and the Bay; the groves of Stillorgan and Dundrum, with part of Dublin, and beyond, the plains of Meath and Kildare; the promontory of Bray and the two Sugar Loafs. The obelisk was erected in 1742, by John Mapas, Esq., of Killiney and Rochestown, to give employment to the poor in that year of famine.

Just beyond Mount Eagle, a road to the left descends steeply to Killiney Strand and Railway Station. On the shore the geologist will identify pieces of Ailsa Craig granite, brought here by glacial action.

The route to the right passes Mount Malpas and ascends towards the gate of Ayesha. Ayesha (formerly Victoria Castle), with towers and crenellated battlements, was built for Provost Lloyd in 1839, the first building in modern Killiney. It was described by the antiquarian Petrie in 1841 as 'a memorial for future ages of one of the most gigantic projects of this speculating nineteenth century of ours.' It remained in the hands of the Lloyd family till about twenty years ago, and has since had several proprietors, including Major Ed. Maunsell, the genealogist, and Robert Warren, who presented the Park to the public. At present it is owned by Colonel Aylmer.

Beyond Ayesha is a descent on the right which leads to the Dalkey tramline and also gives access to Rochestown Avenue (Route 20A). On this descent are the main entrance to Killiney Park, Holy Trinity Church (Protestant) and Killiney Castle, built on the site of the former Mount Mapas. Opposite the entrance of the Park is Knockaderry, a modern house where lives Sean O'Faoláin, the famous novelist.

Mount Eagle and **Mount Malpas** are on the left, and farther on **Ayesha**, which, at time of writing, is in the course of renovation works. It was bought by the singer Enya in 1997 for £2.5 million. The works currently under way, which include the laudable replacement of aluminium windows with timber-framed windows, are reported to be costing a further €630,000.

Knockaderry is extant.

Ayesha

Our route after the ascent past Ayesha turns very sharply to the left, and descends through Killiney village, one of the few hill villages in Ireland, but entirely modern. The hill possesses, however, some pseudo-Druidical remains, and also presents peculiar features of interest to the naturalist and geologist (see Praeger's *The Way That I Went*).

At the bottom of the village, on the right, is Killiney House, parts of which are of the eighteenth century. There are the remains of an old coaching inn in the grounds. Killiney House was formerly the seat of the Nolan family, who are ground landlords of the slopes which once extended precipitously to the strand. These slopes have been laid out and are now occupied by well-built villas, mostly of the 1860s and 1870s, with pretty gardens, a feature of the landscape being the groves of eucalyptus trees which flourish in the mild climate.

At the right of Killiney House is a sharp descent to the golf links and to Kenah Hill. The latter is the largest house in Killiney and was built in about 1890 by du Bedat, a philanthropic stockbroker, whose affairs collapsed disastrously before he could come into residence.

About ½ mile from the village, after another sharp descent, is Marino, the residence of Lady Woods, where a monastery anciently stood.

Marino, one of the older houses in Killiney, was enlarged in 1908 by the Rt Hon. Laurence Waldron, a stockbroker, who lived here for many years and was celebrated for his hospitality and Johnsonian wit. Other noted residents in Killiney have been Michael Davitt, father of the Land League; Caesar Litton Falkiner the historian (Mount Mapas); 'George Birmingham' (Canon Hannay, at the same); William Smith O'Brien (Saintsbury); and Judge Bramley (Stratmore), who provided the village with some of its best cottages.

Opposite Marino, on a by-way, are the ruins of the old church of Killiney, dating from pre-Norman times, when Killiney bore the name of *Cill Inghean Leinin*, the Church of the Daughters of Leinin. It has an early square-headed doorway with a cross on the lintel. Near the west door is a bullaun stone. The north aisle is of a later date. In the enclosing walls of the ruin and churchyard has been placed this inscription:

> Petrie dates this gem of early Irish churches from the 6th century. Its patrons, the five sainted sisters, their festival, March 6th. Petrie and Wakeman loved this sacred sanctuary. Here for a thousand years God was worshipped by Gael, Dane and Norman, united by the one faith.

Cill Iníon Leinin

Killiney village, perched on the south side of the hill, retains a good village ambiance.

Killiney House is still there behind a tall peaked gate.

Kenah Hill is extant, overlooking the bay.

Marino is still there also, densely surrounded by newer villas.

The remains of the ancient **Killiney church**, *Cill Iníon Leinin*, stand in a walled graveyard hemmed in by villas and gardens.

A little below the gate of Marino, an avenue on the right leads to the modern Catholic church, and just beyond is the turn to Ballybrack village on the right (see Route 20A). Here a road to the left leads to the sea and passes the country seat of the Catholic Archbishop of Dublin, formerly Ashurst of the Dobbs family.

The Bray road continues straight on through the pretty vale of Shanganagh, with Loughlinstown on the right, into Shankill. The ruins of Shanganagh Castle (Route 19) are seen on the right about ¾ mile before Shankill.

For Shankill and Bray, see Route 19.

Ashurst is a rather severe building in red brick with granite trimmings, bought by Archbishop John Charles McQuaid from the Dobbs family. Much of the grounds have been sold off for quality housing. The house has a tall and incongruous-looking water tower which was increased in height to provide a viewing room; indeed, it must provide spectacular views.

For **Shanganagh Castle**, see page 207.

Entrance Hall, Shanganagh Castle

ROUTE 20A

BALLYBRACK AND BRAY VIA STRADBROOK

	Miles from the GPO
Stradbrook (Blackrock)as on Route 19	4¾
Village of Kill o' the Grange	5¾
Watson's Nurseries	7½
Ballybrack	7¾
Shankill	9⅓
Bray	11¼

At the Blackrock end of Stradbrook Road is a Friends' Cemetery, beautifully kept. The Meeting-House is at Monkstown, between the church and the castle (see Route 20).

At Rockville House, the residence of Mrs C. O'Reilly, begins Newtown Park Avenue, which joins the Stillorgan to Bray road above Galloping Green (see Route 19). Newtown Park Avenue is about 1½ miles long, and on it are Avoca School (headmaster Cyril Parker Esq.), Newtown Park village and Newtown Park House, recently acquired and magnificently renovated by E. A. McGuire Esq., chairman of Brown Thomas & Co., art connoisseur and painter. Ardagh, the residence of P. J. Ruttledge Esq., TD, a former Cabinet Minister of the Fianna Fáil party, is also on the road.

Continuing along Stradbrook Road, we meet another turn to the right, which leads past Dean's Grange Cemetery to Cabinteely on the Stillorgan Road, a distance of 2½ miles. Our road, always to the left, passes Rockford House, the residence of Herbert Dudgeon Esq., on the right. At Silke's Corner, Kill o' the Grange, is a crossroads. The turn right leads to Cabinteely by Dean's Grange and the Stillorgan Road, and the turn left to Monkstown. On the turn right, just below Silke's Corner, a short path to the right through fields leads to the old cemetery of Kill, where there is a graveyard and the remains of an ancient church. The poet Æ, when a youth, liked to bring his friends here and recite his verses to them. Adjoining the graveyard is Kill Abbey, one of the oldest, still-inhabited houses in County Dublin. It was built in 1695 by George Ussher as a residence for the Deans of Christ Church, but was leased in 1717 to a Huguenot family, the Epinasses, whose representative occupied it until a few years ago. It is now owned by the famous restaurateur family of Jammet.

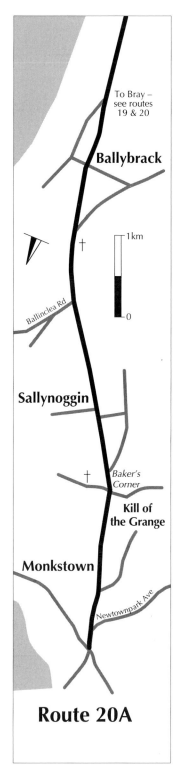

To Bray –
see routes
19 & 20

Ballybrack

1km

Ballinclea Rd

0

Sallynoggin

*Baker's
Corner*

**Kill of
the Grange**

Monkstown

Newtownpark Ave

Route 20A

Beyond the sylvan, peaceful **Quaker Burial Ground**, look out for the **gate lodge of Rockfield House**, a whimsical romantic cottage of 1905.

Rockfield House, today called Cluain Mhuire, is much altered and added-to. Farther on, opposite the Church of the Guardian Angel, housing covers the site of **Rockville House**; only its gate lodge remains.

Avoca School became **Newpark Comprehensive School** in 1972. Many of the old village cottages are still there around the pub, which is now thatched in the in Irish-Disney style.

Newtown Park House has been a retirement home since 1984, surrounded by a well-designed grouping of retirement cottages and retained old trees. The house itself has unfortunately been slighted with plastic windows, and the added porch does not help.

Ardagh Park was demolished and replaced by private housing.

On Stradbrook Road is **Brooklawn**, a fine Victorian villa, once the home of solicitor Charles St George Orpen, brother of the artist Sir William Orpen. The modern housing development in its grounds is laid out sensitively, retaining trees and leaving an appropriate amount of space around the villa.

Rockford House is being converted to apartments at time of writing.

There are no longer fields around Kill o' the Grange; the **old church**, with antae and tall, narrow gables, stands in a locked beer can-strewn graveyard, surrounded by headstones daubed with graffiti. **Kill Abbey** is a modest house, veiled with shrubs and trees and with few external features other than a stone-carved coat of arms surmounted by a knight's helmet on the front elevation.

Jammet's Restaurant closed in April 1967.

Our route enters Rochestown Avenue at Kill and passes a large Sisters of Mercy convent, Lourdes, on the right. About a mile from Kill is Sally-noggin Road, leading into Dunlaoghaire, the bus-route from Dunlaoghaire to Bray by Ballybrack. At the Rochestown turn is Somerton (A. Conor Esq.), and facing it is Woodpark (Edward Kenny Esq.). Half a mile farther is a turn to the right to Cabinteely (see Route 19), and at this turn is Granitefield, the residence of Dermot Coffey Esq. of the Record Office.

Opposite Granitefield is Flower Grove, the residence of a former Lord Mountmorres (1837), now of Dr Oswald Murphy. In the time of the Irish Parliament, Granitefield was occupied by John MacCartney, MP for the Borough of Ferns. These houses on Rochestown Avenue have very pretty views to the south of the Dublin hills and the Sugar Loafs.

At ¼ mile from Granitefield, on the left, are the ruins of Rochestown House, accidentally destroyed by fire about 1920. It bore the date 1750 and was on the site of a much older house built by a member of the Mapas family. In the early period of the Pale, the Talbots of Malahide (see Route 2) were proprietors of the land around Kill and Rochestown, and up the southern side of Killiney Hill. They were later held under the Talbots by John Fagan, from whom descended Patrick Mapas of County Louth, who built the original Rochestown House. The Mapases became Catholics after a marriage with one of the Fitzwilliams of Merrion, but were among those who had their property restored to them at the Restoration, in 1660. They were also connected to the Talbots by marriage, and, at the end of the eighteenth century, Rochestown House came into the ownership of a branch of the Talbot family. Its last occupants were three Misses Kelly, descendants, in the female line, of the Mapases.

At a turn to the left is Ballinclea Road, leading to Dalkey and also to Killiney village (Route 20) past Bellevue Park—the residence of Mrs Mary Belton, widow of Mr Patrick Belton, creator of the Irish Brigade in Spain—also Ballinclea House, built in the nineteenth century by the Talbots when they left Rochestown House. The last of the Talbots of Killiney died here not many years ago, and the house is now let in flats. The grounds were sold for suburban building purposes, which have now been effected.

Our route keeps along the flat and passes Beechwood (now a hotel) and Killiney Golf Links, on the left. On the right are the famous Watson's Nurseries (formerly Kilgobbin Farm). A little farther on is Killiney Avenue on the left, which leads to Killiney village, and facing it are Killiney Church and glebe.

Continuing past Baker's Corner, look out for **Larkin's Forge** with its cut-stone horseshoe-shaped doorway on the left, now derelict and in very poor condition.

Farther on are the buildings of the **National Rehabilitation Centre**, formerly **Lourdes**, which has submerged an old house called the **Cedars**.

Somerton is closely surrounded by recent housing and tightly hemmed inside an oval boundary wall; only the wrought iron balcony screen and graceful window canopies with wrought iron tracery can be admired from the road. The architect Raymond McGrath lived in Somerton until 1978 and subsequently the property was divided into three separate apartments.

Woodpark was demolished in the 1990s.

Flower Grove and its gardens are at time of writing being developed; three apartment blocks are being built in the gardens, and the house itself is also being restored and converted into apartments.

Flower Grove

Opposite Flower Grove, **Rochestown Lodge Hotel** hides the bones of **Granitefield**, but the ruins of **Rochestown House** are gone, and the lands developed with housing.

Towards the end of Ballinclea Road a rustic lodge signals the entrance gates to **Bellevue Park**. There is nothing particularly exceptional about the house's exterior, but it does retain some good internal features. It is now a school run by the order of **St Joseph of Cluny**, who bought the property from Mrs Mary Belton.

Ballinclea House, a late Georgian residence, was demolished in the 1950s, but the stable buildings have been converted into dwellings.

Beechwood was demolished, but its entrance gates survive.

We remain on the flat and, at a short distance, enter the village of Ballybrack.

For Ballybrack to Shankill and Bray, see Routes 19 and 20.

Rockford House

	Miles from the GPO
Grand Canal Dock	1½
Ringsend Park	2
The Pigeon House	3
Half-Moon Battery	3½
Poolbeg Lighthouse	4½

N.B. This route is practicable for pedestrians and cyclists only.

After crossing O'Connell Bridge, the turn left is taken down Burgh Quay. Notice on the right the *Irish Press* office, originally built as a temporary building for one of Daniel O'Connell's meetings over a hundred years ago, and then named Conciliation Hall. Later it was, for many years, the Tivoli Music Hall, and has been re-fronted during the last two or three years. Near it is the old Corn Exchange, of which the interior, though much altered, is worth seeing.

Butt Bridge, the last bridge over the Liffey, is named after Isaac Butt, and was originally a swing-bridge, rebuilt in its present form in 1931–32. Above it is the Loop Line railway bridge, Dublin's most unfortunate disfigurement, built in the late 1880s, and opened in 1891. Passing under it, a fine view is obtained of the magnificent South Front of Gandon's Custom House, built in 1781–91 on recently reclaimed land. In May 1921, the building was burned by National Forces, with the object of destroying Local Government records. The restoration was completed in 1931. Though much (especially internally) was irrecoverably lost, the opportunity was taken to tidy up the building, which had become a forest of unsightly chimneys, girt about with railings now removed, and with the eastern arcade blocked up. The present drum and dome are restoration, built of Irish limestone which does not harmonise over-well with the original Portland stone. The statue of Hope on top, however, survived the fire and was re-erected. The four statues which stood over the central portico have unfortunately never been renewed. Nearly half the windows over the arcades were, before the restoration, hollowed niches.

Sir John Rogerson's Quay is called after Chief Justice Rogerson (d. 1741) to whom was leased a large estate in the South Strand. It succeeds the City

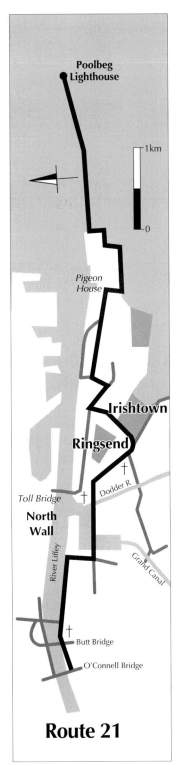

Poolbeg
Lighthouse

1km

0

Pigeon
House

Irishtown

Ringsend

Toll Bridge

Dodder R

North
Wall

River Liffey

Grand Canal

Butt Bridge

O'Connell Bridge

Route 21

Conciliation Hall was replaced by a modern newspaper building in the 1970s, but the *Irish Press* ceased publication in the early 1990s.

The Burgh Quay front of the **Corn Exchange** is extant and the building is in commercial use, although the market hall that backed it, with its tall cast-iron columns, is no more. Four of the original columns, 5.9 m high and cast in a single piece, are now incorporated into the Mount Brandon Hotel in Tralee.

The Corn Exchange cast-iron Tuscan columns

Butt Bridge is no longer the last bridge on the Liffey; **Matt Talbot bridge**, farther downstream, was opened in 1978, and the **Toll Bridge** was opened in 1984.

On the north side of the Liffey, major alterations have occurred in the last fifty years, beginning with the demolition of the original **Liberty Hall** and **Northumberland Buildings** which faced onto Eden Quay and Beresford Place. The new **Liberty Hall**, Dublin's first skyscraper, was formerly opened on May Day 1965.

The **Custom House** underwent considerable refurbishment in the early 1980s when much of the stonework at parapet level and the statues over the pediment were replaced.

Quay, and was built in about 1720, as a first step towards reclaiming the slob-lands which lay between Trinity College and Ringsend. The premises of the Dublin Cold Storage Company on the right embody what is left of the Hibernian Marine School, established in 1766, and designed by Thomas Ivory. The building was abandoned after a fire in the 1870s, and the Marine School now occupies a site at Clontarf. A little farther on, set in the premises of the Tropical Fruit Company, may be seen the two old key-stones of old Carlisle Bridge, widened and rebuilt in 1880 as the present O'Connell Bridge. Replicas of these stones may be seen on the east and west faces of the modern bridge. These heads represent Anna Liffey (female) and the Atlantic Ocean (male), and from their similarity to those on the Custom House seem to be the work of Edward Smith, though the female head is perhaps not up to his usual standard.

At this point there is a passenger motor-ferry operated by the Corporation, plying to the North Wall for one penny. Another ferry also operates from the mouth of the Dodder farther down. In this district too may be seen one or two old-fashioned waterfront taverns, notably the Eight Bells.

The gigantic Waterless Gasholder, built in 1932–1934, which is now the most conspicuous object in any distant view of Dublin, is on the right, towering to a height of 252 feet. In Forbes Street, a turn to the right just beyond it, is the old façade of the Mariners' Church, now embedded in the Gasworks and used as a cooling-house.

Sir John Rogerson's Quay comes to an end at the mouth of the Dodder, which is also the eastern terminus of the Grand Canal. Here there are locks leading from the Liffey to a large dock, in which barges and sea-going steamers can meet on equal terms. The industrial scenery in this region is particularly fine. Between the Dock and the Dodder are the graving docks of the Grand Canal Company.

The Dodder is crossed by Ringsend Bridge, a graceful single arch of stone. Down to the left, at the right-hand side of the mouth of the Dodder, is a tunnel leading under the Liffey to the East Wall, built in 1937 in connection with the Oil Refinery.

Ringsend is, like Stoneybatter or Booterstown, an example of a hybrid Anglo-Irish name, meaning the end of the Ring or Rinn—the Point. Though nearly all of the land around it is reclaimed, it existed as a fishing village in very early times. Cromwell landed here in 1649, and in 1690 it was the scene of a minor naval engagement.

All the buildings on **George's Quay** were demolished in the 1980s and their place taken by the **Ulster Bank Group Centre**. The four Tuscan columns and entablature standing at the north-east corner of the block were rescued from an old house in County Tipperary.

Across the river is the **International Financial Services Centre**, and stretching east from it is a series of new commercial buildings and hotels.

On the south quays the **Dublin Cold Storage Company** is gone, and with it the **Hibernian Marine School**.

The red-brick **Tropical Fruit Company** building now houses **Worldcom**, an IT company; the old Carlisle Bridge sculptures of Anna Livia and Atlantic are still set into the façade.

Keystones from the Old Carlisle Bridge, Anna Livia and Atlantic

There are no dockers left now, and few quayside taverns, and those bars which remain have little of the character of old. The quays have been prettified with cobblestones, trees and railings to create a riverside walkway where cargo ships moored not long ago—a fine bronze scupture of a docker straining at the end of a rope is a reminder of the past. Farther on some of the original quayside buildings remain, such as the **British and Irish Steam Packet Company** building of 1909, and what is now the called **The Ferryman**, an old house with a Gibbsian doorcase.

No buildings remain standing in **Forbes Street**.

The great **gasholder** at Sir John Rogerson's Quay was dismantled about 1996, but the Victorian example dating from 1871 near Shelbourne Road, with its decorative ironwork framework, is still there.

The **Grand Canal Docks** now serve as moorings for luxury yachts, and the sheltered expanse of water is overlooked by new highrise apartments and a café bar, as well as the retained original dockside buildings.

In a work called *The Dublin Scuffle* by John Dunton (1699), there is an allusion to the King's Head Inn at Ringsend where, he says, he was most nobly treated; and about fifty years later the principal inn was the Sign of the Highlander, also the Sign of the Good Woman, which drew good business as the horse races and sea-bathing brought numbers of citizens to Ringsend in summer; and there were also the shrimp and oyster beds.

During the seventeenth and eighteenth centuries, Ringsend profited from the fact that the Pigeon House was the packet-station. The tower (though not the rest) of the present Protestant St Matthew's Church, Irishtown, represents the building of 1703, which was entitled the Royal Chapel of St Matthew, presumably because it was the first church encountered by the Viceroy after landing. In the churchyard are the monuments of many families: Vavasours, Lundy-Footes, Fitzgibbons, Roes, Askins.

The villages of Ringsend and Irishtown are hardly separable. Here, a hundred years ago, were Clark's Iron Works, and glass works which still survive. There was also a ship moored here, *The Floating Chapel*, of the then established church.

Ringsend Park, which lies to the east, is a recent creation, formed, like Fairview Park, by rubbish-dumps. It leads to Pigeonhouse Road, the name given to this part of the South Wall, which was first built of wooden piles in 1717, and in 1735 embanked in stone. A good view is obtained of the entrance to Alexandra Basin, behind the North Wall, but otherwise there is little to note until, at 3 miles, the Pigeon House is approached.

Where the Pigeon House now stands, there was in 1735 a floating lightship. It is said that when the wall was being extended, the caretaker of the watchhouse here developed the place as a resort, and that his name was Pidgeon. The Pigeon House soon developed into the packet-station, and in 1790 was built the hotel which still stands on the right beside the power station. When the packet-station was transferred to Howth in 1813, the hotel and other buildings were turned into a fort; the remains of the fortifications may still be seen. In 1897, it was sold to Dublin Corporation for £65,000, and converted to the purpose of an electrical power station. From this period dates the tall chimney which, until about seven years ago, was such a conspicuous feature of the Bay. The Pigeon House power station has been continually modernised, and still carries a large proportion of Dublin's supply of current.

The path leads to the right behind the power station, and so on to that part of the South Wall which was built during the fifth and sixth decades

Ringsend and **Irishtown** have survived to retain their village character.

The western end of the **South Wall**, together with two coastguard stations, is landlocked today by extensive reclaimed lands.

The **Pigeon House** is extant and in use as offices, and near it stands the old power station, a rusting hulk. The two great red-and-white-striped chimneys of the oil-burning power station have altered the bay skyline for the last few decades.

The Pigeon House

of the eighteenth century. In ½ mile is reached the Half Moon Battery, so named, it seems, from the shape of the spit of land that stretched southwards from it. These sandbanks were sometimes known as the South Bull or the Shelly Banks, and contained an islet near Strand Road called Cock Lake. During the last century, however, the banks here have been disappearing, while the North Bull (see Route 1) has been growing. The Half Moon Battery is now tenanted by a swimming club, and is the scene of bathes on Christmas Day and other unseasonable times.

From now on, the views obtainable from the Wall are very fine indeed: Clontarf, Howth, the Wicklow mountains and the Dalkey hills sort themselves out as the traveller proceeds. In particular, it may be noted that the seaward aspect of Dublin itself appears to be entirely masked by trees, from quite a short distance in this direction. This is mainly because of the number of large trees in the private gardens of Sandymount.

As the walker on the Wall approaches Poolbeg lighthouse, he will observe the Bull Wall converging from the north, not so substantial as the South Wall, and impassable for the outer part of its length, where it is a permeable 'half-tide' wall. It has a lighthouse at its end.

The Poolbeg lighthouse was built in 1762–68, designed by John Smith, architect of some of the Protestant churches. It has been somewhat altered since, but not rebuilt. Round its base are enormous concrete blocks, dumped there to protect the structure from the elements. There is a mark on the base of the lighthouse, 21 feet below which is the low-tide mark, which was taken as the level datum by the Ordnance Survey when it was first surveying Ireland in 1837.

Before returning along the Wall to Dublin, the pedestrian may console himself with the reflection that he has walked more than half-way to Howth.

The **Half Moon Swimming Club** is still frequented by hardy swimmers.

The long promenade of rough granite blocks stretching out into the bay has changed little in the last fifty years, but the area around the **lighthouse** has been tamed by the construction of a new concrete deck with protective walls. The future of the Poolbeg area is uncertain; ownership is divided between the ESB, The Dublin Port Company, Dublin Corporation and various private concerns, all of which seem to have a different vision of how development should proceed here.

The Poolbeg lighthouse

Index